HARD THINKING

The Reintroduction of Logic into Everyday Life

John D. Mullen

ROWMAN & LITTLEFIELD PUBLISHERS, INC.
Lanham • Boulder • New York • Toronto • Oxford

ROWMAN & LITTLEFIELD PUBLISHERS, INC.

Published in the United States of America
by Rowman & Littlefield Publishers, Inc.
A wholly owned subsidiary of The Rowman & Littlefield Publishing Group, Inc.
4501 Forbes Boulevard, Suite 200, Lanham, Maryland 20706
www.rowmanlittlefield.com

PO Box 317
Oxford
OX2 9RU, UK

British Cataloging in Publication Information Available

Library of Congress Cataloging-in-Publication Data
Mullen, John D., 1943–
Hard thinking : the reintroduction of logic into everyday life /
John D. Mullen.
p. cm.
Includes bibliographical references and index.
1. Logic. I. Title.
BC108.M78   1995   160—dc20   94-39420   CIP

ISBN 0–8476–8002–9 (cloth: alk. paper)
ISBN 0–8476–8003–7 (pbk.: alk. paper)

Printed in the United States of America

∞ ™ The paper used in this publication meets the minimum requirements of
American National Standard for Information Sciences—Permanence of
Paper for Printed Library Materials, ANSI Z39.48–1984.

When did I not wish
for a daughter and for a son?

to
Kimberly B. Mullen
and
Alexander M. Mullen

proof in witness
of my life's great fortune.

Contents

Chapter 5: Hard Thinking about Values   93

Chapter 6: Mastering Language   115

Chapter 7: Everyday Fallacies of Reasoning   137

Chapter 10: Modern Formal Logic   237

Preface

This is a text in logic, based upon a course that I have developed and taught over a period of twenty years. My history as a logic teacher is similar to that of many who began teaching in the early 1970s. Formal logic, including quantification, formed the core of these early courses, with a treatment of the syllogism as a side issue. In my case, a treatment of informal fallacies, at first presented as a mere diversion from rigorous matters, gradually elbowed out quantification. I found later that while students were adept at naming fallacies that stood alone in a sentence or two, these same students were unable to uncover the fallacies when they were buried in a longer paragraph. The problem was one of reading; the students had trouble understanding extended arguments in a way that would uncover the structures of the subordinate reasoning. This led to the inclusion of argument tree diagramming as a technique to improve reading-for-structure, and replaced sentential logic (much to my chagrin).

There was one other concern that became apparent—more in my philosophy courses than in logic—and coincided with my experiences during a two-year critical thinking workshop with some middle school teachers. I have become convinced that not only are young students not taught the rudimentary skills of logical argument, they are taught rather systematically to mistrust and indeed to reject their own powers of reasoning. These irrationalist tendencies find their way into thinking not as explicit doctrines, but as tacit attitudes and vaguely understood phrases that function as "argument stoppers," erecting barriers to the practice of logical conversation.

"Who's to say?"

"I have a right to my opinion."

"Value judgments are just subjective."

"Aren't you just imposing your culture's values onto another culture?"

"Hey, what's true for you is not true for everyone."

Although there is some affinity between these mushy verbalizations and some of our contemporary postmodernist thinking, I have no ideas about the direction of causation, if any, between the two. What I understand very well is that as a society we have lost a clear and shared language to evaluate reasoning, and that this loss coincides with a deep distrust of the power of reasoning to settle questions of truth and value. I believe also that this distrust is being systematically, though unwittingly, taught in our public schools.

If this is true, then it becomes important to address issues concerning the limits of reason in a practical manner in logic courses. These are issues that get treated more theoretically in courses in epistemology and the philosophy of science. Logic courses also need to address the pessimistic and suspicious attitudes about reasoning and argumentation that students bring out of high school. It makes little sense to teach solid techniques of argument to someone who has been miseducated into a visceral suspicion of reason itself. "Hard thinking" is the term that I use to describe the attitudes and reasoning of those who have escaped this miseducation. Soft thinking is its obvious counterpart.

Having said this, I do not count myself in the ranks of the antiformalists when it comes to teaching logic. I believe that experience with a formal system of reasoning has an important "sharpening" effect upon thinking. And I believe as well that a sense of the aesthetics of formal reasoning, something that students could but rarely do get from mathematics, is a valuable experience. Finally, a system of formal reasoning is a good way to illustrate some of the core concepts of logic, much the way the Skinner box is used as a paradigm for the language of operant conditioning, or behavior modification. As a result, I have retained syllogistic logic in my own courses and will likely alternate it with sentential logic in the future. I have included treatments of both in this text.

Acknowledgments

By way of acknowledgments, no one who purports to write a logic text can escape a debt to Irving Copi for his remarkable texts, which set a very high standard for those who would aspire to follow. I still treat with fondness my copy of his *Symbolic Logic* in the second edition (1965). Ronald Giere's *Understanding Scientific Inference* (1979) not only influenced my thinking about causal relations, but showed me how results from the philosophy of science could be usefully incorporated into the practical teaching of the logics of the sciences. While I loved formal logic for its beauty, it took the many elegant papers of Patrick Suppes on preference, utility, and subjective probability to show me how this beauty could be put to empirical use. No one has sharpened my thinking on social issues more completely than has my good friend and previous coauthor, Byron M. Roth. I thank him for that, for his friendship, and for graciously allowing me to borrow freely from our *Decision Making: Its Logic and Practice* (1991), particularly from the sections on causation and probability. I acknowledge the support in time and money of the Long Range Planning Committee of Dowling College and of the college's President, Victor P. Meskill. My editors at Rowman and Littlefield, Jennifer K. Ruark and Melissa McNitt, are an author's dream. In regard to this book, the greatest debt is owed to the students of Dowling College, who taught me what and how to teach about logic. Their judgments are reflected in the contents of this text. Their intelligence, seriousness, and good nature have rendered my years of teaching nothing if not a manifest privilege. Finally, the strength and beauty of Constance Hassan Mullen, my wife, friend, inspiration, and sustenance for twenty-eight years, have been the wings that have carried me.

1
What Is Hard Thinking?

Soft thinking in the present age

The human brain is a magnificently powerful organ, an awe-inspiring fact of nature. One of its many functions is to reason, to try to arrive at the best possible understanding both of how the world actually is and of what is good and bad about it. The best possible understanding involves not only having a belief, but also having arrived at that belief in a reasonable way, and being able to provide clear and persuasive reasons why others should share it. The human brain is naturally adapted to "truth tracking,"—to searching for correctness in understanding and the supporting arguments for that correctness. It has the power to separate out weak arguments, foolishness, logical missteps, and fallacies. If it made sense to be proud of things about ourselves for which we are not responsible—something that I don't believe—then we should surely be proud of our brains.

Although some people's brains work a little more efficiently than those of others, as measured by IQ and other tests, when considering the immense power of any normal brain, these differences are largely irrelevant. A boat with 600 horsepower is slightly faster than one with 580 horsepower, but both are plenty fast enough. In fact, since neither boat will use its full capacity in ordinary outings, the difference is irrelevant. Good reasoning has nothing to do with "high IQ" or "being smart." Every person reading this book has a natural wonder resting on his or her shoulders.

Looked at this way, you should be concerned to take good care of your most powerful asset. Caring for your brain does not mean, in this context, wearing a helmet when bicycling. (Would you permit me, though, to call you foolish if you don't?) Here, taking care of your

1

brain means two things: first, developing proper techniques of reasoning through practice and habit, and second, not allowing it to become filled with popular foolishness about its own limitations.

What are we teaching about reasoning?

Human reasoning fills our social environment, in school classrooms, dormitories, and textbooks; on talk shows and in newspapers; arguing in bars; at work and in politics; in sports; and more. Everyone has a viewpoint, and most are ready to tell you what it is. Too often, however, the quality of this reasoning is atrocious. It lacks clarity and logical force, is riddled with cliches, and exhibits blatant logical fallacies. It is mushy reasoning, or what I prefer to call *soft thinking*. This has nothing to do with someone's "not being smart." It's a matter of lack of training and practice. Too many people have not cared enough for their brains to learn to make proper use of their reasoning capacities.

But there is another cause of the pervasiveness of soft thinking. In too many contexts we are literally taught to shut off our brains, to forget about reasoning, to believe that reasoning is inappropriate or inadequate to some task. We are taught that reasoning has no place in "feelings," that "feelings are not right or wrong," and that in many situations feelings must decide. We are taught not to be "judgmental," that values are "opinions" or "matters of taste," that the greatness of art is "in the eye of the beholder," that there really are not any "right answers," that religion is "a matter of faith," that "who's to say what's right," and that "what's true for you may not be true for me." The effect of all of these mushy, soft thinking, cliches is to say, "Don't bother using your brain to reason about that!" I repeat that the second aspect of caring for your brain is not allowing it to be filled with foolishness about its own limitations. Let's look at an example.

First dialogue: Soft thinking on the radio

Rob Randolf is a (fictitious) radio talk show host with the best ratings in the city. His audience appreciates the tolerance and evenhandedness that he brings to issues, a quality not generally found among his competitors. The topic for today's discussion is the problem of what to do with the homeless who panhandle by the dozens in the local commuter railway stations. Rob's producer flashes the name "Harry" and indicates line six.

"Harry? Are you there, Harry?"

"Rob?"

"Yes, Harry."

"Rob, I'm a first time caller. Love your show. Now, I wanted to say that I don't see why I can't sit in Central Station, read my paper, and wait for my train without some bum, smelling like urine, who hasn't worked a day in years, coming up and hassling me for money . . ."

"Harry, don't you think . . ."

"I worked for that money, so I don't see why I should be expected to give it to somebody who won't work, won't wash, and won't live in a regular building like everybody else. And the money that I pay for my ticket goes to maintaining the station so that people like me can use it in peace. The city has shelters for these people with clean beds and toilets, but they insist on living in boxes and soiling all over themselves."

"That's pretty harsh, isn't it Harry? You've got a lot of judgments in there."

"I'm just saying that . . ."

"The point is, Harry, that the homeless are people too. And who are we to be calling them 'bums'? It's these kinds of value judgments that lead the skinheads to go out and beat up on these people."

"Ya, but . . ."

"Harry? Are you listening? This issue isn't so simple; in dealing with people things aren't black and white. And if you were in his boat, you wouldn't be so quick to judge and make all these value judgments imposing your own tastes on other people's lives. Look, Harry, I thank you for the call, we've got to go to a commercial."

(The commercial ends.)

"You know we've got to realize, folks, that life is not like a science where everything is cut and dried, right or wrong. What one person may think is ok, like Harry there living in his comfortable suburban home, someone else may not want. Harry's got a job, he works hard, and that's OK. It works for him, but everybody's not going to be like Harry. Let's lighten up, have a little empathy for others. Harry and his ilk should stop telling people how to live. . . . Ginny? Are you there, Ginny? . . ."

Forget for a minute whether or not you agree with the caller's views. The fact is that Harry has made an argument, however skimpy, that the homeless should not be allowed to panhandle in train stations. His argument is that he, and not they, will be using the train; he, and not they, has paid for a ticket and thus contributed to the station's maintenance; he, and not they, has worked for his money; he, and not they, bathes. He points out as well that the city has alternative living facilities for the homeless, which these particular homeless people have freely rejected.

Rob Randolf, on the other hand, has the logical spine of a marshmallow and reasoning skills to match. He ignores all of Harry's arguments, claiming instead that using the word "bum" could lead to skinhead violence (a claim that is very likely false); that if Harry were homeless he would not believe as he does (a logical fallacy that is entirely irrelevant); that Harry was merely expressing his tastes (another false claim); that as long as a person believes that a lifestyle is OK, then it is OK (another false claim that Rob ought to try in the raising of his teenage children). Rob treats "value judgments" as something that are best avoided (a value judgment in itself), and confuses Harry's clear statement of a position with treating problems as "black or white." Finally, Rob condemns Harry for "telling people how to live," while doing exactly that to Harry. Rob's "tolerance" of alternative viewpoints does not extend to those whose views differ from his own. Rob is a soft thinker not because he is not "smart," but because (1) he has not mastered the techniques of good reasoning, and (2) his brain is filled with false ideas about reasoning itself. Rob would be better off as a hard thinker.

Why is hard thinking important?

Being a hard thinker depends upon both your skills and techniques of reasoning, and your beliefs and attitudes about reasoning. As a preliminary, I will characterize hard thinking as follows:

> *Hard thinking is the confidence, willingness, and skill to use your reasoning powers to develop clear viewpoints, to argue for those viewpoints, to seek and accept others' skilled evaluation of your own positions, and to evaluate intelligently the viewpoints and arguments of others.*

Its importance to the individual

It is a rather simple task to show that there is a direct connection between hard thinking and your own *personal freedom*, being master of your own life. A person whose mind is soft, who is a soft thinker, is at the mercy of every trickster and charlatan who passes his or her way. The soft thinker falls under the control of religious hucksters, of political demagogues, of financial swindlers, medical frauds, and more. The soft thinker cannot stand up to the false expertise of the quack or incom-

petent doctor, cannot protect his or her children from the rampant fad-
dishness in education and the poorly prepared teachers it employs, cannot control the lawyers that he hires to serve his own interests and the
financial planners whose advice he seeks, and cannot formulate clear
decisions about complex issues. Rather than using the expertise of those
consultants in order to make his own decisions, the soft thinker is forced
to place himself in the hands of those with specific expertise.

The soft thinker, in other words, is constantly under the control of others.

Armed with the ability to reason and the confidence that she can make
intelligent judgments, the hard thinker is able to take control of her own
life. Hard thinking, the willingness and the ability to reason, is a necessary prerequisite of personal freedom. It is, in addition, an almost indis-
pensable tool for social and economic success in a free society. Hard
thinkers tend to be winners; soft thinkers tend to be losers.

Its importance to society

From the *societal perspective* rather than that of the individual, the
existence of a public order, commerce, politics, and social relationships
in a free society relies upon a certain level of logical sophistication
among citizens. Once patriarchal tribal relationships are rejected as the
basis of politics, and once notions of the "natural superiority" of aristo-
cratic families, of ethnic or racial groups, and of men over women are
discarded as the basis of other social relations, then it falls to reason,
logic, and the principles of argumentation to resolve issues in dispute.

Where logic fails, the result is chaos and tyranny. Either order breaks
down altogether and the power of the gang rules, or the order is arbitrarily imposed according to the whims of a tyrant. A people's willingness and ability to reason together in public dialogue are prerequisites
of a free society and of egalitarian social relationships.

Reason is the foundation of democracy. A second's glance at the
present age in all levels of life is sufficient to show that both the willingness and the ability to employ reason are dangerously low. It is this
fact—not economic inflation, the deficit, poverty, sexism, racism, or the
entire collection of the earth's petty tyrants—that is the greatest present
threat to civilization. Without the effective public use of reason, none
of these terrible problems can be solved.

Characteristics of hard and soft thinking

This early discussion must remain preliminary and somewhat abstract. The best way to explain what hard thinking is, is to look at examples of both it and its counterpart, soft thinking. For now, hard and soft thinking need to be contrasted on two different levels. The first level concerns the thinker's attitudes and beliefs about reasoning itself, about its powers and limits. This level is like the attitudes and knowledge that the gymnastic coach has about gymnastics. For example, the coach respects and loves the sport (attitudes) and knows a great deal about it and how to teach it (knowledge). The second level has to do with the different abilities to reason that each displays, the capacity to use this powerful tool. This is like the coach's actual ability to do, for example, a back flip on a balance beam. The chances are that the coach is not very good at this second level, but expert at the first.

In the area of reasoning the first level, called the *meta level*, concerns the attitudes and beliefs that you have about reasoning in general. The second level, called the *performance level*, concerns your actual performance as a reasoner. Rob Randolf was weak at both levels. He believed that when reasoning we should avoid value judgments, an absurd belief about reasoning. When he argued, performed as a reasoner, he employed logically fallacious (erroneous) arguments, rather like the performance of a gymnast who constantly falls off the balance beam.

Hard thinkers are strong at both levels. Of course, the concepts of hard and soft thinking are quantitative and not discrete; that is, everyone is more or less a hard or soft thinker. But for the purposes of our preliminary discussion, we will pretend that a person is either one or the other.

Soft thinking at the meta level

This section involves not how well a person actually reasons, but rather what the person believes *about* reasoning in general and about his or her own reasoning in particular. Reasoning involves clearly stating a claim or position on some issue and backing up that claim with statements that tend to imply its truth. This process includes the evaluation of the reasoning of others. The claim that receives the support is the *conclusion*, or point of the argument or of the reasoning, and the claims that provide the support are the *premises*. People have a whole range of beliefs and attitudes that they display about reasoning, which affect when and how they reason.

Soft thinkers do not trust reasoning; indeed, they fear it.

Soft thinkers are eager to cut off reasoning at its earliest appearance. Thus they will have developed a long list of areas that are off limits to reasoning and a long list of verbalizations to do the job. These verbalizations function in discourse as "argument stoppers." If they have a message, it is, "Enough! I will reason no more." Here are some examples: "Who's to say?" "Your opinion is your opinion." "You have a right to your belief." "Let's just agree to disagree." "There's really no right or wrong here." "What's true for you may not be true for me." "Isn't it all just faith?" "Heh, it's all relative, right?" "If it works for you." "That may be your truth, but it's not mine!" "Things aren't that black and white." "Who are we to judge?" "Isn't it just all words, semantics?"

These phrases that are heard so often in discourse are, in a literal or descriptive sense, meaningless. Their repetition begins to resemble an incantation. Nonetheless, they play an important role in our dialogue with others; they cut off further discussion. "We have reached the point," these phrases say, "to put away the power of our reason. Reason should proceed no further."

To think of some of the areas that the soft thinker insists are beyond the power of reason is to list the most crucial judgments that any human being has to make. Religion is just faith. Values are all relative. Emotions are never right or wrong. Politics is just a matter of power. Beauty is in the eye of the beholder. Morality is just social acceptance. Your philosophy is personal opinion. And so the list goes on.

Hard thinkers, since they trust reason, tend to rely upon their own judgments both in formulating their beliefs, and in evaluating the beliefs of others. Soft thinkers are forced to use reason substitutes.

Hard thinkers know that reasoning conveys power. Hard thinkers can rely upon their own judgment because they believe in the tool of reasoning in general and in their own ability to employ it. Soft thinkers reject either their own ability to reason or the capacity of reasoning in general to decide issues. And often, of course, they reject the general capacity because they mistrust their own ability to use it. This mistrust, in view of their miseducation to reasoning, is not wholly unjustified.

We are constantly being bombarded with messages suggesting that we ought to believe something. These come from advertisers, politicians, talk shows, friends, teachers, family members, newspaper reports and editorials, religious teachers, sales personnel, purported experts of all kinds; the list is endless. And we are constantly faced with the need to state what we believe, and why we believe it. Hard thinkers have no problem with this. What do soft thinkers use to replace this power of reasoning that they so fear and mistrust? How do hard thinkers arrive at their beliefs, and what do they say when asked to justify what they believe and do? The answer is that in the initial formation of their beliefs they are forced to rely upon reason substitutes.

Reason Substitutes

A reason substitute is any tactic or approach to arriving at a belief that avoids or replaces the use of intelligent argumentation.

The arsenal of reason substitutes is in fact quite extensive, involving all sorts of illogical ways of arriving at and defending beliefs:

She will believe what her society or subgroup believes.
He will believe what his master or leader tells him to believe.
He will believe what has traditionally been believed, rejecting any new proposals.
She will believe whatever seems to fit the way she would like things to be.
He will believe whatever seems to be common sense, that is, seems on the surface to be true.
She will believe whatever is good for the cause to which she is devoted, and reject whatever seems to undermine that cause.
He will believe whatever appears in newspapers, or in one particular newspaper.
She will select a particular book and believe whatever she thinks that it states.
He will wait to find out what the majority believes and then believe that.
She will find out what the majority believes and then, being an individualist, believe the opposite.
He will believe whatever fits his already established beliefs, without ever thinking of revising these.

And so the list goes on. What is common to all these substitutes is relinquishing reason as an attempt to come to the truth.

Naive pragmatism

One of the most common and pernicious categories of reason substitutes that we find in contemporary discourse is naive pragmatism. There is a reputable philosophical tradition, American Pragmatism, in which the truth of an idea is connected in complicated and interesting ways to the idea's use-value, its ability to effectively guide action. But there is also a naive version of this, *naive pragmatism*, which is the view that a person should base his belief upon what he would want the truth to be rather than upon what evidence and reasoning indicate ought to be believed.

Suppose that you are managing a political campaign. Your candidate issues a statement, for example, about her financial dealings. There are two questions that you could ask about it. The first is whether the statement is true, or whether good evidence could be provided to support it. This is a claim's *epistemic value*. The term comes from the Greek "episteme," meaning "knowledge." A claim has high epistemic value if it is true and also is adequately supported with evidence. The epistemic value of a claim depends upon how well reasoned it is.

The second concern that you have concerning your candidate's statement is whether the campaign will garner more votes as a result of its having been stated. Holding beliefs and making public claims have the ability to serve our interests well or poorly, to make us feel good or bad, to help us or to hurt us. This ability of statements and beliefs to improve our lives, regardless of their truth, is their *pragmatic value*.

Naive pragmatism is the view that the only value a belief or a statement has is it ability to help you get your way. It follows from this that the only purpose of engaging in public debate is to convince others to believe something, whether or not you believe it. During the Nixon years presidential statements were judged by the White House as "operative" or "inoperative," depending upon whether they tended to help or hurt the president's popularity. The truth of the statements was irrelevant. A Marxist friend once called this the "materialist theory of truth," stating, "It doesn't matter if it's true or false, but whether it furthers the revolution or not."

In the 1980s a young black woman, Tawana Brawley, claimed that she was imprisoned and raped by a gang of white men. The crime as described was horrendous and brutal, and fostered much discussion about the depth of American racism. When the incident was shown, after a lengthy grand jury investigation, to have been a hoax, some supporters called the findings irrelevant. The important point was that Tawana Brawley was a symbol of the oppression of black women by white men. It was considered better for the cause of black Americans if we continued to believe that the rape occurred, or at least to act as if it occurred, even if the facts proved otherwise.

Conscious naive pragmatists will ignore any fact, distort any claim, rearrange any belief, or tell any lie under the guise of helping the cause. Concern for the truth of beliefs and of public statements falls victim to the importance of the cause.

The unconscious naive pragmatist will believe what it makes him feel good to believe and reject what it would make him feel bad to believe. If it makes him feel warm all over to believe in God, then he will confidently assert that God exists. If the demands of his chosen religion become too strenuous, he will confidently assert that religious belief is outmoded. Epistemic values are totally dominated by pragmatic values.

When his beliefs are challenged, the naive pragmatist falls back on what social psychologists call "confirmation bias"; that is, when forced to reason or discuss, he will focus his attention solely upon the evidence that tends to confirm his belief and away from the facts that tend to undermine it (Brown 1986). The point is not that the naive pragmatist is a liar, though he may be. He may simply lack the courage to face unpleasant facts. Or he may be firmly convinced that the importance of his "cause" overshadows any commitment to the truth.

Hard thinkers give priority to the epistemic value (the truth and well-reasonedness) of beliefs. Soft thinkers are not interested.

Hard thinkers believe that in the long run, at least, it's better to know what the truth is. Soft thinkers fear the truth as an impediment to their goals.

Argument stoppers

How do soft thinkers rationalize the rejection of reasoning when their thinking or their conclusions are challenged? What do they do when challenged? One tactic is to resort to argument stoppers.

An argument stopper is a verbal response to argumentation that is intended to, and has the effect of, ending rational debate.

Some of these tactics, those of the "naive soft thinkers," are just the crude "incantations" that were described above. Naive soft thinkers are victims of soft thinking environments, particularly in their homes, in their schools, and in the media that they choose to enjoy. They learn to employ reason substitutes as systematically and naturally as they learn to eat junk food and to hate school. When faced with a clear, well-reasoned challenge to one of their beloved and ill-understood beliefs, they respond in barely literate fashion: "Don't mess with my mind!" "I have a right to my opinion!" "What's true for you may not be true for everyone." "That's your truth, but it's not mine." "It's all subjective anyway." "Truth is in the eye of the beholder." "Isn't it all just a matter of belief?" "Who's to say?"

What these and other like expressions have in common is that they stop rational discussion in its tracks, which is how the soft thinker prefers it. Their attempts at using speech to express disagreement deteriorate in the most extreme cases to pathetic exchanges: "*&%$# you!" "No, *&%$# you, man!" So it goes, with finger pointing, fist pounding, and the assumption of threatening physical postures. Added complexity enters in only when the "you" is replaced by "your mother," "your girl," etc.

The sadness here derives from watching any person trying to perform completely out of his element, to engage in a subtle task for which he has not the least training or experience. The result is clumsy, humorous, and sad, but in this case especially sad because the vast power of the brain and its reasoning capacity is being so completely wasted.

On the other hand, there are more sophisticated soft thinkers. This is a group with quite well-developed analytical, or "verbal," skills. They can talk until their faces are the color of the midday sky. But try to pin them to a conviction, proceed to challenge a view that they have (ever so reticently) expressed, and they bring out a ready arsenal of logical systematic or theoretical argument stoppers to use in justification of their rejection of reasoning. These are theories about reasoning, its limits, and its dangers. They are ways of avoiding the power of reason.

A useful digression about belief

What does it mean "to believe" something? Believing is not the same as having ideas roaming around our brains. Surely we can allow ideas to roam through our brains as we think of them, enjoy them, let them please or scare us, analyze them, gather evidence for and against them, or laugh at them. None of what has been described is the same as believing them. To believe an idea is related to entertaining it as marrying someone is to casual dating. Casual dating involves sampling and evaluation, marriage involves commitment. To believe an idea is to commit oneself to it, to accept the idea as part of you, as being a reflection of you. The more important the idea is, the more it speaks of the kind of person that you are.

In discussing ways to avoid reasoning, it is useful to recall the following four features about "believing." First, as was mentioned, to consciously come to believe something is to make a choice, a commitment to that idea. It is an action that we perform. Second, we all have a natural tendency to avoid believing ideas that cause us pain. What do we say upon witnessing something that is for us a tragedy? "I must be dreaming!" "This can't be happening!" Third, there is a natural tendency to assent to beliefs that are well supported by evidence; the human mind is a "truth tracker." This tracking trait is probably both "wired in" by evolution, and learned through our development. Finally, going against either of these two tendencies will create anxiety, or what some psychologists have called *cognitive dissonance* (Festinger 1957).

The expression, cognitive dissonance, does not convey the depth of fear, desperation, pain, or dread that we can feel when cherished beliefs are challenged, when that seed of doubt begins to creep into one or more of the foundations on which our lives are built. This foundation could be something as complex as our belief in a cherished religious tradition, or as simple as our belief that one whom we love is alive and well. To have these beliefs challenged can cause us to be terrified to the core. And since to believe is to choose, it is within our power to choose not to believe what causes us pain.

The philosopher Soren Kierkegaard notes that there is in believing, "a dialectical interplay of knowledge and will" (1849, 1968, p. 181). The dialectic is something like this: If an idea is a pleasure to believe and is well supported, or if it is painful and unsupported, there is no problem. But if it is a pleasure to believe and unsupported by evidence, or if it is painful to believe and supported by evidence, then it becomes a question of will power, courage, and integrity, to determine whether one will "face the facts," as they say.

The important point about belief that we must keep in mind is that to believe is to choose, and that we all have plenty of maneuvering power concerning what and when to believe. This *maneuvering power* is the psychological capacity to resist beliefs that are well supported, or to accept beliefs that are contradicted by evidence. Just as we have the power to refuse to do what we don't want to do, since believing is a form of doing, we have the power to believe what we want to believe regardless of reasoning. Reason substitutes are ways of arriving at beliefs without reasoning. Argument stoppers are ways of handling the challenge that the soft thinker receives concerning his refusal to reason. Unlike the crude argument stoppers mentioned above, some argument stoppers are quite sophisticated and subtle.

Argument stopping relativism

Foremost in the weaponry of the reasoning avoider are the various forms of relativism. In general, relativism is the view that the truth of some claim is to be judged not on the basis of whether it is supported by good evidence or reasons that are subject to public scrutiny, but upon some feature of the person or group that believes in the claim. If a society believes that slaying the firstborn female is a good thing to do, then that belief is true. What makes it true? The very fact that the society accepts it as true, since "truth is relative to society." If a person believes that four enemas a day will cure his cancer, then that belief is true. Truth is relative to the individual. In this case, here's how the conversation goes between the hard and soft thinker:

> HT: "But is it true that the enemas will be beneficial?"
> ST: "It's his belief."
> HT: (excitedly) "But is it TRUE? Is there any evidence?"
> ST: (calmly) "It's true for him."
> HT: (on the verge of apoplexy) "I know that he *believes* that it's true, but that's not the same as its *being* true!"
> ST: (unperturbed) "Hey, he's got a right to his belief."

Another form of relativism claims that truth is relative to broad and intricate belief systems (*systems relativism*). The Canon Law of Roman Catholicism reasons from natural law principles to the conclusion that the ultimate purpose of marriage is the creation of a family, and from that premise to the further conclusion that prior impotence is a "diriment" impediment to marriage, rendering such marriages null and void (Catholic University of America 1967). The systems relativist will claim that the belief system of Catholic religious and moral law is so well developed that it cannot be critiqued from the outside. Whatever logically follows within the system is true (within the system). Truth is relative to the belief system that contains the claim.

The coherence of some forms of relativism will be discussed in a later chapter. Note, however, that the common feature of these relativisms is that if I am on the outside, then I can't reason about or dispute a claim made by someone on the inside. If truth is relative to the individual, then I can't reason with you or dispute your views since I am not you. If it is relative to the group, then I can reason with you only if I'm in your group. If there is male, female, Black, white, Asian, native American, gay, and straight truth, then I can reason only with those I am lumped with. Whatever the beliefs of the others, no matter how absurd, poorly reasoned, vicious, or foolish, they are just as good as mine if I am on the outside. Turn off your brain because reason is irrelevant to the views of those who are (to you) outsiders.

Soft thinkers, when not fanatics, tend to be relativists; hard thinkers do not.

Most sophisticated soft thinkers are not relativists in all regards, or at least they don't live their relativism, even if they talk it. Most are ready to admit that the claims of modern Western medicine are a great deal more likely to be true than the archaic practices of a witch doctor, despite the fact that these medical traditions emanate from radically different belief systems, within radically different societies. Even if our relativists don't admit the point in theory or in speech, they concede it in practice when their children become ill.

But when matters turn to questions of *value*, of deciding what is good or bad in some regard, or in deciding whether one thing is better or worse in some way than another, the relativism gushes out unchecked. Ask them if Matisse was a better artist than their two year old neighbor. "Who are we to say what's good or bad?" they ask, as if making such a judgment were a form of social oppression. Relativism loves to mask itself as tolerance.

In some societies, especially those that practice polygamy, young girls are subjected to a mutilation of their sexual organs (a clitoridectomy or female circumcision) as a way of preserving their virginity until marriage and assuring that any children that she will produce (if she still is able) will be those of her husband. Ask the relativist whether such a practice is not in fact child abuse. "What's right in one society may not be right in some other society!" he will insist, thereby confusing what *is* right with what is *believed to be* right. "We should not impose our western values on other cultures."

I once asked an evening class of adult students to state whether the following statements were true or false, and to state how much confidence they had in their judgments.

1. Hitler was a German. Reply: True, with confidence.
2. Hitler caused World War II. Reply: True, with less confidence.
3. Mother Teresa is a better person than Hitler was. Reply: Hesitation.

Why the hesitation? Hitler ordered the extermination of millions and Mother Teresa has spent an entire life reducing the suffering of the poorest outcasts on earth. Surely they ought to reply with as confident a "true" to the third case as they gave to the first. If I had asked them to write down as many reasons as they could muster why #1 and #3 were true, they would have had a much easier time with #3. Where did they learn this hesitation on questions of values? "Aren't value judgments just opinions?"

Soft thinkers believe that value judgments are not subject to reasoning, and so soft thinkers lack confidence in their own value commitments.

Misplaced tolerance

Another view about reasoning that leads people to shut off their reasoning power is the idea that criticism of someone else's claims is an attack upon him, or is in some way dogmatic behavior, a show of disrespect, or just plain bad manners. In this view every questioning or critique of the views of another is ". . . just trying to impose your views on another person." The following is a principle of logic. If someone else's belief contradicts yours, and you are confident that your belief is true, then you must be just as confident that the other person's contradictory belief is false. To hold as a firm conviction that the other's view is false is not being "judgmental," at least not in any negative sense; it's being logical. The decision of if and when to state publicly that the other person is in error is a matter of subtle social skill.

The idea that it is bad manners, dogmatic, judgmental, overbearing, aggressive, and *intolerant* to state a conviction that contradicts another's, and to be clear that this implies that the other is wrong, stems from a lack of respect for the epistemic goal of reasoning. It implies that sensitivity to even the most trivial affront to the feelings or self-esteem of others is more important than speaking the truth.

This tolerance for falsehood out of fear of offending others is misplaced. It misses the point that, for the hard thinker at least, the purpose of reasoning is to discover the truth, and so an act of criticism is an assist in that endeavor. There will always be those who will fear or be insulted by challenges to their beliefs, but these responses are consequences of their own soft thinking and so need not impede the uses of reason.

Soft thinkers equate confident argumentation with dogmatism; hard thinkers recognize the distinction between the two.

Hard thinkers welcome and encourage challenges to their own views; soft thinkers fear criticism as blows to self-esteem.

Fanatical closure

It is not what a person believes that makes him a fanatic, it is how he believes it. Nor is a fanatic a person whose belief is very strong. One does not become a fanatic on the basis of what one believes or on the basis of how strong one's belief is. A fanatic is a person who refuses to subject his or her beliefs to questioning. A belief is fanatical if it is held and protected by closing off one's mind to investigation and inquiry. This closing off is *fanatical closure.*

There may be some beliefs that are so outrageously false, so lacking in evidence, that they could only be believed on the basis of fanaticism. In this case the content of the belief forces the believer to hold it fanatically. But these types of belief are rare, though the numbers of people who hold them are not. The religious cultist, the virulent racist, and the doctrinaire anti-Semite are examples of this. Most acts of fanatical closure concern ordinary beliefs, and are performed out of fear of losing these beliefs as well as out of a lack of confidence in the ability to defend them.

It is wrong, therefore, to think of the fanatic as having strong beliefs because the move of fanatical closure, of becoming fanatical, is most prompted by the fear that the belief cannot stand up under scrutiny. Fanatics are weak in their beliefs, and so mask that weakness by fanatical closure.

It is common to find the fanatical closure rationalized by some doctrine expressing paranoid claims about the outsider, about those who are not believers. The outsider is the great Satan, the red menace, the bourgeois counterrevolutionary, the force of evil, or a seducer of minds. The outsider has some magical power to overcome the belief of the insider, and so the insider must be shielded from his treachery. To open one's mind to the reasoning of the outsider is to risk having one's convictions overwhelmed by power or trickery. Fanatics generally congregate in groups.

Fanatics are soft thinkers, and hard thinkers are never fanatics.

Hard thinkers have the courage to subject their beliefs to investigation; soft thinking fanatics live in fear of scrutiny.

Argument stopping relativism, misplaced tolerance, and fanatical closure are three of the most common argument stoppers. It is their function to prevent you from using that great and powerful brain that rests upon your shoulders eagerly awaiting your command to Reason!!!

From those who suggest in so many different ways that we put aside our reason, the hard thinker demands reasons.

The view from the performance level

The issue here is very simple: hard thinkers know how to reason, have the skills of reasoning; and soft thinkers do not. Recall that this has nothing to do with "being smart," if that phrase is taken to refer to some innate ability. It is merely a matter of whether a certain set of skills has been learned.

Exceptions to the claim that soft thinkers lack the skill of reasoning are those soft thinkers who know how to reason quite well, but who reject that ability because of some form of relativism masking as tolerance, or as a result of some fanaticism that masks a frightened attempt to cling to some doctrine. But in general, soft thinkers are reasoning illiterates. They never learned to think clearly, to argue logically and persuasively, and they never learned to reason dialogically, with others in groups.

To distinguish hard and soft thinkers by means of what the hard thinkers can do and the soft thinkers cannot do must again be preliminary at this point. It is after all a major function of this book to draw that distinction and to induce soft thinkers to mend their ways. This brief discussion will proceed from differences that the two have in regard to *language*, then to *argument recognition*, and then to *argument evaluation*.

Use and misuse of language

Language is a fluid, ever changing tool of communication. Understanding this point motivates the hard thinker to develop the proper skills for mastering language, skills of definition, of demand for clarification, of the recognition of emotive power and of the metamessages that accompany literal speech. In this regard the signs of a hard thinker in conversation are, "What exactly do you mean by (for example) 'fitness' in this context?" or "You could mean by 'fitness' just physical strength, or you could mean something broader like the old Greek idea of 'virtue'." Hard thinkers never assume that key words in a discussion, even familiar words, mean the same thing to all parties involved.

Hard thinkers are conscious of language as they use it; soft thinkers take language for granted.

Hard thinkers are the masters of their own communication, whereas soft thinkers are the victims of the tool of language that they do not understand.

Argument recognition

Argument recognition is the ability to recognize when an argument is being offered, what the point of the argument is, and how the arguer is supporting that point. To be able to reason well with others, a person must be able to know the point that the other is trying to support and how she is arguing for it.

Even the briefest of arguments tend to have structures that are quite complex, being made up of many subordinate arguments. Thus a paragraph-length newspaper editorial making the point that the city needs to hire more police officers will in fact be a chain of smaller arguments, and the logical force of the editorial will depend upon the strength of these subsidiary arguments. The hard thinker will be able to isolate the main point and the subsidiary arguments. She will be able to focus upon these smaller points individually, while keeping in mind their connection to the whole. This is nothing other than good reading or good listening.

It is common to hear people claim after having read a complicated argument, "It's just a lot of words." "It keeps going around in circles." "It's all just semantics." In fact, the author has presented an organized, logically interrelated chain of reasoning that the reader has simply not been able to follow. To the designer of a maze in an English garden, the walkways are logically and systematically laid out. To the newcomer caught in the maze, it's just a lot of paths leading nowhere.

The hard thinker can "read" the structure of an argument, whether written or oral. The soft thinker experiences the same argument as a set of blurry manipulations.

Argument evaluation

The area of *argument evaluation* is the most important in logic. Ultimately we want to be able to decide, assuming we have recognized the argument that is staring us in the face, whether it is a good argument or not. We want to know whether the argument deserves our assent or does not. To decide this, we must be able to evaluate it.

The hard thinker possesses tools of argument evaluation, and is thus able to distinguish good from bad arguments; the soft thinker must resort to reasoning substitutes.

The hard thinker can distinguish the trickster from the reasonable person; the soft thinker is at the mercy of the charlatan.

The hard thinker can recognize fallacies of reasoning; the soft thinker cannot.

The hard thinker is comfortable with probabilities; the soft thinker is reduced to irrelevant possibilities.

The hard thinker is comfortable evaluating popular scientific and medical reports; the soft thinker is not.

The hard thinker is very careful in drawing conclusions about what the causes of things are; the soft thinker rushes into such conclusions, and often into superstition.

These are just some of the elements of hard thinking and of its degenerate counterpart, soft thinking. Many more will follow in the text. There is no question that one of the major sources of soft thinking is the school system. Teachers are not trained to be clear, logical thinkers. In fact, the reverse is often true; teachers are systematically taught false ideas about reasoning, which they dutifully impart upon their students. The following section is about teaching.

Second dialogue—Social studies class

It's only November, and already Ms. Thayer is getting those feelings after fifth period. Her legs seem draped with ankle weights, and a familiar pressure is building in her chest. Her lungs are refusing to fill, her head is permeated with fog. By this time the coffee in the teachers' room is muck, but it makes sixth period social studies possible. Thank God for social studies after five straight classes of Spanish. Why didn't they tell her about that in all those education courses she had to take? At least in social studies she can relax, let *them* do some of the work. Especially today, because that clever Anne Marie Winters is going to square off against Bobby Mannaro. The dexter against the jock; this should be good.

"OK, let's settle down. We've got work to do today. Remember we've been talking about the *Bill of Rights*, what it means to us all, how it protects us from the powers of the government. Today Anne Marie and Bobby are going to discuss the question of whether we should have mandatory and random urinalysis here at Lincoln, to test for illegal drug use. Some people say that this is a question of civil rights. Anne Marie, it's ladies first, and try not to be too hard on poor Bobby." . . . (laughter)

"Yah! If she gets too excited she'll pop her retainer," says Bobby in *sotto voce*, grinning to Frank behind him.

Suppressed laughter from the class. Anne Marie seems unperturbed. Her index cards in order, she begins.

"Yesterday I walked from the school to the deli during lunch and I saw, just in that brief time, four students smoking pot. And I know from friends that students do that and more at parties. This shows how serious the drug problem is, and last night the President said that it was increasing.

"It's clear that we have not been able to stop drugs from coming into the country, because attempts at border interdiction have been a failure. So we have to stop them from being used.

"There was a time when we didn't have this kind of problem in America. According to a recent *Newsweek* cover story, drugs did not become a problem in our schools until the 1960s. It has been pointed out that it was in the sixties that the liberal Supreme Court and the American Civil Liberties Union tied the hands of the police and the schools. They said they were protecting our rights, but what we have now is the result of that permissiveness."

Anne Marie looked up from her cards. The class stared back without expression. Quickly she looked down and continued reading.

"Statistics from our book in health class show that about three-quarters of all heroin users and ninety percent of cocaine users started out using pot, the same way as those students I saw yesterday. The school has a responsibility to stop them from going on to hard drugs.

"The liberals who think that children are really adults don't realize that children need guidance. To leave them to just fend for themselves is not good child raising policy. Every child psychologist believes that children need guidance in their lives.

"So I think that we need to find out who these students are who are using drugs and see to it that they don't get others involved. They should be expelled if they are found with drugs. So I think that not only is drug testing OK—after all, even the president had testing—but I think it is a necessity."

Anne Marie returns quickly to her seat.

"Take her, Bobby," grins Frank.

Bobby saunters to the front of the class, hitching up his jeans. Trying to look serious, he clears his throat and begins.

"I have only one question to ask my esteemed opponent. Anne Marie, when's the last time you smoked a joint?"

The class roars; Anne Marie doesn't look up.

"OK, never, right? Here we have someone who never even tried marijuana, telling us that the school nurse should go around grabbing us by the collars, pulling us into the john, standing over us and watching while we pee into her little plastic cups."

The class roars approvingly.

"Now I have a question for the class. How many here know people who smoke . . . you know . . . a little grass now and then?"

Most raise their hands.

"And how many of you know people who use heroin?"

One in the back sticks up his hand.

"So that takes care of Anne Marie's claim that marijuana leads to bad drugs. Now I don't do any drugs myself . . . unless of course you consider a few brews in the off-season . . ."

"Kegs are more like it," yells Frank.

The class laughs; Bobby smiles his boyish good looks and continues.

"I'll bet even the President himself takes a drink or two, once in a while. Anyway, the kids around here aren't into bad drugs, so there's no reason to start all this stuff about testing. And besides, like Miss Thayer there says, this is a free country, we've got rights against self-recrimination. I guess that about does it."

Bobby takes his seat.

"OK, Bobby!" says Frank.

"Anne Marie, would you like to respond to Bobby's discussion?"

Anne Marie's eyes were glued to the desk. For a long time she said nothing. The students begin to fidget, looking her way and then at each other.

"Anne Marie?"

Slowly Anne Marie stood up. Her cards were on the desk. She spoke quietly, her voice halting.

"Before we moved here we lived in Freeport. My brother was in high school, and I was in seventh grade. I knew then that he was doing drugs. I asked him not to, but he made me promise not to tell. I knew then I should have told, but I didn't. He's dead now."

Anne Marie sat down. The room was very quiet.

"Well class, this . . . ah . . . this is a very difficult issue and as we've said many times, there are no right or wrong answers. These questions have to do with people's values. Anne Marie's points were very good, that young people need guidance. And Bobby was right that we do have certain rights. I think that we can call this one a draw, what do you say? Yes, Barbara?"

"I knew a guy who took so many drugs, his brain now is all messed up. I don't think that hard drugs are as harmless as Bobby there says."

Sue broke in.

"All he said was that a little grass wouldn't hurt anyone."

Leroy stated, "But what happened to Anne Marie's brother can happen to anyone."

Things went on in this vein until the end of the period. Students taking sides and relating the discussion to personal experiences. Ms. Thayer sat in the back of the room, pleased with the class, with the enthusiasm of the debate. It's this kind of classes that give her the strength to go on. That night she repeated it all to Pete.

"They really got into it, especially after poor Anne Marie dropped that bombshell."

She felt good about things.

Ms. Thayer should not have "felt good about things." The class period was a disaster from the standpoint either of clarifying the issue of mandatory drug testing, or of teaching the students about reasoning. The issues remained shrouded in a verbal and rhetorical fog, and the "lessons" about reasoning were all wrong. One more seed from Miss Thayer's soft thinking was planted in the minds of her students. I once asked for an evaluation of this fictitious class period from a group of middle school teachers, chosen because they were among the best in their building. To a person, they thought that the class was a success.

Meta level confusions

1. The atmosphere of the class experience was one of a contest. Reasoning was understood as a move in a game in which there were winners and losers. This was evident in the teacher's mind as she categorized the event as the dexter vs. the jock. This was conveyed to the students by the teacher's remark that Anne Marie should not be too hard on Bobby. This was clearly in the minds of the students, as shown by the remarks of Bobby's friends. The mood did not become serious until Anne Marie "dropped her bombshell." But this seriousness had nothing to do with respect for dialogue or for the truth, and it was followed by students simply relating their own personal experiences and impressions, rather than by cogent reasoning. Students should be taught that reasoning in the best sense is a cooperative endeavor in which the purpose is to develop ideas that are more and more well-reasoned.

2. The view was expressed that on complicated issues, especially issues involving values, there are no right answers. This attitude leads to a lack of respect for reasoning, since it fosters the idea that in the

area of value judgments anyone's views are as worthy of belief as anyone else's. Not only is this clearly not the case, but it leads ultimately to a dangerous social nihilism in which power is the only determinant of right. A later chapter will argue that value issues can be argued well and poorly in the same manner and to the same degree of precision as purely empirical issues. Some value issues remain controversial with no general consensus. This, however, is a consequence of their being difficult, and not of their being value issues. Students should be taught that reasoning can be evaluated as to its success, including reasoning about values.

3. In the absence of a *logical* criterion to determine whose point of view was most well argued, the approval of the audience became the criterion. This was evident from the manner in which Bobby played to the audience, and from the teacher's asking the class to agree that it was a draw. It was also evident from the loose manner in which the teacher evaluated the arguments, citing only that each had made a good point. It is a logical fallacy to determine the adequacy of an argument by an ''appeal to popularity.'' An argument can be evaluated for logical adequacy only by appeal to principles of logic. A clear distinction should be drawn between logical and rhetorical adequacy.

4. The teacher made the assumption that a discussion or class experience is a success if it is enthusiastic. While enthusiasm may be a desirable feature of a class experience, it is not sufficient to guarantee that the experience was a success. In particular, if the students learned the wrong things while being enthusiastic, the experience was a failure. Enthusiasm can be used as the sole judge of an experience only if the sole purpose of the experience is to create enthusiasm. If the purpose is to investigate an issue, clarify positions, and improve understanding, then enthusiasm must be seen only as a means and so not be used in the evaluation of the end product.

Performance level errors

1. The issue was not clearly delineated. For example, was the question whether such searches would be useful? Whether such searches were a violation of first amendment rights? What should be done to students caught using drugs?
2. The language used in the debate was vague and sloppy. There were missing quantifiers, and emotively loaded terms.
3. Both sides in the dialogue committed numerous logical fallacies, including straw man, false authority, post hoc, circular reasoning,

small sample, biased sample, etc. There was no recognition of this fact by the teacher, the audience, or the participants.

The two dialogues in this chapter displayed numerous examples of soft thinking. The chapters to follow will show that this is the case, and will present principles and skills that are useful in the avoidance of such logical mush.

2

The Core Language of Reasoning

Introduction: Talking about reasoning

Reasoning is not only something that we *do*, it is also something that we *talk about*, and in fact it is something that we cannot avoid talking about if we are to do it. We talk about reasoning when we are evaluating whether a point has or has not been sufficiently proven. For example, in American law the prosecution at a trial has the burden of proving guilt "beyond a reasonable doubt." At a preliminary hearing to determine whether a trial should take place the burden of proof is less; it may be summarized by phrases like "probable cause" or "preponderance of evidence." When the prosecution and the defense dispute in their closing arguments about whether the relevant burden of proof has been met, they are using the language of reasoning to talk about reasoning. In this regard reasoning is somewhat like drinking wine; sometimes we do it, sometimes we talk about doing it, and generally we talk about it as we are doing it.

Discussions in which people are reasoning together are necessarily interspersed with comments about whether conclusions are well founded ("OK, you've proved your point!"); whether they are absurd ("Accepting your point implies that evolutionary biology is a huge anti-religious conspiracy."); whether they need further investigation ("You've got an interesting point, but I'm still not convinced."); whether they are well stated ("I'm not sure that I understand your point."); and so forth. The process of reasoning and the commenting upon that reasoning, though logically distinct, in fact occur simultaneously.

25

A common language

As with wine, if we are to communicate clearly about reasoning, we will need to share a common language. If I describe a wine as "hollow," you will know that I'm referring to a lack of "middle flavor." Knowing that, you can either dispute or agree with the claim. You may find the same wine more "lean" than hollow, claiming that what it needs is more "mouth-filling flavors." If you and I don't share the language of "hollow," "middle flavor," "lean," and "mouth-filling flavors," then our communication will break down.

Not sharing this language does not mean necessarily that we do not both use these terms, but perhaps you learned them from a professional vintner, and I learned them by eavesdropping on conversations in restaurants. We will both use the terms, but in different ways, with different paradigm cases for each term. A paradigm case is an example to which a word or phrase clearly and unambiguously applies, and it is one of the ways that we attach meaning to language.

The same is true about the language of reasoning. Terms like "proof," "fact," "opinion," "objectivity," and even "reasoning" are used by everyone. Unfortunately the common sharing of such a language is not widespread, resulting in problems of communication when assessing reasoning. This lack of sharing is not merely a linguistic phenomenon. It betrays serious differences in the understanding of the nature, power, and limits of reasoning. On the most elementary points about, for example, whether proving a point means the same thing as convincing an audience, or whether value claims are "mere opinions," there are widespread and serious misunderstandings.

Compounding the problem is the fact that there is no source that we can consult that will give us the "real," "true" meanings of these terms. The dictionary is merely a report about how most people use them, and experts such as logicians and rhetoricians will disagree among themselves. There is no expert to legislate how we should talk about reasoning. So the only solution is for me to propose to you that these terms mean what is described below. In no case are these accounts far off from common usages, but they are somewhat more clear, less ambiguous, and they seek to avoid some common misconceptions about reasoning. The terms treated below form only the core of the terminology of reasoning. Other important terms will be introduced in later chapters.

The slipperiness of language

The last few paragraphs illustrate the point that was suggested in Chapter 1 about language. The English that I am using in this book is a tremendously powerful but slippery communication tool. I will not assume that what I mean by "truth," "fact," "opinion," "well-reasoned," "conclusion," "assumption," "objective," "subjective," etc., is what you mean by these terms, even though they are ordinary words that we all use in everyday contexts.

In not making this assumption I am not implying that my meanings are better than yours, only that they are likely to be different. So I don't trust the language to take care of itself, to remain a satisfactory tool for precise communication. I will assume instead that in order for me to communicate clearly to you in the following pages, I need to take a portion of this English language (the part that is used to talk about reasoning) and reconstruct it, nail it down, shrink or stretch it, define and delimit it, and hope that you will accept these modifications, at least while reading this book.

If you and I were together in a room, we would do this together. This points up the attitude of the hard thinker toward language. It won't take care of itself when precise communication is desired. The hard thinker reasons and speaks in the language, but remains aware of it as she is doing her reasoning. Language is an immensely complicated set of tools. Like the good mechanic who is constantly recalibrating instruments, the hard thinker is constantly recalibrating language.

The central concepts

Suppose that everything that any person believed to be true was always true, that the brains of human beings had infallible "truth tracking" powers that were exercised unconsciously and produced only true beliefs. Successful lying would, of course, be impossible because any attempted lie would immediately be found out. In such a world, everything that anyone said would be taken as true at face value, without question, and anything that we recognized in ourselves as a belief would be accepted automatically as true without further inquiry. For better or worse, this is not our world. In our world people often believe what is false, or state what is false even when they believe what is true. People make errors and people lie. As a result, we cannot take statements at face value. We need to require that people give us reasons to believe the claims that they want us to believe.

Claims, premises, conclusions, arguments

A *claim* is any idea, proposal, proposition, statement, or sentence that a person suggests ought to be accepted, believed, adopted, or assented to. Here are some examples of what could be claims were anyone to propose them:

1. There is intelligent life on the sun.
2. George Washington was the U.S.'s first president.
3. You should see a doctor about that rash.
4. Human life evolved through natural selection.

The sentences above are not claims in the context of this chapter since no one is asking you to believe or accept them. All but the first have been claims at some point (perhaps even the first). In order for a claim to exist, there must be someone making the claim, someone to whom the claim is made, and the idea or proposition that forms the content of the claim (that which is claimed).

The person who makes the claim is usually different from the person to whom the claim is addressed, though not always. The fact that they are most often different indicates that the making of claims is a social process, a process that goes on among people. As with any social process, there will be principles of propriety, ethics, and reasonableness that govern reasoning. For example, the social process of buying goods in a store is governed by rules such as: unless you have paid for the goods you should not harm them, remove them from the store, or take them from the hands of someone else who is examining them. So also the social process of making and justifying claims is governed by rules. You should not make claims that you don't believe, you should give evidence to support claims that others are likely to doubt, the evidence that you give should be able to be checked by others, you should not withhold from others relevant evidence just because it does not agree with your conclusions, you should try to clearly understand the positions that others assert, etc.

The use of the term "claim" rather than "proposition," "sentence," or "statement" brings out the fact that assent is being requested of and by persons, and it emphasizes the tentative nature of human knowledge. Since we do not accept claims at face value, we demand that they be supported with reasons. We demand that the person state why it would be reasonable for us to assent to the claims, or unreasonable for us to reject them.

To fulfill this demand, at least one more claim must be asserted that provides us with a reason why we should accept the original claim. We now have at least two claims, one which gives support, the *premise,* and one which receives support, the *conclusion.* In logic, this combination of premise(s) and conclusion is called an *argument.* The existence of an argument does not imply anger, acrimony, or even disagreement when the term is used in this restricted sense.

An argument is any series of two or more claims, one of which, the conclusion, is supposed or alleged to receive support for its truth from the others, the premises.

In this way of looking at it, a claim becomes a premise or a conclusion as a result of the role it plays in the person's thinking or use of language. Premises have a reason-giving (or support-providing) role and conclusions have a support-receiving role. The degree to which premises and conclusions *succeed* in their roles is a matter of logic.

How are we to know what a claim's role is, since people rarely label their premises and conclusions? The fact is that arguers do label their premises and/or their conclusion by using logical *indicator words.* Suppose that I want to convince you of the truth of the claim that Christopher Columbus did not discover America. I could argue:

There is plenty of archaeological evidence to the effect that the American continents were visited by Europeans long before the late fifteenth century. So, it's clearly false that Columbus discovered America. Another reason for this conclusion is that before any Europeans arrived, both American continents were already populated, and one cannot "discover" an already inhabited land.

In this argument the conclusion is announced by the presence of the conclusion indicator, "so." A *conclusion indicator* is a word or phrase that announces that a conclusion is about to follow. Other conclusion indicators are "thus," "therefore," "ergo," "it follows that," "we can conclude that," and more. A *premise indicator* is a term or phrase that announces that a premise is about to follow. Premise indicators include "since," "because," "from the fact that," and "another reason is."

We can think of an argument as having a logical direction from premise to conclusion, and the indicator words are the signposts of that direction. It is important to realize that this direction is logical, and not physical or temporal. Thus the conclusion of an argument may be at the end (in time or on the page), but it may just as well be at the beginning or anywhere else in the argument.

In long arguments it is not possible to rely solely on indicator words to determine logical direction, that is, to determine which claims are supposed to support which. It is often necessary in real life (as opposed to logic book examples) to guess at the arguer's intention. When one guess seems as good as another, apply the *principle of charity* and assume that what the arguer intended were the relationships between premises and conclusion that makes the argument strongest. Hard thinkers will do this since what interests them is not making some easy rhetorical point, but determining the truth. The truth is more likely to be discovered by building up strong arguments than by knocking down weak ones.

The form and content of arguments

What does it mean to say that one argument is stronger than another? Let's think first of a bridge, and what the ingredients of a strong bridge are. Suppose that the first time an eighteen wheeler attempts to cross a new bridge, the structure collapses. What is the first question that we need to answer? Nowadays the first question seems to be, who should we sue? The architect? The construction firm? Both? You could say that if the design or abstract structure of the bridge were faulty, we would sue the architect. If the materials that went into the construction were faulty, we would sue the construction firm. If both were shoddy, we would sue both. A bridge is well built, we could say, if its structure as revealed in the plans is acceptable, and if the materials that go into the structure are of good quality. Good abstract structure plus good materials will give us a good bridge.

The same is true of an argument. Arguments have abstract structures just as bridges do. Let's take some simple cases:

(1)	(2)
All animals are mortal	All living things need oxygen
All people are mortal	All growing trees need oxygen
so,	so,
All people are animals	All growing trees are living

(3)
All animals are mortal
All people are animals
so,
All people are mortal

We can reveal the logical structure of these three arguments in several different ways, depending upon the logical system and logical notation that we choose. The simplest way to do it is to remove all the nouns and adjectives, and replace them with variables. A *variable* is a symbol that can stand in for many different words, numbers, and other things. If we substitute variables for the nouns and adjectives in the first two arguments we get:

(structure 1)

All X is Y
All Z is Y
so,
All Z is X

If we do the same for the third argument, we get:

(structure 2)

All X is Y
All Z is X
so,
All Z is Y

It's simple to see that there are different structures here. In the first, the second variables in the two premises are both the same. In the second, this is not the case.

Validity and soundness

Structures are an important element of good arguments. In structure 2, if you put words in for the variables in such a way that both premises are true, then the conclusion absolutely must be true. The structure alone guarantees that a true conclusion will result from all true premises. This fact about structure 2 can be proven within the system of logic of Aristotle, as well as within modern logic. This means that the structure is valid.

An argument is valid if it has a structure that guarantees that whenever the premises are all true, the conclusion will necessarily be true.

With a valid structure, if even one premise is not true, then nothing is guaranteed about the conclusion (though, of course, the structure may still be valid). No such guarantee exists for structure 1 above. For example, below is an instance of structure 1, in which the premises are all true, but the conclusion is false.

(structure 1)

All snakes are mortal	(true)
All people are mortal	(true)
so,	
All people are snakes	(false)

To have an argument with a valid structure is like having a bridge with a perfect set of blueprints. The argument (or the bridge) can still fail if the materials used to build the argument (or the bridge) are no good. In an argument, faulty materials refers to premises that are false. Here is an argument that has a perfect structure (is valid), but has faulty materials.

(structure 2)

All people are mortal	(true)
All animals are people	(false)
so,	
All animals are mortal	· (true)

In the above argument the second premise is false, so the argument is faulty. This imperfect content does not affect the fact that the structure is still perfect. We can still say that had all the premises been true, the conclusion would necessarily have been true. You wonder why, since the conclusion "All animals are mortal" is true, should we care that the argument is faulty? The answer is that the point of the argument was to give good reasons to believe that the conclusion is true. To the degree that the premises are false, those reasons are weak.

So, an argument can fail by having a poor structure, by having false premises, or both. If an argument has a valid structure and has all true premises, then it is said to be *sound*. This is as good as an argument can get. A *deductive argument* is one that is intended to be valid. *Deductive logic* is an investigation of the successful logical structures or patterns of deductive reasoning. The deductive logical systems of Aristotle and of modern formal logic are described in chapters 9 and 10. An *inductive argument* is one that is not intended to be valid, but that is still intended to provide strong support for the conclusion. Most of the arguments that you will experience in everyday discourse are inductive arguments, though they will usually contain deductive patterns as parts or subordinate arguments. The closest that we have come to developing a formal system of inductive logic with the precision of a deductive system, is in the very restricted areas of sampling and hypothesis testing developed by statisticians.

Most important arguments are, as a whole, inductive. This is because soundness, with its ingredient of structural validity, is much too high a standard to strive for in most circumstances. In arguments of more than four or five premises, it is impractical to attempt strictly valid forms. Such *extended arguments* have the form of chains of simpler arguments. An extended argument is one that is made up of more than one simple argument. The argument above concerning Columbus is an extended argument. Here is another brief example. The parenthetical letters serve to identify the claims in the argument.

(A) In the past whenever the capital gains tax has been reduced, there has been an increase of economic activity, so (B) reducing the capital gains taxes is one way to boost the economy. Since (C) the economy is now in a slump, and since (B) reducing capital gains will boost the economy, then (D) we should now reduce the rate of the capital gains tax. Of course, some say that (E) reducing the capital gains tax is just a payoff for the rich, but they don't realize that (F) you can't make the poor richer by making the rich poorer.

In the argument above, D is the *final conclusion*. The final conclusion of an argument is the claim that receives support from one or more other claims, but gives no support in that argument to any other claims. Sentence B is an intermediate conclusion. An *intermediate conclusion* is a claim that receives support from one claim and gives support to another. Sentence B supports the final conclusion, D, and receives support from A. Sentence A is a premise or assumption of the argument.

A *premise* in an extended argument is a claim that gives support to another claim but receives no support in that argument. The structure of extended arguments is best revealed with the aid of argument tree diagrams. The construction of argument trees will be treated in detail in chapter 3.

It may seem like a defect in an argument if it contains premises in this sense—that is, assumptions that are unproven in the argument. But in fact every argument must have such assumptions. If it did not, it would be infinitely long or would go around in circles. But it is important to note that a claim like A above is an assumption only relative to this particular argument; it could be a final conclusion of some other argument. Some have argued that the premises or assumptions of an argument, since they are not supported in that argument, must be in some sense "self-supporting." This is to require that all arguments must ultimately rest upon claims that by their very nature do not need any further proof. Such claims could be said to be indubitable. This requirement, which we call the *foundationalist fallacy*, will be criticized in chapter 4.

Truth and well-reasonedness

If it is too much to ask that our arguments be sound in the strict sense defined above (that is, that they be structurally valid and that all their premises be true), we can and should demand that our arguments be well-reasoned. A *well-reasoned argument* is one that provides adequate support for its final conclusion. It is impossible to give a general and also precise definition of "adequate support," since the situations in which reasoning takes place and the types of reasoning that are appropriate to these situations are so varied.

For example, in a standard sampling study that tries to determine the degree to which some population has some characteristic, the reasoning is considered adequate if the population could be said to reflect the sample in ninety-five percent or more of the cases (within some interval of plus or minus n%). This gives a five percent chance of error, that is somewhat arbitrarily selected as the cut-off for adequate reasoning. In other situations the margin could be a good deal greater. In courts of law in the United States, prosecutors are required to meet a burden of proof summarized in the phrase, "beyond a reasonable doubt." This is a very rigorous standard, much more difficult to meet than what is necessary for a grand jury indictment.

Not only do the degrees of required support vary with circumstances, but the type of reasoning that is appropriate varies as well. Scientific approaches to reasoning, which are so powerful when dealing with the causes of phenomena revealed in statistical correlations, are irrelevant when arguing the merits of works of art. It is not that one type of reasoning is more objective or certain than the other, but rather that different situations call for different reasoning strategies. The reasoning strategies and the standards of adequate proof for various areas of research are defined by the communities that engage in that research. It is the physicists who determine for physics what are adequate reasoning strategies and burdens of proof, and similarly for the historians, anthropologists, legal scholars, etc.

Having said this, there is enough overlap among the different areas of knowledge that research communities can and should be held accountable also to outsiders. Thus if an area of research does not meet some central core standards of good reasoning, it can legitimately be criticized by outsiders. This is certainly the case with astrologers, palm readers, and the like, but may also be the case with psychoanalytic theorists, futurists, some theologians, and others. Let's set some requirements for a well-reasoned argument in general as follows.

A well-reasoned extended argument should at least (1) clearly state a final conclusion, (2) develop premises that are true and that are logically relevant to the conclusion, (3) avoid fallacies of reasoning in the simpler arguments that make up the extended argument, and (4) neutralize any serious counterarguments that may arise to the final conclusion, or to any of the important premises or intermediate conclusions.

We can define a *fact* as any claim that has been supported by an argument that is well-reasoned in this sense. An *opinion* ("mere" opinion), then, is any claim that has not been supported by a well-reasoned argument. We often hear people exclaim, "I have a right to my opinion!" If the word "opinion" means a claim that is not well-reasoned, then in many circumstances we do *not* have a right to opinions. This is because, since our important beliefs almost always affect how we act toward other people, we have a moral duty to try to reason them out. This means that we have a moral duty to avoid committing ourselves to mere opinions. Does a young father have a right to the opinion that shaking a newborn is a good way to get it to stop crying?

Perhaps when people say "I have a right to my opinion!" they just mean that I have a right to state whatever it is that I believe, as an expression of free speech. But while governments should protect speech of almost all kinds against suppression, the fact that some speech is legal does not mean that you have a *moral* right to state it. While we have the legal protection to make racist comments about groups that reflect pure ignorance about those groups, it's also true that we have a moral obligation to investigate the truth of claims that may be hurtful to others when stated.

Perhaps the claim to have the right to my opinion just means that I have the right to believe what I want or choose to believe. This is generally true, as long as I don't act upon those beliefs in ways that affect others. When I do act upon beliefs in ways that affect others, then I have a right only to those beliefs that are well-reasoned. My beliefs are not personal matters that reside somewhere inside my brain. They are commitments that I make, which provide me with rules and directives about what I should do, how I should live my life. Since I don't have the right to *live* any way that I choose, so I don't have the right to *believe* whatever I want or choose to believe. Put another way, each of us has a moral obligation to be a hard thinker, and if any of us were appointed trustee for another, the obligation would be legal as well.

It should be noted that the term "fact" is not defined in terms of what is true, but rather in terms of what is well-reasoned. The word "fact" is more slippery in its meaning than the others we are discussing, so this way of defining "fact" may seem a little unusual. It follows from this definition of "fact" that a claim can be a fact at one time and later become an opinion with the addition of serious counterarguments. With this approach to defining "facts," the claim that the earth is at rest and orbited by the sun was a fact in A.D. 1300, since there was a great deal of evidence for it and no serious evidence against it. It would be wrong to state that this claim was *true* in A.D. 1300. A claim is *true* when it adequately describes the world. The claim that the earth is orbited by the sun, when stated in A.D. 1300, did not adequately describe the world of A.D. 1300, though there was at that time every reason to think that it did.

Here is an abstract but important way of describing the difference between truth and well-reasonedness. The well-reasonedness of an argument is a relation between the supporting premises and the claim that is the conclusion, whereas the truth of a claim is a relation between the claim and what it describes in the world.

WELL-REASONED   TRUE

                    adequately   adequately
                    support   describes
PREMISES   ———>   A CLAIM   ———>   THE WORLD

Since there is often abundant evidence that a claim adequately describes the world when in fact it does not adequately describe the world, claims can be very well-reasoned but false. If well-reasonedness can some-times lead us to falsehood, why should we be concerned with it? Why not be concerned just with truth? The answer is that our brains, as pow-erful as they are, are not automatic and infallible "truth trackers." The only access that we have to truth (outside of pure luck) is through deter-mining what is well reasoned. We cannot first check to see if a claim is well-reasoned and then, through independent means having nothing to do with well-reasonedness, check to see if it is also true. The only way to check if a claim is true is to check if it is well-reasoned. *Well-rea-sonedness is our only road to truth.*

This means that we ought to believe in the truth only of those claims that are well-reasoned, especially for beliefs that affect ourselves and others. This is the mark of a hard thinker. And not only can facts be-come opinions with the addition of new information, but opinions can become facts with the addition of new information. Finally, it is not possible in this view that two contradictory beliefs could be well-rea-soned given the same body of evidence, since in that case each of the two would constitute significant counterarguments to the other.

I have avoided the term "proven" in the above discussion. The rea-son is that the word has taken on a sense of finality, as if to have "proven" something to be true means that it must remain proven for all time, and there is no longer a need to question. Few claims have this status, and to think in these terms risks fanatical closure. I would not object to the use of the term "proven" if it were taken to mean "sup-ported by a well-reasoned argument."

Hard thinking and mastered irony

I emphasized in chapter 1 that the hard thinker should have confi-dence in his or her beliefs and not shrink from being equally confident that those with opposing views are wrong. It's simply a matter of logic;

two contradictory beliefs cannot both be true. But now I have shrunk from the term "proven" when that is taken to imply finality. If I have confidence in my beliefs and in the arguments that support them, shouldn't I expect that they will remain unrefuted for all time? If I leave open the possibility that they might at some future time be disproved, doesn't this mean that I am not really confident about them? Suppose I have just voted on a jury to convict a defendant for armed robbery. If I am still open to the possibility that new evidence could prove innocence, do I lack confidence in my vote?

The answer to these questions rests with one of the most subtle and powerful capacities of our great brains, the capacity for irony. *Irony* is my ability to consciously remove myself from my own convictions (from what I believe) and from my commitments (including the feelings I have for others), to pretend in a sense that I am not me. It is irony that allows us to feel another's pain, pain that is not ours. It is irony that allows a novelist to create characters entirely different from himself or herself, and make them come alive as real people. It is irony that allows me to fairly and objectively judge a science fair in which my child is participating, even when I desperately want my child to win. It is irony that allows one to passionately believe in God, while recognizing the merits of the nonbeliever's case.

In irony I am able to "ironically withdraw" from myself to achieve a perspective that is different from *my* perspective. As a hard thinker I must cultivate the power of irony so that I can "ironically withdraw" from even my deepest convictions, and from that perspective constantly monitor the arguments that support them. If I can do this without weakening my beliefs (unless evidence requires it), then I have achieved what the philosopher Soren Kierkegaard calls "mastered irony" (Kierkegaard 1989). Mastered irony is a subtle condition of my mind. Hard thinkers can live with this subtlety; soft thinkers prefer to retreat into fanatical closure.

True for you and true for me

Since claims are either true or false, then my conviction that a claim is true requires me to believe with equal strength that opposing views are false. Some seem to believe that there is a way around this. There is a common and misleading habit on some people's part to place the word "for" after the word "true." Thus someone may say, "Well, what's true for you may not be true for me" or "What's true for the Chinese may not be true for the French." What's wrong with these expressions is that they blur a distinction that is crucial for any clear thinking about reasoning. Since the human brain is not an automatic and infallible truth tracker, there is a difference between *believing* that something is true and its *being* true. Think of the following two sentences:

A. In A.D. 1300 European astronomers believed that the sun orbited the earth.

B. In A.D. 1300 it was true that the sun orbited the earth.

Let's agree that these are different sentences. Let's agree further that sentence A is true, based upon what we know from the history of science, and that sentence B is false, based upon what we know from astronomy and physics. We can conclude then that believing that something is true does not make it true. Whether or not you *believe* a claim is a matter between you and the claim. Whether the claim is *true* is a matter between the claim and the world. How then shall we understand sentence C below?

C. In A.D. 1300 it was true for European astronomers that the sun orbited the earth.

Is sentence C stating something different from A or from B? Or is sentence C stating something that is the same as either A or B? On the surface it seems to be stating something about truth, yet it's not stating everything that B is stating. Does C just repeat what was stated in A? Or is there some middle ground between something's merely being believed and actually being true? Here's a slice of conversation.

Terry: "Did you know that in A.D. 1300 they believed that the sun orbited the earth?"

Fran: "I know, and they were dead wrong."

Terry: "Well, it was true for them."

Terry's second comment seems to add something to the first, and it seems intended to rebut Fran's comment, but it fails on both counts. The only clear meaning that "_____ is true for them" can have is as a repetition of "they believed _____." There is an appearance that Terry's second comment advanced the conversation, but it only took it back to step one. Since there is no useful purpose served by the "true for

_____'' expression, and since it creates false appearances, clarity would require that it best be avoided. The expression "true for them" is not the mark of a hard thinker.

To say that we should believe only those claims that are well-reasoned points up the fact that we have some freedom concerning which claims we come to believe. It was noted in chapter 1 that to believe a claim is to make a choice to add that claim to our belief system. In general the process is that we first entertain ideas and only later do we make the commitment to believe them, to make them part of us. Since our identities as individuals are defined in large measure by what we believe, these choices are often difficult and painful.

Although humans are not automatic "truth trackers," we do have a characteristic that makes us uncomfortable when we become aware of contradictions among our ideas. It creates cognitive dissonance, along with the urge to eliminate this dissonance. On the other hand, we also have the tendency to believe what will create in us the least anxiety or pain, regardless of the truth. There are, then, constant temptations to believe what is easiest on us, even if the painful belief is well-reasoned. This anxiety-avoidance tendency is a very strong motivating force for soft thinking, for as our thinking becomes softer it becomes less likely that we will experience cognitive dissonance. As hard thinkers we should be concerned with truth, and we should learn to detect in our feelings even the slightest twinges of cognitive dissonance.

Hard thinking and arrogance

Let's suppose that I have done significant research into the U.S. policy in Vietnam (1964–72) and conclude after considerable thought that the policy was tragically in error from the very beginning. Of course there are those who disagree with my conclusion. What does logic require that I believe about their equally strong conviction? Logic requires that I believe that their belief is false, wrong, in error. Here's another slice of conversation.

Fran: "My research shows clearly that the decision in 1964 to escalate the commitment of American forces in Vietnam was a tragic mistake, strategically, tactically, and morally."

Terry: "There are plenty who would disagree [stating the obvious]."

Fran: "I know."

Terry: "They have their beliefs, too [implying perhaps that all beliefs, regardless of the thought that went into them, are equal]."

Fran: "My view is not merely a belief; it's a conclusion from my evaluation of the evidence [drawing the distinction between beliefs regardless of support and well-reasoned beliefs]."

Terry: "But who are you to say you're so right? Do you think you're so much smarter than all the rest [implying that whether an idea should be believed or not depends upon who says it]? When did you get so arrogant?"

Logic does not require that I judge the beliefs of those with whom I disagree to be irrational, or in any way foolish. If they have drawn their conclusions as a result of reasonable inquiry, then their beliefs can be judged reasonable—although wrong.

Terry suggests that it's arrogant of me to believe that I'm right on some issue and that those who disagree are wrong. But this confuses arrogance with confidence or conviction. Arrogance is an obnoxious assertion of one's superiority. Certainly if I flaunted my rightness, taking pleasure in the ignorance of others on some issue that I happen to understand, or if I used my rightness simply to boost my self-esteem, I could justly be accused of arrogance. But the mere judgment, or even the public statement, that another is wrong on an issue could be considered arrogance only by one severely afflicted with misplaced tolerance.

To inform another of his or her errors and the reasoning that led to that conclusion is, to the hard thinker, an act of assistance. How could one be a boss, teacher, parent, coach, or friend without being willing to correct the errors of others? Finally, what are the alternatives to judging that those who disagree with my reasoned judgments are wrong? There are two. One alternative is to claim that everyone is right no matter what they believe, which is logically incoherent. The other is to never form a confident conviction that I am right, which is an impossible way to live.

Objectivity and subjectivity

It was argued above that to be deeply committed to the truth of a claim does not imply that you should not continue to evaluate arguments and evidence about it. It does not follow as well that the believer cannot be objective in the evaluation of deeply held claims. To be *objective* means to be willing to consider honestly the arguments both for and against some claim, giving the arguments on all sides the weight that they deserve. The possibility of objectivity stems from the power of mastered irony. To be objective, therefore, does not require that one's mind be blank, or that one's commitments be nonexistent. It only requires that one not be biased on the issue.

To be *biased* concerning some claim is to refuse to consider honestly one or another of the sides of the issue. In the extreme, bias involves fanatical closure. Being committed to a belief does not imply that one is biased. If on the basis of press reports I believe that a defendant in a trial is guilty, it is still possible for me to serve objectively on a jury, and to evaluate his or her guilt or innocence based only upon the evidence presented in the trial. It is possible, in other words, for me to put aside the information that I have previously learned about the case and the belief that I have formed, to focus only upon the issue of whether the prosecution has met the burden of proof.

Some have argued that nominees for the Supreme Court should not have convictions concerning the constitutionality of antiabortion laws since that would prevent such nominees from objectively evaluating the briefs on either side. Some have argued that a juror in a well-publicized trial can be objective only if the juror has no previous knowledge of the case. This produces a peculiar jury pool of people who neither read newspapers nor watch the evening news. These ideas rest upon the mistaken belief that one cannot be both committed to a viewpoint and objective at the same time. Since each of us carries around a system of belief commitments, if we could be objective only about issues on which we had no beliefs, we could never objectively revise our beliefs or change our minds. To be biased in the extreme is to employ fanatical closure.

One form of being biased is to be subjective. The word "subjective" in this context stems from a rather technical use of the word "subject." In this technical use, the "subject" in the process of a person's being conscious of something refers to the person's conscious or intentional states. My beliefs or claims are *subjective* to the degree that they express or are about my own affective states or feelings. Sometimes it is entirely appropriate to be subjective as, for example, when I express that I am sad about the coming death of a loved one. Other times, the states of my feelings interfere with judgments that are *not about* my feelings, as when I refuse to admit, despite overwhelming evidence, that my loved one is about to die. Subjectivity in this bad sense is a failure of irony, and turns me away from well-reasonedness and hard thinking. In chapter 4 it will be argued that it is false to claim that value judgments must be subjective.

The proper goals of argument

We have seen that an argument is an attempt to use one set of claims (the premises) to support the truth of some other claim (the conclusion). What is it that we should be trying to do when we argue? There are at least three things that people often try to accomplish through arguing a point.

Conquest

Some argue solely for the pleasure of *conquest by surrender*. In this case, argument is a sport, the object of which is to defeat an opponent. The opponent is defeated when he or she is reduced to silence or incoherence. The sure-fire sign that you have won the arguing game is when your opponent is reduced to one of the white flags of surrender:

> "That's your opinion!"
> "That's what you say!"
> "I still say I'm right!"
> "No matter what you say, you'll never change my mind!"
> "You have your view, I have mine."

Since people are competitive creatures and argument is a pervasive human activity, it is natural that it should become competitive, and it would be foolish to claim that this should cease. It does, however, make some sense to try to encourage people to change the criteria that they use to determine victory. To think that you should try to win an argument by getting your opponent to emit one of the surrender signals is rather like trying to win a tennis match by breaking the opponent's legs. It's true that he or she can't continue, but by the rules of good tennis you still have failed to win.

Once conquest by surrender is the main goal of the activity, it makes little difference whether what you say is true or whether your conclusions logically support the premises. Any lie, mystification, arcane jargon, deceptive definition, fallacious argument form, or intimidation tactic is an effective form of argument if it elicits surrender. But if you do take pleasure in competition and want to use the practice of argument as a playing field, then at least you should accept the rules of logic, of hard thinking, to define victory. In this case, at least the victory will be real rather than fraudulent.

Persuasion

The second reason that people argue is to convince an audience. Rhetoric, as defined by Aristotle, is the art of persuasion, and so this is the *rhetorical goal* of argumentation. Since it is a necessary human ability to be able to convince others to believe what you want them to believe, this goal of argument must not be disparaged. But we have seen already that there is an ethics involved in the practice of reasoning together. We should not try to convince others of what we know to be false. We should not try to convince others of something about which we ourselves are unsure. We should not try to implant in others a level of certainty about some claim that is greater or less than our own level.

To do any of these things is to be a liar, and the fact that politicians, advertisers, and others do these things does not make it any more acceptable. As with any human activity, arguing has its own ethics. The avoidance of bullying and intimidation is important in arguing for competition. The avoidance of lying is important in arguing for persuasion.

Truth

The ethics of arguing implies then that there is a third goal of argument that ought to take precedence over the first two. This is arguing to establish the truth of a claim, the *epistemic goal* of argument. With this goal the purpose of argument is to discover which competing claim is true, or to act together to prove the point. If you ask, "Prove a point to whom?" then you have missed the point.

In an argument, a point is either well-supported (proven) or it is not. When a player in tennis is victorious, she may be victorious *over* someone, but she is not victorious *to* someone. She is victorious, period. And so, when a claim has been proven, it may have swept aside someone else's competing claim, but it has not been proven *to someone*, it has been proven, period. To say that proving a point means proving it to someone would mean that logical success is a matter of ratings; it would be to confuse the epistemic goal with the rhetorical goal. This should not be done. Logical success is a matter of following the rules of good argumentation.

The epistemic goal of argument should take precedence over the competitive goal because reducing someone to incoherence (victory by surrender) is hollow if the rules of good argumentation are not followed, if the point has not in fact been proven. And the epistemic goal takes precedence over the rhetorical goal since the ethics of argumentation require us to have logically established a conclusion before trying to convince others of its truth. Finally, it goes without saying that arguing is most often done in the context of trying to discover which course of action will be most beneficial. In these contexts, adopting the epistemic goal is more likely to lead to successful action than either the competitive or the rhetorical goal.

Third dialogue: thinking softly about abortion

Frank is a nurse who works in the outpatient surgical ward of a large urban teaching hospital. Much of the surgery that he assists involves Medicaid-funded abortions. Yvette is a devout Catholic, single mother of two, and the charge nurse of the pediatric ward. Frank has been trying to go out with Yvette since he began working at the hospital. He has finally succeeded, but finds himself in the middle of quite an emotional argument on the issue of abortion.

Yvette: "If you worked all day with these sick kids and watched them cling to life, you wouldn't be so quick to back the termination of life."

Frank: "That's not a very convincing case. I could say the same about you seeing some of the suffering of these young girls—and I mean girls, not women—who come in needing to end their pregnancies."

Y: "Who are you to tell me what's convincing? This is the conclusion I've come to. Don't I have a right to my opinion?"

F: "I didn't say that, but the fact that you're a Catholic isn't irrelevant to this. This is the way you were brought up, so I can understand it. If I had been brought up Catholic I would probably be against abortion too. People are different. Their truths are different. We are who we are."

Y: "So what you're saying is that I don't think for myself, the Bishop made me do it. I knew from the first time you came on to me that seeing you was a bad idea."

F: "You're not hearing me. For you abortion is wrong. That's what's true for you, it's your opinion. I would never criticize that. I respect your beliefs on this because they're true for you. I just think that freedom of choice is what's most important for a woman. Especially if she has been raped or abused. I just can't see how anyone could want to force them to have a kid after all that. But I respect your view. Who am I to criticize another person's religion? People have every right to believe whatever gets them through the day. Hey, let's have another drink and forget it.''

Y: "So, I'm a Catholic because I'm too weak to get through a day of my miserable life, is that it?"

F: "Oh God . . .''

From a hard thinking perspective, just about everything is wrong with this conversation. Yvette's first point is irrelevant. What motivates a person to argue a particular point is not relevant to whether the argument is any good. "Motive mongering" is an epidemic of illogic in contemporary conversational reasoning. Her claim to have a right to her opinion is also false if it means that whatever we believe, we have a right to believe. Frank's point about Yvette's being a Catholic is irrelevant, and saying that people's "truths" are different is a confusing way of stating the obvious, which is that people disagree on issues. Frank throws around some "true for you" phrases that add nothing to the conversation. He claims to respect Yvette's views but then states that he can't understand how anyone could think that way. There is a great confusion between respecting a viewpoint vs. respecting the person who has the viewpoint. From the hard thinking perspective, to criticize a person's arguments is to serve that person's interests, to do them a favor, and is no more of a mark of disrespect than the dentist telling you that you have seven cavities.

In chapter 3 we will work on the skill of argument recognition, including the technique of tree diagrams to reveal the structures of extended arguments.

3

How to Read Arguments

Simple argument trees

One of the skills of hard thinking is ability to evaluate reasoning (that is, arguments) effectively. The first step of this process is *argument recognition*, the ability to read arguments for their structure. This means the ability to identify exactly what the main point of an argument is, as well as the structure of the premises supporting that conclusion.

Technique

One technique for representing the logical direction or structure of arguments is the argument tree diagram. It is particularly useful in the case of an extended argument in which there are intermediate conclusions, counterpremises, premises to counterpremises, and other complicating structures. The technique is quite simple. Let's think of a tree standing vertically, as it should. The final conclusion of the argument is at the bottom of the tree. The final conclusion, you will recall, is a claim in an argument that is supported by one or more other statements in the argument, and does not itself support any other claims in the argument. A simple tree could look like the diagram immediately following:

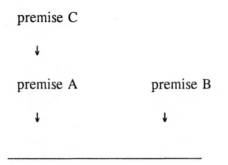

premise C

↓

premise A   premise B

↓   ↓

_____

final conclusion

Note that going *down* a level always indicates that you are going from a premise to a claim that is being supported (or from a counterpremise to a claim that is being undermined, as we will see). Premise C supports the truth of premise A, which itself supports the truth of the final conclusion. Premise B is itself unsupported, while it supports the conclusion. It must make sense to say "since . . . therefore . . ." when going down a level from a premise to what is immediately below (even though in actual conversation we often do not speak this completely). Here are some very simple examples. The indicator expressions are in *italics*.

Argument #1. *Since* Mary was good at fielding, she was a valuable asset to the team. *Another reason was* her team spirit.

(Tree #1)

Mary was a good fielder.   Mary had good team spirit.

↓   ↓

_____

So, Mary was a valuable asset to the team.

In argument 1, the final conclusion or point of the argument is the claim that Mary was a valuable asset to the team. The truth of this claim is supported by two other claims, that she was good at fielding, and that she had good team spirit. The reasoning is complicated slightly in argument 2.

Argument #2. Mary's record of only three fielding errors all season *indicates that* she was a good fielder. Her constant cheering on the sidelines *was evidence of* her team spirit, *as was* her very determined playing style. *From these two facts we can assert that* she was a valuable asset to the team.

(Tree #2)

Mary made only three errors.	Mary cheered on the sidelines.	Mary played hard.
↓	↓	↓

Mary was a good fielder.   Mary had good team spirit.

↓   ↓

_____

So, Mary was a valuable asset to the team.

In the more complicated argument 2, there are two intermediate conclusions. These are defined as claims that follow in the argument from some other claim(s), but serve also as premises to some further claims. The claims that Mary was a good fielder and that Mary had good team spirit are both intermediate claims. Each gives support to the conclusion, and each receives support from one or more premises. There are three claims that only give support, but do not receive any support. These are premises, or assumptions. They are the claims that Mary made only three errors, Mary cheered on the sidelines, and Mary played hard.

It is important to note that for the sentences that are *on the same level* in the argument tree and are supporting the same sentence, it does not matter whether they are to the left or right of each other. So in tree 2, it would make no difference if the claims "Mary cheered on the sidelines" and "Mary played hard" were to switch positions. The same is true for "Mary was a good fielder" and "Mary had team spirit," though if these were switched everything leading to them would need to be switched with them.

First exercises

A. Below are listed five distinct claims. Beneath them is a simple argument tree diagram with a conclusion written in. Select the two claims that best fit the conclusion, and fill in the uppercase letter.

1. Q. The weather yesterday was very cold.
   R. I have been to many concerts before.
   S. Bruce Springsteen is from New Jersey.
   T. I have been saving money for this concert since the summer.
   P. In the past there have been problems with drugs at these concerts.

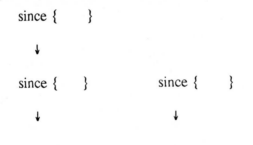

            since {   }   since {   }

                ↓   ↓

So, I should be allowed to go to the
Bruce Springsteen concert next week.

2. Q. My family lives in the United States.
   R. The United States and China are both strong military powers.
   S. The United States' capital is in Washington D.C.
   T. There is more freedom in the United States than in China.
   P. In China political speech is restricted.

        since {   }

          ↓

        since {   }   since {   }

          ↓   ↓

So, I should prefer to live in the U.S.
rather than in China.

B. Same directions as numbers 1 and 2, except that all the claims will be relevant, they will be labeled with uppercase letters, and the indicators are again in italics.

3. (A) Even people who don't smoke, but are around smokers, can get some of the bad effects of smoking. (B) *I know this because* studies have shown that children of smoking parents have more colds. (C) Another bad effect is smokey clothes, and just being around smokers gets your clothes and hair all smokey. (D) *It is also true that* teachers should set an example to their students. (E) These are the reasons for the conclusion that teachers should not smoke at school.

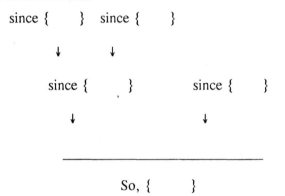

4. I believe that (A) young men and women who are eighteen should be allowed to buy beer and other alcoholic drinks. *There are two very important reasons for this. The first is that* (B) it is the only fair thing to do. *It is fair because* (C) eighteen year olds have to pay taxes. *And it is fair because* (D) eighteen year olds can join the army. *The other major reason is that* (E) it will teach the eighteen year olds to be adults. *This is true because* (F) adults won't treat you like one of them until you can drink. *It is also true because* (G) it will force eighteen year olds to use will power.

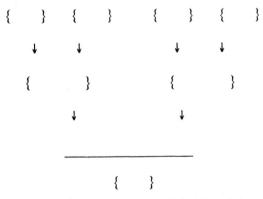

C. In the two arguments below you are to label the claims in such a way that they fit the structure of the tree below the argument.

5. (＿＿) Since the weather is beautiful and (＿＿) the people are more relaxed, (＿＿) Santa Barbara, California, is a better place to start a business than Long Island, New York. (＿＿) They say that there are on average 160 days of sunlight per year in Santa Barbara. (＿＿) It's also true that Santa Barbara provides a very good business environment, since (＿＿) the taxes are low and (＿＿) labor is not expensive. (＿＿) The average hourly rate for unskilled labor in Santa Barbara is $5.25.

{ H }

↓

{ E }   { G } { F }

↓   ↓   ↓

{ D } { B }   {   C   }

↓   ↓   ↓

_____

{ A }

6. (＿＿) Without a proper water supply communities become undesirable to live in, which is reason to believe that (＿＿) without clean, safe drinking water communities die. (＿＿) In the County of Suffolk all of the drinking water is taken from a vast underground source known as the aquifer. (＿＿) Increasing housing and industrial development on top of the aquifer will result in its becoming polluted. We know this because (＿＿) as development has increased over the aquifer, more reports of pollution have been registered. All this leads to the conclusion that (＿＿) unless we restrict development on the aquifer, Suffolk County will die. (＿＿) We have no right to allow Suffolk County to die, so (＿＿) we should begin immediately to halt the development of the aquifer region.

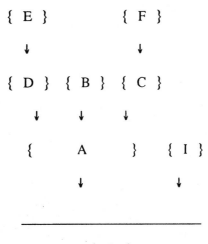

{ G }

D. Create your own trees for the arguments below. Note that when an argument begins with a question there's a good chance that the final conclusion of the argument is an answer to that question. Note also that the final conclusion of an argument is not always stated *explicitly* in the argument. You have to watch for *suppressed (that is, implicit or unstated) conclusions.*

7. The question of whether adultery is immoral is not difficult to answer. It destroys marriages that could have flourished, a fact that is known from the high rate of divorces that involve adultery. Adultery also harms the fabric of society since it seriously weakens the family structure, and everyone knows that the family structure is the foundation of our social structure. How do we know that our family structure is the foundation of society? Just look at the rate of crime and how it has increased since the family has declined.

8. People have long faced the issue of whether boys should be raised any differently than girls in important matters such as schooling and family responsibilities. There is certainly no evidence that there are biological differences between the sexes that would justify different treatment. There have been many reviews of the literature that show this. And when women have been given jobs that have traditionally gone to men they have performed splendidly, as for example in the armed services, even in combat situations. Finally, it is only a matter of justice that gender discrimination not be practiced. It is also un-American to discriminate since the *Declaration of Independence* states that all men (including women) are created equal. Why are we still even debating this issue?

Trees with counterpremises

Argument #2 above, about Mary's value as a player, can be further complicated by the addition of counterpremises. A *counterpremise* is any claim added to the argument that tends to undermine some other claim in the argument. A counterpremise may attempt to directly undermine the conclusion, or it may be aimed at a premise or an intermediate conclusion. Finally, a counterpremise may be intended to neutralize another counterpremise, and thus be a counterpremise to a counterpremise. A counterpremise is a claim that some opponent of your argument might make to undermine your argument. There are two very good reasons to include counterpremises in your arguments even though, if left unchallenged, they will weaken your case.

The first reason is to counteract your tendency toward confirmation bias. Social psychologists use the term *confirmation bias* to refer to the tendency in all of us to prefer and to pay more attention to reasoning that confirms or supports our beliefs than to reasoning that undermines them (Ross and Anderson 1982, pp. 149–51). Put simply, we like to be right, and there's nothing wrong with this. We would avoid, for example, a doctor who preferred to be wrong over being right. But our preference for being right should not lead us to avoid evidence or reasoning that tends to show that we are wrong. To practice such avoidance in the extreme is fanatical closure, something the hard thinker rejects at all cost.

One way to avoid confirmation bias is to get into the habit of including in your argument-construction the counterarguments that the opponents of your view are likely to offer. You will of course attempt to answer these counterarguments with your own reasoning (counterpremises to the opponent's potential counterpremises). If you succeed, then your position will be all the stronger. If you find that you have no satisfactory answer to your imagined opponent's counters, then it is time that you considered changing your own position to one that is more defensible. The hard thinker's interest in constructing an argument is in finding the truth, and the best method of doing that is by finding the strongest arguments.

The second reason for including counterpremises is rhetorical rather than epistemic. Rhetoric is the art of persuasion, and one of the legitimate reasons that we create arguments is to persuade others of our views. By including potential opponents' arguments in your own argument, and by answering these counters with your own reasoning, you cut off avenues of attack before the opponent can develop them. This has the rhetorical effect of keeping yourself always on the offensive in debate, and making it seem that you are in control of the issue.

Of course you have the obligation as part of the ethics of argumentation to represent the opponents' arguments as strongly and clearly as possible. To offer counterpremises that are "puff-balls," and to imply that these are your opponents' views, is to commit the fallacy of straw person, to be discussed in chapter 7. Since the hard thinker is interested in truth before persuasion, it is in her interest to create the strongest possible counterpremises to her own views.

Example

Argument #3 is an elaboration of Argument #2 with counterpremises added. The counterpremise indicators are in italics.

Argument #3. Mary's record of only three fielding errors all season indicates that she was a good fielder. *Some argue, of course, that* first base is not a difficult position to play, *but* they are people who have never played the position. Her constant cheering on the sidelines was evidence of her team spirit, as was her very determined playing style. These two things made her a valuable asset to the team.

(Tree #3)

(CP)Those who say this have
have not played the position.

↓

(CP)Some say her position
was not difficult to play.

↓

Mary made only   Mary cheered on   Mary played hard.
three errors.   the sidelines.

↓   ↓   ↓

Mary was a good fielder.   Mary had good team spirit.

↓   ↓

_____

Mary was a valuable asset to the team.

The claim that first base (Mary's position) is not a difficult position to play was meant to undermine the importance of her having only three errors in the season, thus undermining the claim that she was a good fielder. This counterpremise was then neutralized by the further claim that those who believe that first base is an easy position have never played it, and thus have no basis on which to make their judgment.

Second exercises

A. The following arguments have the claims labeled. They are followed by tree structures. Fill in the tree structures with the claim labels. Indicator words are in italics.

1. (M) Dogs are easily trainable. *It follows that* (N) they can be made to perform many useful tasks for our society. (O) Any animal that can be so useful to our society should be respected. (P) To respect animals implies that you do not kill them as a matter of mere convenience. *So* (Q) it's time

that we stopped "putting dogs to sleep." *True,* (R) the problem of strays is a difficult one to solve, *but* (S) we put a man on the moon, *so* (T) we ought to be able to solve this minor problem.

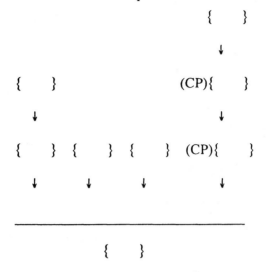

2. *It has been said that* (L) it is good for a child to raise him or her religiously, *because* (M) it gives the child a moral system to live by. *But surely* (N) we can teach morals to a child independently of any religion. Also, (O) to teach a child a religion interferes with the freedom of the child to choose his or her own religious beliefs later on *since* (P) religious education biases the child toward one particular religion. (Q) It's time that we stopped teaching our religions to our children.

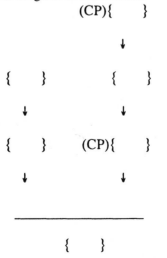

3. (H) The new tax bill will tax the middle class at lower rates. *This is a reason to think that* (G) there will be more money at the disposal of the middle class, *and so* (C) Government's programs supporting the middle class should be cut. In fact, (F) the whole idea of government programs was never intended to support any class other than the very poor. (B) One of the most costly of the middle class welfare programs is student aid. *It follows that* (A) student aid programs should be cut. *Sure,* (I) some students will have to work harder in order to graduate from college, *but* (J) there's a long tradition in America of students working their way through school. In any case, (D) if college students would settle for Ford Escorts rather than Camaros, they wouldn't need these giveaways. (E) The President has said as much.

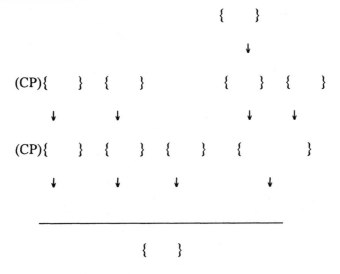

4. (A) Most of the people that I know who are married wish that they were not. *So it seems that* (B) marriage is not a step that is likely to bring lasting happiness. *It is also true that since* (C) I have not finished my degree, (D) I am not in a position to support myself, let alone another. *Yet* (E) it's true that Pat's father is rich and has (F) offered to give us enough money. And (G) it's likely that those who claim to wish that they were not married would not choose to be single if given the chance. *So* I think (H) I should marry Pat. (I) I do love Pat. *I can tell by* (J) the tingling feeling that I get whenever we're together. And after all, (K) love is the most important thing. *Sure,* (L) my mother thinks that Pat is not good enough for me, *but* (M) I have the right to make up my own mind on some things.

(CP){   }

↓

{   } {   } (CP){   } (CP){   } {   } (CP){   }

↓   ↓   ↓   ↓   ↓   ↓

{   } (CP){   }   (CP){   }   (CP){   } {   }

↓   ↓   ↓   ↓   ↓

{   }

B. The following arguments have the indicators in italics. Construct your own argument trees below each of them.

5. M is false. *This is clear from the fact that* Z is true, *which we can tell from* J being false. *Another reason that M is false is because* T is false.

6. *Because* M is true, *it follows that* F is true. *Since* F is true, then L is true. *Sure*, some people say that F can't be true because W is false, *but* W is not false since B is false. *From the fact that* L is true, *it follows that* D is false.

7. *Since* Z is Y and Q is M, *then* T is D. *Since* T is D, *then* M is L. *Some say* P is L *and so* M is not L. *But* B is not S, *so* it is false that P is L. R is W *because* M is L, and *since* R is W, *we can finally conclude* that D is H.

8. (M) In Boston you are able to get around a lot better than in New York City. (N) The public transportation is better, and (O) many things are within walking distance. *Another reason why* (P) Boston is a more livable city is that (Q) it is safer. (R) There are fewer incidents of crime, and (S) the accident rate from automobiles is less. Finally, (T) anyone who has been to both cities will agree that Boston is a more beautiful place. *Oh sure,* (U) New York has Central Park, which is a pretty place, *but* (V) it's hard to appreciate its beauty while you're being mugged.

9. (M) Soren Kierkegaard was the greatest philosopher of the nineteenth century. *This is clear from* (N) the insightfulness of his writings *and from* (O) their originality. *The latter quality is attested by* (Q) his application of the concept of "ressentiment" *and by* (R) his use of the idea of unconscious motivation long before Sigmund Freud. (S) Nietzsche has been said to be the greatest, especially *since* (T) he is so popular at present. *However,* (U) Nietzsche was neither a serious person (V) nor a disciplined thinker. And (W) to those who want to hand this mantle to Karl Marx, (X) I would only point to what has been done in his name around the world.

10. (A) The United States was built from the beginning on the principle of liberty. *That reason by itself is enough to show that* (B) government should leave smokers alone. (C) The principle of liberty states that each person has a right to determine the course of his own life, as long as he gives that right to others as well. *So* (D) government has no jurisdiction over the consenting actions of adults who are not violating another's rights. *It follows then that* (E) any attempt to ban cigarettes would be a violation of the principle of liberty. (F) I have no doubt that cigarettes are harmful to the health of the smoker. *But* (G) sky diving is harmful to the health of the diver and we would not ban that. *True,* (H) some claim to have evidence that smoking endangers the health of nonsmokers, *but* (I) the evidence so far brought forth is very flimsy at best.

C. In the following, the labels of the claims and the italics for the indicator expressions are gone. You are on your own in the construction of the trees.

> 11. Should you accept God into your life? More and more people today are testifying to the fact that a world without God is a world not worth caring about. This should convince even the most defiant atheist that a life with God is better than a life of empty, fruitless, and ultimately unsuccessful striving. Some will say that God is an illusion. Is it an illusion to be able to know where the world came from? Is it an illusion to be able to answer the question of why you or I are here at all? To believe in God is quite simply to face the facts. It is a fact that the world with all of its infinite complexity and orderliness could not have just come about by chance. It is a fact that many people, millions in fact, experience God directly in their lives, as directly as they experience their families and friends. Is your choice so difficult?

NOTE: In this argument "rhetorical questions" are used. A rhetorical question is a statement or claim that is not intended to be a question but still has the grammatical form of a question. A parent says heatedly to the child while telling it not to run into the street, "Do you want to be killed?" This is not a request for information. When you encounter a rhetorical question in an argument, you must translate it into the claim that it is. Put your tree below.

12. Should I teach my children to avoid ethnocentrism? I say no! Ethnocentrism is defined as the belief that one's own culture is superior to someone else's, or that some feature of one's own culture is superior to a similar feature of another's culture. You mean that I can't teach my child that democracy as we have it is better than the tyranny that exists all around the world? Am I supposed to pretend that having indoor plumbing with pure running water is not really better than trenches in the back yard? Isn't a society with a vibrant book publishing industry, free libraries, and freedom of expression superior in that regard to one that suppresses ideas? In other words, I am supposed to lie to my children in order to avoid ethnocentrism. I won't do it!

13. Some people say that beauty is in the eye of the beholder, because our judgments about art are subjective. For a judgment to be subjective means that it is about the person himself (his feelings, for example) rather than about the thing that is judged. This would imply that no person's artistic judgments are better than anyone else's. This seems to be a ridiculous view about art. It would imply that a child's kindergarten crayon scribblings would be as representative of great art as a Monet. But that can't be true, because who would pay ten million dollars for such scribblings?

14. No one will dispute that it is your moral obligation to vote for the candidate who represents the ideas that most closely approximate justice in the country. In the U.S. today there is starvation and degradation that is so bad that children are growing up permanently brain damaged. It is impossible to claim that a system that condones this is a just system, yet capitalism not only condones it, but necessitates it. As Karl Marx said, capitalism needs a permanent army of the unemployed. There are societies today in which vast differences in the quality of life do not exist. To name some of these—Sweden, Cuba, Denmark, and China—is to point out that every one is socialist. Of course it is true that under capitalism you are more likely to become a millionaire. But how likely in fact are you? Not very. It is also true that under capitalism you are more likely to starve to death while others prosper. Little more needs to be said as to which system is more fair. On your ballot in November, there will be only one candidate who represents the ideals of socialism. Don't let the fact that she is a representative of the American Communist Party frighten you away from doing your moral duty.

15. Many people look forward to the day when medical researchers will find a cure for Alzheimer's disease. It kills thousands of elderly every year and costs hundreds of millions of dollars in medical expenses. These are financial figures supplied by reputable university researchers. On the other hand, this disease is a relatively painless way to end one's life as I know from watching my neighbor who had it. And everyone must eventually end his or her life. If Alzheimer's disease did not exist, older people would be more likely to die of cancer, and cancer is far more painful. It used to be that the elderly died of pneumonia (the old person's friend it was called), but now antibiotics prevent this. It is simply a fact that unless we are willing to institute a system of euthanasia, which is unlikely, we as a species need some way for those of us who are elderly to die. I think therefore that the money now spent on Alzheimer's research would be better spent on diseases of the young.

16. Since the time of the New Deal, Americans have been led to believe that it is the responsibility of government to take care of the needy and the helpless in this country. When I consult the dictionary, I find that stealing is defined as the removing from another's possession of things that are justly theirs without their consent. In order to carry out this program of handouts and freebies to all the losers of the country, it is necessary to remove from the possession of the working people of America a good deal of the fruits of their labor. There is nothing that a person has more of a legitimate right to than that which derives from the fruits of his or her labor. This is a first principle of ethics and a law of the jungle. If two wolves fight for a piece of meat, it is unnatural to take it away from the victor because you think that the weaker of the two may have a pang of hunger. It follows that the welfare state that has existed since FDR has its foundation in plain and simple theft. Finally, since student aid is part of that program, student aid is theft. Sure, some will argue that student aid benefits the country, but it never benefits a nation in the long run to commit crimes of the state, no matter how pure the motive.

ı

Argument construction using trees

Tree diagrams can be used to aid in the construction of arguments, as well as in their recognition and analysis. It is often the case that we have a good idea of the position that we want to take on an issue, the final conclusion, but are blocked when it comes to constructing the argument. In this case, simply construct a tree diagram relatively arbitrarily, with your position as the final conclusion. Then proceed to "fill in the tree" with your reasoning. Don't forget to include counterpremises, for the reasons that were discussed above. You will probably find that the tree will easily fill in, and that you will then go beyond the simple tree that you began with to construct a much more complicated argument.

Third exercises

In this case you have to think up some reasons to believe the sentences directly below on the tree. You are given the major conclusion. You need to supply premises and intermediate conclusions that fit into the appropriate places on the tree. Put these claims that you create on the lines on page 69.

1.

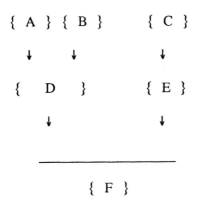

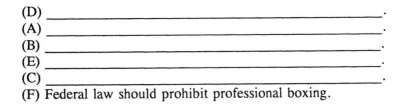

(D) _____.
(A) _____.
(B) _____.
(E) _____.
(C) _____.
(F) Federal law should prohibit professional boxing.

2.

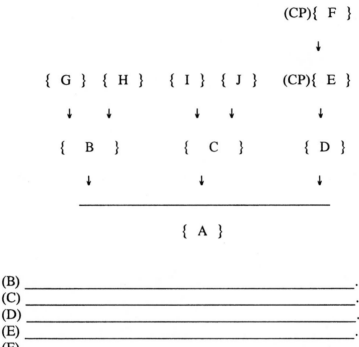

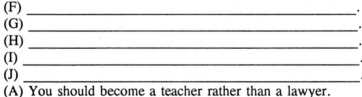

(B) _____.
(C) _____.
(D) _____.
(E) _____.
(F) _____.
(G) _____.
(H) _____.
(I) _____.
(J) _____.
(A) You should become a teacher rather than a lawyer.

Conclusion

This concludes the discussion of argument tree diagramming. It is a very simple technique that, when mastered through practice, will tremendously improve your comprehension of the extended arguments that are found in newspaper editorials, legal reasoning, business proposals, and everyday arguments. Of course, it is not thought that you will sit down with paper and pencil to diagram newspaper editorials in your everyday life. But practice with doing it formally will result in your doing it informally, "in your head," as a reading practice.

4
Myths of Privileged Sources

Childhood certainties

Early childhood, for the lucky ones at least, is a time of security and certainty. The certainty of childhood stems not from having the answers, but from the firm belief that there are answers ready at hand. We learn early in life to seek answers from others, mainly from adults, and to believe firmly in those answers. This lesson misleads us in at least two ways. The first is to make us think that answers to questions are not to be developed by our own reasoning but are to be received from authoritative sources. The second bad lesson is to believe that the truth of issues is absolute, resting upon some firm foundation, some *privileged source, that should not be questioned.*

In this chapter we explore the idea that there is one privileged source of knowledge, that this source provides the ultimate justification for all knowledge, and that if our beliefs are to be rational, then they must rest upon this privileged source. This is a bad idea, not only because there is no such source and no such basis, but also because believing that there is becomes a barrier to the use of our own reasoning powers. Believing that there is only one legitimate source of knowledge means that in the absence of that source, we don't have the ability to reason issues ourselves. The hard thinker, recall, has confidence in her own reasoning ability, and so is reluctant to hand over the job to someone else or to wait for some infallible source to appear.

Belief systems

Each of us lives our life with an understanding of what the world is like and what it would be good or bad for the world to be like. This *belief system* includes what we believe about the natural sciences, psychology, politics, geography, sports, our families, the arts, and so forth. It also includes principles and judgments about proper behavior, good art, fairness of societies, and other value issues. Our general belief system is composed of many subsystems—for examples our ideas about religion, the environment, ethics, computers, exercise, and wine. These subsystems may be very tightly or just loosely connected to each other.

One of the major differences between a philosopher and others is that the philosopher tends over a lifetime to integrate the various subsystems of belief into one very large system. For example, her political system influences her ideas on family life, and her ideas about her career are influenced by her ideas about the moral implications of world hunger, and so forth. This makes philosophers very difficult to argue with.

In addition to the beliefs that inhabit this system, there are a host of ideas that we have thought about including, but did not. As each of us proceeds through life, we leave behind a trail of discarded ideas. Some of these were at one time part of our belief system—for example, that Santa brought the holiday gifts. Some were contenders that never made it, for example, the claim of our Marxist sociology professor that American capitalism is on the verge of collapse. This collection of rejected ideas we could perhaps call our *disbelief system*, although it's unlikely that there is anything very systematic about it.

There must be some rules that each of us employs to decide which ideas to include and which ideas to exclude from our belief system. A system of belief is a huge tangle of interconnected, overlapping claims. Think of a length of rope made of hemp and spliced into a circle. There is no one strand that runs the entire length of the rope, and yet the circle is incredibly strong, and each strand is connected at many points to the circle. If we try to pry loose a strand from the circle, numerous other strands are there to hold it in.

When one belief in our circle of beliefs is called upon to buttress another or to exclude a third, it is a premise or a counterpremise. This premise or counterpremise could be a principle, something someone told us, something we read in a textbook, a report about what the majority believes, something we saw with our own eyes, something we inferred from a mass of evidence, an interpretation of intentions, or other types of claims. To become part of what we believe, a claim must be spliced into this belief system in the sense that other strands support it, and so it does not weaken or undermine areas of the circle.

As with our circle of rope, there will always be strands that are barely connected to the circle, that can be detached relatively easily, and that provide little added strength to the circle. There are other strands that are woven into the core of the rope, that would threaten the entire circle if they were removed, and that are very difficult to detach.

In our belief systems, there are central ideas that are supported by many other ideas and provide strength to the entire system. These we consider highly certain and will not give up without a complete re-arrangement of the system, a revolution in our ideas. Since the way we live and act is determined to a great degree by what we believe, this complete rearrangement would imply a radical change in how we live, and for this reason is not a frequent occurrence. There are other ideas that we believe that are on the surface of our system, that are relatively unsupported, and that we could relinquish without significant changes in how we live.

The foundational myth

There is a temptation to think of our system of belief as more like a building than like a circle of rope. The reason for this is to emphasize the point that just as a building rests upon a firm foundation, so must our beliefs. And just as there is no part of the building that supports the foundation, so our belief system must ultimately rest on a set of foundational beliefs that are not supported by any other. Since these foundational beliefs are not justified by any other beliefs, they must be self-supporting, or self-evident. These self-evident beliefs are the privileged sources of our entire system of beliefs.

To think this way is to claim that no argument has succeeded in justi-fying or supporting its conclusion unless its premises (or assumptions) are self-supporting. That is, the argument below could not prove that G is true unless A, B, and D were all self-evident, or self-supporting. The self-evident, indubitable nature of A, B, and D would then be passed down through C, E, and F to G, and so G would be justified.

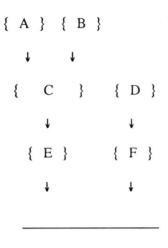

This has been a common view in the history of philosophy. In its modern incarnation it's usually associated with the philosopher Rene Descartes (1596–1654), the first of the great European rationalists, but it is equally a part of the classical empiricist philosophy of John Locke (1632–1704). What seems to motivate this search for privileged, foundational sources is a distaste for any uncertainty or ambiguity. This "quest for certainty," as it was called by the philosopher John Dewey (1859–1952), requires that these privileged claims themselves need no support, because either they are divinely inspired or, in some sense self-evident. This idea is wrong. These foundational claims are supposed to be self-evident because they are of a certain type, they represent a certain privileged source of ready-made knowledge.

Privileged texts

In ancient Mesopotamia (3000 B.C.) the written alphabet contained over 2000 characters and so was incredibly difficult to use. Only very few members of the priestly class could write or read the sacred and other texts that were developed. It is understandable in this circumstance that common people would come to believe that these temple priests possessed a kind of knowledge that was far beyond ordinary understanding. We would expect that on matters unrelated to their routine daily tasks, the common people would come to rely upon these learned priests for answers, and would believe that the sacred texts contained these answers.

While circumstances today are quite different, sacred texts still function as the foundation for the belief systems of many people. I refer particularly here to the Hebrew *Torah*, the Christian *Gospels*, and the Muslim *Koran*, while for others the works of Karl Marx, Sigmund Freud, or Joseph Smith provide the same foundation.

The point here is not to call into question the truth of any of the claims made in any of these works. There are many claims in the scriptures mentioned that have been shown to be accurate. The Hebrew presence in ancient Egypt, described in *Exodus*, is well confirmed. The Roman procedure of crucifixion mentioned in the *Gospels* is equally accurate. There are other claims about events that seem to violate nature's laws as we now understand them, and so cannot be confirmed. This is not the point. We are concerned here with whether it is reasonable to use privileged texts as the foundation of knowledge in the following sense.

> To use a privileged text as a *foundation of knowledge* is to claim that: (1) something ought to be believed merely because it is asserted to be true in a privileged text, and (2) no argument needs to be made as to why that text ought to be believed.

There are many problems with this approach to knowledge. If we confine ourselves to the three great religious texts, there are contradictions within them, between them, between varying interpretations of them, and between them and our most widely accepted sciences. Modern scriptural scholarship has identified the broad outlines of when the *Torah*, the *Gospels,* and the *Koran* were written into their present forms, the fact that they were composed as well as translated over time, and that no original compositions are known to exist.

These considerations are not presented as reasons against accepting any of these as sacred texts, only as *foundational* texts. What this means is that anyone who wishes to use scriptural citations as support for a claim—for example, concerning abortion or the miracles of Jesus or the legitimacy of polygamy—has an additional burden of showing why that particular text ought to be believed rather than some other. In addition to this there is another burden in most cases of showing that the text actually means what you claim it to mean. Does *Exodus* really state that the fleeing Hebrews crossed the Red Sea (in the south) or the Sea of Reeds (the northern Nile delta)? This is a matter of scriptural scholarship.

One may be tempted to argue that a particular scripture ought to be believed without question because it is the revealed word of God. Indeed, if any one of the scriptures does represent the ideas of the great monotheistic God, that would be good reason to use it as an authoritative source. But note that this line of reasoning is used to provide an argument in support of the reliability of scripture, and so scripture itself is not treated as a foundational source. But further, since different scriptures make similar claims about being the revealed word of God, there is still the burden of showing that this particular scripture, and not some others, is God's word.

Finally, some may argue that no reasons are needed as to why a particular scripture is true because the truth of scripture is "based upon faith." The nature of religious faith is both a subtle and a complex topic. But the use of "based upon faith" to ward off sincere and reasonable requests for support for claims concerning the credibility of a text has little to do with religious faith. None of the three religions mentioned here claim that no support can be given for the truth of their scriptures except "based upon faith." The use of this expression in this context to prevent reasonable inquiry is an example of fanatical closure. It is to say, "This is what I have chosen to believe and I'm not going to question it." This is not the mark of a hard thinker, nor is it the mark of one who has confidence in his or her own beliefs. It is a sign of fear. There is a further reason to reject this "based upon faith" maneuver when done in order to close down inquiry. It is very dangerous to allow the rejection of reason to enter public dialogue as an acceptable conversational device. Once fanatical closure becomes respectable, all manner of dangerous behaviors, terror, intimidation, and coercion will appear under its cover. Public order within a democratic framework cannot exist except in an atmosphere in which the public use of reason is respected as the most fundamental decision-making procedure.

Seeing is believing

The most common candidate for self-evidence is what we see with our own eyes, hear, smell, taste, or feel with our touch. We could refer to these as our "observations," and the claims that we make about what we see, hear, smell, taste, or touch as "observation claims." There is a tradition in philosophy as well as within common sense, to think that what we observe with our five senses is the foundation of the rest of our knowledge. The idea is that I can be confident that what I observe to be true is true, and the truth of what I do not observe must ultimately rest upon the direct truth of what I do observe. This is often presented as a hard-nosed, skeptical attitude, so it may perhaps be thought to be a characteristic of the hard thinker to claim that "seeing is believing." This cliche admits of many different meanings. Some of these are discussed below.

Believe whatever you see

I should always believe what I see (or hear, taste, smell, or touch). Observation claims are never mistaken.

Those who promote observation as the one certain form of knowledge most often do so in order to discredit claims to knowledge from some other source. This idea is perhaps behind the story of when Galileo, having just constructed the first astronomical telescope in 1609, invited the Pope's astronomers to view the newly discovered moons around Jupiter. According to the earth-centered astronomy that was accepted by the Church in Rome (and by just about everyone else), such moons literally could not exist. The astronomers from the Vatican (the Pope's enclave) declined to look through the instrument, declaring such an action a waste of time.

This story, part of the new science's propaganda barrage against the "old thought" of Aristotle and the Church, is meant to depict the clash between the open-minded acceptance of pure observation and the dogmatic reliance upon theory. The term "theory" is notoriously slippery, but for our purposes we can define *theory* as any claim that contains elements that have been *inferred* rather than *directly experienced* by one or more of the five senses. During a trial the prosecutor may ask the witness:

Prosecutor: "Did you see the defendant enter the house to kill the victim?"

Defense attorney: "Objection! Calls for an inference on the part of the witness."

Prosecutor: "I will rephrase the question. Did you see the defendant enter the house?"

Witness: "Yes, I saw the defendant enter the house."

In this case, the courts will allow the witness to report what was seen (the defendant entering the house), but it will not allow the witness to report any inferences from what was seen (that the defendant had in mind to murder the victim). Theory, in this sense, is a belief that contains inferences, conclusions, or interpretations about matters not presently being experienced. For example, the prosecutor in a case may have a theory that the husband killed his wife. This sense of theory should not imply uncertainty, as when we say "it's only a theory," since in our sense of the term we can on occasion be perfectly sure that some theory is true. In the trial, the jury will be asked to decide if the prosecutor's *theory* is true "beyond a reasonable doubt," a very high degree of certainty. Even purely theoretical claims, claims about something that has not been directly observed at all, can be very well-founded in the sense that they are supported by other claims that are themselves very well reasoned.

It should be noted that on the basis of our definitions, theoretical claims are sharply contrasted with direct experience claims, but not with observation claims. Reports of what we observe (observation claims) almost always contain theoretical elements. So there are at least the following categories.

Pure experience claims: Claims about what we are directly experiencing, which contain no inferential elements.

Mixed theoretical claims: Claims in which some part of what we are claiming has been inferred, and some part has been directly experienced.

Purely theoretical claims: Claims in which what we are claiming is beyond any possible direct experience.

Observation claims: Claims about what we are now or have in the past seen, heard, tasted, smelled, or felt.

This way of looking at it allows a spectrum among the first three types of claims.

Pure experience claims	Mixed theoretical claims	Purely theoretical claims
↓	↓	↓
No inferential elements	Some inferential elements	Only inferential elements
↓	↓	↓
"I feel pain"	"Sirhan shot Kennedy"	"Humans evolved."

Observation reports are almost always mixed theoretical claims in the sense described above. When Joe Friday in the old *Dragnet* series says to the woman witness, "Just give me the facts, Ma'am," he does not require direct experience claims. What he means is, "Don't include any inferential elements that I, as a professional in this context, would not immediately accept as true." Observation claims often fulfill this requirement, but not always.

In the case of the exchange between the prosecutor and defense attorney above, the witness's answer that he saw the defendant enter the house did in fact contain inferential elements. Suppose, for example, that the defendant had an identical twin. In that context, the defense attorney would have objected to the reformulated question since it called for the inference that the man who looked like the defendant was not the twin. The prosecutor would then be forced to reply:

> Prosecutor: "I will again rephrase the question. Did you see a person enter the house who resembled exactly the defendant?"

> Witness: "Yes, I saw a person enter the house who resembled exactly the defendant."

The inferential elements have been further reduced, but not entirely eliminated. If you use your imagination you can think of a context in which even to this response, the defense attorney would be justified in objecting that the question called for a conclusion or inference on the part of the witness.

This leads us to reject the absolute distinction between observation and theory as claims that do not vs. claims that do contain inferences. We can define observations as claims that do not contain inferences that are questionable, given the context and the prevailing requirements of reliability. Theories, in this view, are claims that, when taken alone, without their evidentiary support, contain questionable inferences. These questions can of course be resolved by further evidence, in which case the theory will be very well supported. This way of distinguishing observation and theory is consistent with our earlier claims that what counts as a "well-reasoned argument" will depend to some degree upon the level of certainty that the context demands.

The Church's astronomers had a theory that Jupiter orbited the earth and was attached to an invisible crystalline sphere that carried Jupiter along on its orbit and could not be penetrated by orbiting moons. This theory was supported by astronomical data, by successful predictions, and by the laws of motion as then understood. This general earth-centered (geocentric, Ptolemaic) astronomy was being used successfully at this time by all the great explorers to navigate the globe.

In the Galileo story, theory is depicted as a type of prejudice that should, for any objective person, have given way in the face of contrary observation. And the telescopic observation is depicted as being in conflict with this geocentric theory (which it was), free of theoretical elements (which it was not), and self-evidently accurate (which it was not).

The problem with the idea that claims about what we see provide a certain basis for knowledge, and with the supposed point of the Galileo story, is that reports of what we see are very often incorrect. I report having seen a deer print on the golf course when in fact it was a dog print. I report having seen a Buick when it was a Pontiac. The witness reports having seen a Japanese man when in fact he was Korean. The astronomer reports having tracked the orbit of the planet Mars around the Earth when in fact Mars orbits the Sun.

The claim that reports of what we see are self-evident is obviously incorrect. They are no doubt more often correct than not, but they are not candidates for self-evident foundations, since they most often need corroboration. When I say "This is a deer print," I am saying that a deer was here some time ago and that its hoof made this mark. These are things that I did not experience, but that I inferred from what I did experience, and are contained in my observation claims. When the astronomer reports tracking the orbit of Mercury around the Sun, the whole investigation is carried out on the basis of the heliocentric system, with all of its components. The claim is not, therefore, reporting "bare facts."

Some philosophers have countered the claim that observation reports contain theoretical elements with the argument that we can describe what we see in such a way that the description contains no theoretical or inferential elements. We can reduce observation claims to direct experience claims. We can do this by distinguishing claims about what *is* from claims about what *appears* to us. Rather than saying "This is a deer print," I can say, "This has the appearance of a sand colored, oval mark." By restricting my claim only to what *appears* to be rather than to what *is*, I have removed the inferential elements and increased the level of certainty. I am describing only "sense data," and so my observation claims are indubitable (cannot be reasonably doubted).

There is reason to think that even such seemingly direct appearance claims can be wrong under some very unusual circumstances, but this point need not be argued. The important fact is that even if the foundationalist has found a type of claim that is self-evident, he has not found victory. This is because there is no way of using these appearance claims as the foundation of a system of knowledge about what actually is. There is no way of inferring in a certain fashion from the way things appear, in this artificial language of sense data descriptions, to the way things really are in the actual world with all of its variety and complexity. And even if, contrary to fact, such inferences could be made, the process would be enormously too complex to be practical for human problems in human life. Here then is our conclusion:

> *If an observation claim has the level of certainty that is characteristic of direct experience claims, then it cannot be used to support systematic claims about how the world is. If the observation claim is the kind that can be used to support claims about how the world is, then it will contain theoretical elements and will not be self-evident.*

Useful observation claims need the support of other observation claims in order to be believable. They need as well to fit into the framework of some theory, without which they will simply make no sense.

Let's get back to the Galileo incident. Does it in fact depict a conflict between open-mindedness (Galileo's reliance on observation) and dogmatism (the Church's astronomers' reliance on theory)? The answer, of course, is no. The story is pure propaganda, developed at a time when the spirit of the new science of Copernicus and Galileo was still under attack.

There was no evidence that the telescope presented to the human eyes the world as it would actually be seen upon closer inspection. There was no theory of optics at this time to explain the workings of the magnifying lenses. No one had first seen the craters on the moon with the telescope, as Galileo did, and then gone to the moon to check that it was really like that. There was no explanation for how the moons could be orbiting Jupiter while Jupiter itself orbited either the earth or the sun, depending upon which system you accepted. So in the face of a working astronomy (the geocentric system of Aristotle, one that sailors were successfully using to circumnavigate the earth), how convincing should some spots on a newly created instrument be? Given the times, there was no reasonable basis to say that Galileo *observed* Jupiter's moons. Whose prejudices were greater: Galileo's whose commitment to the sun-centered system (heliocentrism) was firm but as of yet ill-reasoned, or the Church's astronomers, whose commitment to geocentrism was equally firm but better reasoned? Galileo's side later prevailed, but not because direct experience claims overwhelmed the older theories of Aristotle. Galileo's views prevailed only when observations could be incorporated into, and interpreted by, a new general theory, the one provided by Isaac Newton (1642–1727).

The conclusion is that observation claims are a very reliable basis for our knowledge, but only when they themselves have the support of other observation claims and of the theoretical framework of our belief systems. They are surely not self-supporting in the sense that the foundationalist demands.

The cliche that seeing is believing no doubt has other meanings. Perhaps what is intended is not that we should believe everything that we appear to have seen, but rather that we should not believe something unless we have seen it.

Believe only observation claims

Perhaps it's true that observations sometimes lead us astray. You could still argue that they are all we have, and so it's wrong to believe in something unless you have seen it. But this can't be right since we have not seen most of what we believe to exist. There are countries, mountains, rivers, species, people, and much more that we have not seen, but which we have good reasons to believe exist. These good reasons are descriptions in books, the words of trusted observers, pictures, movies, etc., all of which we have seen. It would be ridiculous to say that I believe in the existence of pictures of Japan (since I've seen them), but not in Japan itself (since I've never been there). And recall that most observation reports contain elements that refer to unseen events, in any case.

Perhaps then what we should say is that I should not believe in something that I could never see if I tried.

Believe only in what could be observed

We often hear someone claim not to believe in God because he has never seen God and never could see God, or perhaps that he would believe in God if he did see God. But this can't be right either, since our entire past, once it is in the past, cannot be observed in any direct way. Are we to doubt that we were once four days old, since we can't observe our four-day-old selves, and can't even remember being that young age? Rather, we argue, unless we were once four days old we could not be the age we now observe ourselves to be.

But note what has happened when we reason this way. We have appealed to unobservable events (our four-day-old selves) in order to explain the existence of observable events (our present-day selves). This is in fact the procedure that all mature thinking, including any mature science, must take. When you drop a rock on your foot, you observe the rock fall onto your foot and you observe the pain in your toes. You explain this observable event by appeal to a largely unobservable force of attraction (gravitational pull) between the rock and the planet earth (and your foot as well). Without confidence in the existence of this largely unobservable and theoretical force, we could not understand the more directly observable event that led to your sore toe.

Once again, the conclusion about observation is that it plays an important role in deciding if some claim belongs in my belief system or in my disbelief system. But observation is only one element, an element that is often wrong and often properly overruled by more theoretical considerations. Observation claims, like any others, are open to the requirement that they be supported by arguments. The arguments that support observation claims will involve both other such claims and a theoretical framework within which the claims make sense. To paraphrase the philosopher Immanuel Kant (1724–1804), observations without theories are blind, theories without observations are empty. Observation claims do not and could never provide the self-evident foundation of our knowledge. They are strands of the ''rope'' that makes up our belief system.

The myth of the truth teller

How many times have we been in a discussion or argument when someone asks, ''Who's to say what's right or wrong?'' ''Who's to say what's in a person's mind when they act as they do?'' ''Who's to say that you wouldn't have done the same?'' The effect of these apparent questions is to halt the discussion. They are not really questions, of course, since the person is not in fact asking you to give the name of someone ''who *can* say.'' The question is rhetorical. It is a claim to the effect that there is no authority, no official truth teller on this issue, and so there is no way to resolve it.

Believe only what the truth teller says

But note the underlying assumption of this claim: that issues get resolved by appeal to some official truth teller and, in the absence of the truth teller, one person's guess is as good as another's. This bad idea fits into the foundationalist's view that all beliefs must ultimately rest upon a firm foundation of indubitable claims. Here the certainty of the foundational claims comes from the official truth telling status of those who make them. The principle is:

> Believe only those claims that have been made by an official truth teller.
> Claims for which there is no official truth teller cannot be resolved with
> reason.

This idea is perhaps understandable in young people who, because of
their youth, have spent most of their lives being told "the truth" by
other, older people. And it is understandable in the ancient Mesopota-
mians who had no access to the "information" that was tightly controlled by the priestly class. Both have gotten used to the idea that the
way to know if something is true is to ask. This implies that when a
situation arises in which there seems to be no one to ask, the truth
cannot be determined. And so they throw up their hands and emit the
plaintive, "Who's to say?" Perhaps living in a society such as ours, in
which there seems to be a professional expert for every conceivable
task, is further temptation to mistrust our reason while awaiting the
expert's pronouncements. But we will soon see that the existence of
experts does not relieve us of the need to exercise our own hard-think-
ing judgments.

Well-reasoned judgments

To await the truth teller's pronouncements betrays a mistrust or lack
of confidence in one's own powers of reasoning. It also evidences a
lack of understanding of the fact that, from the standpoint of sound
reasoning, questions of who made a claim are almost always irrelevant
to the truth of the claim.

> *It does not matter who says what. What matters is whether it is possible
> to support a claim with well-reasoned arguments.*

If I claim that the widely practiced ritual of mutilating the sexual
organs of young females is morally wrong, the retort "Who are you to
judge another culture?" is irrelevant. It assumes that something ought
to be believed or rejected depending upon *who* says it. It assumes further that I am asking you to believe it on the basis of the fact that it was
I who said it. While there are very limited circumstances when expert
testimony can be used to support a conclusion, in general, the credibility of a belief should not rest upon who said it. Hard thinking demands
that beliefs rest upon the strongest available argument, regardless of
whose arguments they are. In the few instances in which expert testimony is relevant to the truth of a claim, that testimony must be supported by arguments for the relevance and legitimacy of the expertise.

It follows, then, that the expert's claims are not foundational. They need to be further justified.

Areas of expertise

If we could rest our claims only upon who said them, how would we determine which people to choose to be our truth tellers? The recognized experts most often disagree among themselves on complicated matters. In our own lives we are required to consult doctors, lawyers, investment counselors, scientists, auto mechanics, and the like. When we do, it is very important to consciously restrict the use of advice to the areas of their expertise.

In most complicated questions for which we seek expert advice, the issues to be decided go far beyond the areas of the expert's particular knowledge. An investment counselor will explain the risks of an investment (within the area of expertise) and then recommend that in your circumstance you should take the risk (outside of the area of expertise). A doctor will describe the possible consequences of leaving a kidney stone lodged in your left ureter (within expertise) and then recommend that your style of living will not be unduly disrupted by leaving it there for a couple of months (outside of expertise). A lawyer will explain the divorce laws concerning community property (within expertise) and then recommend that you forget the spouse's infidelities and accept the settlement (outside of expertise). The school psychologist will test your child for a learning disability (within expertise) and then recommend that he or she be removed from the mainstream classroom (outside of expertise).

To put ourselves blindly in their hands as if theirs is the only reasonable solution to our problem, is to ignore the fact that had we selected a different set of expert hands we would have gotten different advice. So rather than "Who's to say?" let's ask, "What reasons do you have to support that claim?" Here are two principles regarding the use of experts.

Keep experts on a very short leash, being careful to regard as particularly credible only those judgments that concern their specific area of expertise.

Never be reticent to challenge the judgment of an expert, and never trust an expert who is not willing to defend his or her conclusions.

In the case of the often-heard "Who am I to judge?" the situation is similar. Logic considers it irrelevant who is doing the judging; only the judger's reasons or arguments are relevant. There is, of course, a *moral* reluctance to judge others for things that one has himself done, but this understandable aversion to hypocrisy is irrelevant to logic. In fact, sinners are probably the best judges of who the other sinners are.

Scientism and the myth of the truth teller

A variation of the truth teller myth is scientism. This is the idea that scientists have in their possession a sure-fire method for obtaining the truth, and that any claim that has not been "proven scientifically" should not be believed.

Scientific method
Scientism would amount to the following rule:

> Believe a claim if a scientist has made it, and do not believe any claim that has not been proven by a scientist using the scientific method.

Just about everything is wrong with this rule. First of all, there is no such thing as "the scientific method." For there to be such a thing there would have to be a set of procedures that all scientists use, which are different from the procedures that nonscientists use. The fact is that very different sciences use very different procedures. Some are very mathematical (physics, decision theory), some are not (zoology, archaeology). Some are experimental (chemistry, social psychology), some are not (evolutionary biology, astronomy). Some are historical (anthropology), some are not (management science). Some are statistical (epidemiology), some are not (price theory). Some seek explanations by mechanistic causes (fluid dynamics), some seek explanations by motives (consumer demand theory), and some seek explanations by general functional analysis (anthropology).

But surely, you may argue, all scientists analyze problems, form hypotheses, collect data, reformulate the hypotheses, make predictions, discard hypotheses, and when there is almost no data remaining that works against a hypothesis, the scientist accepts it for the time being. This is more or less true, but this can't be called the scientific method because almost every other thinking person in the world, certainly the hard thinker, does the same. How else should executives decide to close a plant, fathers decide if the baby is sick enough to call the doctor, detectives investigate a murder, spouses decide whether to file for divorce, presidents decide that war is the only plausible alternative, coaches decide not to renew a player's contract, sports writers decide who will win the Superbowl, philosophers debate the fairness of capitalism, and biographers explain what made the famous person tick?

You may argue that there must be some set of characteristics that all scientists have and that no nonscientists have, otherwise we could not have the idea of "scientist," or a definition of the word "scientist". To argue this demonstrates a mistaken notion of how concepts are formed and held together. This will be discussed in chapter 6. Since there is no discernable procedure that is unique to the scientist, there is no reason to place one's faith uniquely in him or her.

It is also true that just because one person who is a scientist makes a claim, that is no reason to believe that the relevant community of scientists will back up this claim over the long run. Thus when one hears from a scientist that oat bran lowers cholesterol, or saccharin is carcinogenic, or the universe began in a big bang, or IQ tests measure intelligence, or spanking children produces aggressiveness, or nuclear power is inherently unsafe, or reducing capital gains tax rates increases tax revenues, or megadoses of vitamin C will ward off the common cold, the important question should be, "What does the relevant scientific community believe on this issue?" Should the scientific community be in general agreement, then you have about the best reason that you can get to believe it.

But you should also keep in mind that if history is any guide, the scientific community will later turn against that very claim. And further, the circumstances in which the scientific community is in general agreement are quite rare, occurring most often for simpler and uninteresting questions. The more common situation is when scientists themselves disagree, in which case you need to reason about which claim seems to you to be best supported. This often means reasoning about whose word you are more willing to believe in the debate.

Is science based on facts?

But isn't science "based on facts?" To the degree that it is true to say that science is based on facts, it is also true that detective work, legal briefs, market surveys, and the decisions of Little League coaches are based on facts.

And it is not true to say that observation claims are the indubitable, or even the final basis of scientific knowledge. If a scientific community (say of physicists) is committed to a theoretical framework (say the principle of universal gravitation (UG) as formulated by Newton), that community will not *and should not* give up that framework on the basis of conflicting observations. It is never the case that either the framework is wrong or the observation is wrong.

The way theories get tested is far more complex. Suppose we are testing the gravitational hypothesis (UG) by seeing if it can accurately predict the orbit of Mercury (which Newton's system never did). We argue:

> If UG is true,
> and
> if the masses of the Sun, Earth, and
> Mercury are as we understand them to be,
> and
> if the distances between these planets
> are as we understand them to be,
> and
> if there are no other unobserved bodies
> that are sufficiently close to Mercury to
> affect its orbit in a noticeable way,
> and
> if all of our calculations are correct,
> and
> if we have not missed anything else,
>
> _____
>
> then
> Mercury should have observed orbit X.
> But
> Mercury's orbit is different from X,
>
> _____
>
> So
> something is wrong, but what????

It would be entirely irrational at this point to throw out UG. This principle made possible the predictability of Halley's comet; predicted the existence of the previously unnoticed planet Neptune on the basis of the surprising behavior of Uranus; allowed for the logical derivation of Kepler's laws; and provided a coherent explanation for the orbits of all other known planets. Observed problems in predicting Mercury's orbit are far from sufficient as a reason to throw out a cornerstone of our system of physical principles (Putnam 1977).

The most that we can conclude is that something in this reasoning has to give. But the last thing ought to be UG, because UG is so central to our belief system. Scientific hypotheses are not tested by *comparing* them with the facts, as one would compare a photo of the dog to the dog. The relation between observation claims and the broad theoretical frameworks that make up science is very complex. The point here is that each relies upon the other for support; observation reports are not the bedrock or the foundation of science. They are strands in the rope circle.

Value judgments in science

Finally, it is often claimed that one of the sources of the particular credibility of science, of the unique ability of science to establish the truth, is that science is *value free*. To be value free is depicted as ''sticking to the facts as they are,'' rather than getting entangled in value questions that are claimed to deal with how we *feel*. This claim is mistaken in a number of ways. First, value questions are not about how we feel, but are about judgments of good, bad, better, or worse, based upon relevant criteria. In chapter 5 it will be argued that the idea that values cannot be objectively argued is false. But for now it suffices to point out that it is false to claim that science is value free. Values enter science both as an absolutely necessary element, without which there could be no science, and as an unfortunate but perhaps unavoidable element resulting from personal and political biases.

If scientists were to refuse to make value judgments about what is good, bad, better, or worse, then there could be no such thing as science. In order for there to be this human practice of science, there must be two ''languages'' spoken. The first is the language *of* the scientific theory, whether in anthropology, chemistry, social psychology, or genetics.

The second is the language *about* that theory, which is used to evaluate that theory. This second language is explicitly and necessarily a value language. The practice of science is a human activity, performed in communities, and therefore governed by necessary rules of behavior. Without this second evaluative language, without the ability to distinguish good from bad science, sloppy from elegant research design, adequate from inadequate margins of error, honest from fraudulent mistakes, sufficient from insufficient data, clearly formulated from vague theoretical constructions, interesting from uninteresting problems, and much more, science as we understand it could not take place. Yet all these are value judgments.

The fact is that no organized human practice can take place except within a set of normative rules that justify specific value judgments in individual cases. Science is such a practice, and so science rests upon such a set of normative rules. The application of these rules in practice generates a set of value judgments. It is also true that scientists are constantly refining and arguing about these rules, and arguing for value judgments about their proper application to specific cases.

Values also enter science in a less appropriate way from the fact that scientists, like other people, have personal and political agendas to which they are committed. If a psychologist is a feminist and is investigating the effect of day care upon children, there is a very strong urge to want the results to show that such care is the equivalent of maternal home care. If a physicist works for the nuclear power industry, there is a strong urge to believe that nuclear waste disposal is not an environmental threat. If a sociologist is a liberal, there is a strong urge to believe that racism accounts for the high dropout rate among minority students. If a chemist works for a drug company, there is a strong urge to ignore as trivial those few cases in the test run where serious side effects seemed to take place. If an ecologist is an environmentalist, there is a strong urge to ignore potential threshold effects and claim that any level of pesticides is polluting. If a political scientist is a conservative, there is strong urge to give credence to the poll showing Republican support, despite its broad margin of error.

What's the point here? That scientists are people too. It is usually claimed that the communal process of duplication and reduplication of results will correct for personal or political biases. But in fact whole communities of scientists, or large subcommunities within a particular science, can be equally under the sway of such commitments. The communities of sociologists and psychologists in fact tend to be politically liberal. The community of nuclear scientists tends to be pro nuclear power. The community of environmental scientists tends to be environmentalists. Economists tend to be split between conservatives and liberals. If scientists are human too, then these political commitments will be likely to affect the results of their science. The conclusion is that in one sense science should not, and could not, be value free. In another sense, we would wish that it were free of interfering biases, but it most likely is not.

None of the above statements should be read as antiscience or as a rejection of what scientists do. It has been said already that if the relevant community of scientists is agreed on a particular scientific issue, this is about the best that any person could want as a justification for her belief, short of becoming a scientist herself. The claim of the above discussion is that we cannot rely upon the scientist as an official truth teller, and thus must accept his or her results with caution and analysis.

So, beware of the claim, "Scientists have shown that . . ."; it's probably not true. What is usually true instead is that, "A scientist has some results that seem to suggest that . . .'' This is a far cry from providing an indubitable foundation for our belief systems. It is sufficient to point out that we cannot give away our own requirement to reason about issues to some official truth teller, even if he or she is a scientist.

What has been argued here about scientists applies equally to all areas of expertise, to lawyers, doctors, engineers, teachers, foreign policy experts, politicians, psychologists, and more. The hard thinker will use experts, but will refuse to "put herself into the hands" of experts.

The focus of this chapter has been to debunk the idea that the immediate goal of reasoning is to identify and rest upon some privileged source of knowledge. If there were such a source, and if we could base our claims upon it, then we could rest our brains, turn them off, and think no more. No such luck! As hard thinkers we need to reason out the issues that confront us, while at the same time allowing our ironic sense to remind us of the possibility of error in even our firmest convictions. It would be easier if there were a privileged source of information or an official truth teller who could relieve us of the need to do this. This, though, is not the nature of the world in which we live. Truth is acquired through struggle, where victories come in small pieces. Battles are won, but never the war.

Fourth dialogue: arguing about God

Henry and Jan are new-found college friends arguing for the first time about religion. Henry has never had any significant exposure to religion, whereas Jan was raised in an evangelical Christian household.

> Henry: "It just seems to me that if all this talk about God were true, then after all these years people would have come to believe it. But most people I know aren't religious at all. How can you believe in something that is, as you say, pure spirit?"
>
> Jan: "If I used your logic we could say the same for atheism, since most people are not atheists by any means. The Spirit of God is not something that I can point to like a basketball, but it's something that I feel in my spirit, and in my life."
>
> H: "Well, I'm what is known as a "doubting Thomas," if I can steal an expression from your *Bible*. Put it in front of my eyes and I'll believe it.
>
> J: "But you believe in black holes in space, you told me about them yesterday. You certainly can't see collapsed stars of immense mass billions of miles away. They're not right in front of your eyes."

H: "Yah, but that's science. That's fact. Science is based on facts, proven mathematically. That's scientific proof. With God you're dealing with opinion. The Buddhists have their God, the Muslims have their God, the Hindus have their God. Who's to say which God is real?"

J: "But who's to say what's proof and what's opinion? Maybe everything that scientists believe today will be disproven tomorrow; it's all opinion. And I have as much right to my opinion as you do. All I know is that when I needed God, God was there for me. Two years ago I was pinned under a car. I was dying. All of a sudden I saw this force around me, and I knew God wanted me to live. I pushed once more on the car and was able to move it, despite my injuries. Nothing anyone can say will convince me that God was not at my side that day. I saw God with my own eyes."

H: "The mind can work what seem to be miracles when people are threatened. You'll never convince me that all that God stuff is true; it just doesn't make any sense. Don't you see that people made up these stories about God just to have some way of explaining things they didn't understand? Now we have science, we don't need these stories any longer."

I think you'll agree that this conversation made very little headway. Go back over the argument above and note (1) the idea that a claim can't be true unless many people believe it, (2) the part played by observation in both the sides, (3) the part played by the theoretical context to provide meaning to the more specific claims, (4) the motive mongering toward the end, (5) some flirting with fanatical closure, and (6) find some successful pieces of reasoning in the dialogue.

5

Hard Thinking about Values

Introduction: The importance of hard thinking about values

One of the most serious failures of our educational system, particularly in social studies and the social sciences, is the teaching of subjectivism and relativism about value judgments. Our lives are organized around our values. It is our values that tell us what is worth pursuing and what should be avoided. Our values determine whom we should emulate and who is deserving of condemnation. Our values direct the smallest items of life, such as what wine to purchase, what films to praise, what computers to buy, and where to go on vacation. They also determine the most important commitments we are required to make, whether to get married, have children, what political party to join, which if any religion to practice, and what occupation to accept. We make hundreds of value judgments each day, mostly small and easy, sometimes momentous.

If we don't have confidence in our ability to reason about our value judgments, then one of two things will happen. Either we will be wafflers, switching back and forth between options and not knowing what we really stand for, or we will be fanatics, deciding upon our commitments and then folding our arms and refusing to discuss it any further. The hard thinker has confidence in his or her value judgments and in the reasoning that led to their adoption. Unlike the waffler, the hard thinker has convictions. Unlike the fanatic, those convictions are based upon reasoning and remain open to revision. The hard thinker has confidence not only in his or her own value commitments, but also in the general ability of reasoning to settle value disputes.

One sure feature of a soft thinker is the suggestion that in matters of values we should disconnect our brains. Value judgments, the soft thinker wants you to believe, are not proper subject matter for our reasoning power. The soft thinker has numerous strategies, all of them unsuccessful, to get you on his side. Here are some cliches from the soft thinker.

1. Values are only opinions, so it makes no sense to argue about them.

2. Since values are subjective, one person is not really in a position to challenge anyone else's values.

3. Since one person's tastes may very well be different from another's, and since people have a right to their own tastes, it is wrong to criticize the values judgments of another.

4. Since what's right and wrong will depend upon the society, who am I to claim that a practice that is widespread in some other society is wrong?

5. Since each of us gets his or her values from society, if I criticize another society's practice, then I'm just imposing my society's values onto another society.

These five cliches, and many more like them, represent a tangle of confusions. The effect of these confusions is to pass down to our children a lack of confidence concerning their value judgments—the most important judgments they will ever make.

The supposed subjectivity of values

Contrary to any of the above, the hard thinker believes that it is perfectly possible to be objective in reasoning about value claims. This can be stated as follows:

The Principle of the Objectivity of Values: *Our reasoning about value issues, if it is done with care, can be every bit as credible as the best scientific reasoning. There is simply no good reason to denigrate the ability of reasoning to come to objective and well-reasoned conclusions on issue of values.*

Let's begin by clarifying some of the major concepts in this issue. Value claims are often distinguished from factual claims. This is a central mistake that biases the issue of the objectivity of value claims right from the beginning. We have seen already in chapter 2 that the best way to define a *fact* is as a claim that is the conclusion of a well-reasoned argument. To distinguish value from fact is to assume at the beginning that value claims cannot be well-reasoned. In fact, value claims should be distinguished from empirical claims. Here are the definitions that we need:

> A value claim *is any explicit or implied claim about how it would be good, bad, better, or worse for something to be, in the past, present, or the future, based upon some criteria.*

On the basis of this definition, the following are value claims:

  a. Kindness is a more moral approach to parenting than cruelty.

  b. Michael Jordan was a better basketball player than Danny Ainge.

  c. Michael Jordan was a better baseball player than Willie Mays.

  d. The dentist: "You have six seriously decayed teeth."

  e. I decided to be an atheist rather than be immature.

  f. Joseph Stalin was a more moral person than Mother Teresa.

  g. Capitalism is more fair than socialism.

In each of the above claims there is either an explicit (a, b, c, f, g) or implied (d, e) claim about something's being good, bad, better, or worse. Some are easily supportable with well-reasoned arguments (a, b, d), and some are easily refutable with well-reasoned arguments (c, f). One remains an open question (g). So ability to prove or disprove a claim has no relevance to whether or not it is a value claim.

> An empirical claim *is any explicit or implied claim about how something is, was, or will be.*

On the basis of this definition, the following are empirical claims:

  h. Michael Jordan played basketball.

  i. All people who are not atheists are Muslims.

  j. The planets travel in elliptical orbits around the earth.

  k. The outside of the White House is painted white.

l. The universe is infinite but bounded.

m. Reducing the rate of the capital gains tax increases tax revenues.

Some of the above empirical claims are easily supportable (h, k), some are easily refutable (i, j), and two are still open questions (l, m). So, *the truth or the well-reasonedness of a claim does not affect whether it is a value claim or an empirical claim*. It should be clear that some claims are mixtures of value claims and empirical claims. For example, the value claim that Michael Jordan was a better basketball player than Danny Ainge (b) implies the empirical claim that Michael Jordan played basketball (h). In fact all but the most abstract value claims will imply some empirical claim, and thus be mixtures of the two. On the other hand, purely empirical claims are quite common, such as (h), or (i), or (j) above. The idea is that (h), (i), and (j) do not state or imply that anything is good or bad, or that anything is better or worse than anything else. If I had stated (kk) in place of (k):

kk. The outside of the White House is painted a disgusting white.

then there would be a clear implication that the color of the White House was below some standard of good or bad colors. This would be a value judgment or value claim.

Empirical claims are also called "descriptive" claims, and value claims are then termed "prescriptive." The distinction that we are discussing relies upon a recognition that how the world *is* and how it *ought to be*, or how it would be *good for it to be*, are different. There *is* tremendous hunger among people in the world; there *should not be* such hunger. Value claims (prescriptions) are about what ought to be; empirical claims (descriptions) are about what is.

What makes value issues difficult?

Most value issues are not difficult at all. Whether it is better to serve your child pure arsenic or bran flakes for breakfast is not a value issue of great complication. When value issues *are* difficult to solve, it can be for one or more of two reasons, there are unresolved empirical issues, or adequate criteria have not been established. Whether a fetus in the first trimester of pregnancy feels pain during an abortion is a difficult and unresolved empirical question that further complicates the value issue of the morality of abortion. Whether socialism or capitalism is the fairer economic system is complicated by the issue of what criteria an economic system should fulfill and what priorities these criteria should have. If great priority is placed upon the ability of a system to provide employment, this would be a boost for socialism. If emphasis is placed upon the right to control one's privately held wealth, then capitalism benefits.

The point is, however, that arguing over the appropriate criteria for an economic system is the same type of value issue as arguing over the specific systems of capitalism vs. socialism. The criteria issue is just one step more general than the specific issue of the fairness of the two economic systems. Value issues about economic systems are very complicated, involving very difficult empirical questions as well. But there is no theoretical reason to conclude that they are unresolvable. The fact that there is no generally held resolution on the capitalism vs. socialism fairness debate after about 150 years is not a reason to think that this or any other value issue is unresolvable. No one would claim that there is no possible answer to the question of the ultimate constituents of matter just because there is not yet an answer after the 2600 years since Thales initiated the search. In both cases there has been great progress, with many issues remaining to be resolved.

In general, for adequate criteria to be developed, there must be some definable human practice within which the criteria function and make sense. There is no difficulty in stating that one infant is more healthy than another because clear criteria of health exist that make sense within the practice of human living. To try to develop criteria for the cuteness of infants would be difficult in the absence of a human practice within which such judgments could serve some purpose. In the absence of appropriate criteria to make value judgments, either because we are not familiar with them or because they don't exist, we generally fall back upon our or our group's tastes (see below in this chapter).

What is subjective knowledge?

It is common to hear that value claims are subjective. What does it mean to say that some claim is *subjective*? The language of subjectivity and objectivity comes from a particular way of looking at the parts of what makes up the process of knowing something. For example, Frank knows that the World Trade Center is in New York City. When we analyze what went into that act of knowing, it breaks down into Frank or his consciousness, called "the knowing *subject*," and the World Trade Center, the *object* of Frank's knowledge. Frank's thinking about the World Trade Center is a state of Frank's consciousness which, in this language, is a state of the thinking subject. It is, therefore, called a *subjective state*, a state that the consciousness of some conscious being is in. In this case, the object of knowledge, the World Trade Center, is entirely distinct from the thinking subject. The World Trade Center (the object) is one thing and Frank's consciousness (the subject) is something else. Since Frank is thinking about an objective state (the World Trade Center), and so his claims can be tested by others besides Frank, his knowledge is called *objective*.

But Frank's consciousness, one of the powers of his great brain, has the remarkable ability to direct itself back to itself. In other words, he can think about himself, and about the states of his consciousness. He can think about his own sadness, joy, pleasure, pain, confusion, confidence, and more. When he does this the *object* of his thinking is a state of the *subject* of his thinking. When we have knowledge about our own thinking and our own feeling, then we have, in the strict sense of the term, subjective knowledge.

Subjective knowledge *is knowledge about the cognitive (thinking) or affective (feeling) states of our own consciousness.*

In this discussion we have distinguished between subjective and objective knowledge in terms of what they are *about* (subjective states vs. objective states). But this is not the whole meaning of the phrase, "subjective knowledge," as it is usually used. The second ingredient of the idea is the view that our subjective states, the states of our consciousness, are knowable only by those whose states they are, that each of us has both a privileged access and the only direct access to these states. In this view, subjective states (1) can be known with direct and absolute certainty by each of us, and (2) can be known only indirectly by others. They are private, not public. Since the fact that the World Trade Center is in New York can be known by others in the same way that it can be known by Frank, his claims about it can enter the public domain of knowledge and be confirmed or falsified by others. Claims about the World Trade Center can be challenged because (1) they could be wrong, and (2) they are as knowable by others as they are by Frank.

Some have stated that it makes no sense to challenge subjective claims since (1) beliefs about them are automatically true, and (2) no one but the person making the claim has access to that truth. In this view there is something very good and something very bad about subjective knowledge. It is good in that it cannot be wrong. If I am in a subjective state, then I know it directly and indubitably. It is bad in that I am the only one who can know it; others can only guess.

It follows that my subjective claims cannot enter the domain of public knowledge to be checked by others. Assuming my honesty, the truth of my claim that I love Terry cannot be reasoned about. That claim is subjective since my love for Terry is a state of my consciousness, and only I have access to that state. Your indirect access, based on inferences from my behavior, cannot compete with my "privileged" access. Let's complete the definition of subjective knowledge as understood by those who would claim that value judgments are subjective.

Subjective knowledge *is knowledge about the cognitive or affective states of our own consciousness and is not open to public testing or reasoning.*

A complication about subjective knowledge

The common view about subjective states as described above is not accurate. Subjective states like love are not defined by feelings alone, but by a combination of inner feeling and public context. Whether what I feel is properly characterized as "anger," "jealousy," "hatred," "disgust," or indeed as "love" will depend not only on what type of inner feeling it is, but also on the context in which that inner feeling arose. For example, fear and jealousy are different, but do they feel different? Most likely not. In fact, jealousy is a form of fear; it is the fear of being replaced by another from some position that we value. So the feeling of jealousy is composed of two elements: (1) an unpleasant sensation (2) arising in the context of the belief that we might be replaced from a valued position.

The fact that feelings are not defined only by the quality of the inner sensation has two important consequences. The first is that we can be, and often are, wrong about our feelings. We think we are in love, when we desire only sex. We think we hate someone whom we really love. We think we are disgusted by someone's behavior when we are really jealous of it. The reason that it is so easy to be wrong is that the criteria that are used to apply these judgments about love, hate, jealousy, and disgust involve a reference to the *cause* of the feelings. If we get the cause wrong, we get the feeling wrong.

The second consequence of thinking of feelings in this different way is that feelings *can* be reasoned about and can be judged to be appropriate, inappropriate, wrong, foolish, irrational, and more. Such judgments can be very well-reasoned. We often hear people say, "Who are you to judge my feelings?" As I once heard a high school teacher say, "Feelings are never right or wrong." Others will say, "I have a right to my feelings." This is a mistake.

A person cannot be jealous unless he believes that another person is threatening to replace him in some desired situation. Thus the negative feelings that a boss has for his subordinate may lead him to think that he disapproves of the subordinate's personal life, when in fact the feeling is motivated by fear of being replaced by that subordinate. In this case, jealousy is mistaken by the boss for personal disapproval. But the jealousy itself may be entirely unfounded, since the subordinate may be planning to move to another company. So the boss is mistaken about what he feels, and the feeling that he does have is unfounded.

It should not be surprising, since it is consistent with our own experience, that other people are often in a better position to know what I am feeling than I am. And further, learning about what it is that I am feeling is a perfectly fit subject for reasoning among others, and between myself and others. This is one of the reasons that people seek therapists.

Since feelings are based upon what we believe, we have a great deal of control over our feelings, and thus we have a responsibility to see that they are appropriate. We do not have a "right to our own feelings" if that means feeling hatred, jealousy, envy, or disgust for other people when those feelings are based upon false or irrational beliefs. And since feelings like jealousy are partly a consequence of our reasoning ("She could come to love him more than me"), they are not off limits to the powers of our reasoning. ("It's stupid to be jealous of him; she is a completely faithful person.")

To conclude this section: Knowledge of our own feelings is subjective knowledge, but this does not imply that it can never be wrong, nor that it is off limits to reasoning, nor that others have no contribution to make concerning the understanding of what I am feeling.

Are value judgments subjective?

We have isolated two ideas that are commonly associated with *subjective knowledge*. The first is that it is *about* the states of the knower's consciousness, and the second is that is not open to public testing and reasoning. The previous section called the second of these ideas into question. *Objective knowledge*, in this common view, is knowledge of things that are distinct from the consciousness of the knower, and therefore is open to public testing and reason. What is the meaning of the statement that value claims are subjective? It seems to be the following:

The principle of the subjectivity of values

Any value judgment is only about, or an expression of, the subjective states of the person making the judgment. As a consequence, it makes no sense either to claim that value judgments are wrong, or to try to reason about them.

Just about everything is wrong with this principle. First, let us suppose that, contrary to fact, value claims were always claims about, or expressions of, the subjective states of the claimer. It would not follow from this that it makes no sense to dispute or reason about them, since it often makes sense to reason about both the truth and the appropriateness of subjective claims. As we have already seen, our claims about what we feel are often incorrect, and even when correct, the feelings are often inappropriate. Second, why would anyone believe that value claims are really about the subjective states of the person making the claim? Some have argued as follows.

A bad argument for the subjectivity of value claims

Empirical statements talk about how the world is, was, or will be. We can observe the way the world is, was, or will be, and so we can test through observation whether the empirical statements are true. Value claims are about how the world ought to be or ought not to be. We cannot observe how the world ought to be and we cannot observe the goodness or badness of the world, so we cannot test through observation how the world ought to be. So, we cannot publicly test any value claims. So, value claims must be subjective.

This is a very bad argument. We have already seen in a previous chapter that observation plays an important but not a foundational role in testing empirical claims. Scientific claims, for example the principle of universal gravitation, are tested with the assistance of observations, but do not *reduce* to observation statements. Observations can be used to test the principle of universal gravitation only in conjunction with other theoretical claims. Even the empirical observation of the earth's rotation that occurs at dusk requires a commitment to the theoretical framework of the heliocentric astronomy. Assume a geocentric astronomy, and you are observing the movement of the sun.

Thus the fact that we cannot observe the goodness of Mother Teresa's actions in the same way that we observe her complexion is no reason to claim that we cannot observe that goodness at all. We can observe the goodness of Mother Teresa's actions in the same way that we can observe the rotation of the earth, namely, within the context of some more general framework. We establish, first, the criterion that anyone who spends the better part of her life caring for the poor and the sick is a good person. (Call this PG for "principle of goodness," and note that it does not say that this is the *only* way to be a good person.) We can then observe Mother Teresa's goodness with our own eyes. As we observe her caring actions, we are observing her goodness. Observation plays a crucial role in value claims. It makes perfectly good sense to say, in the presence of her ministering to the poor, "Look at what a good person she is, you can see it with your own eyes."

You may object that I can observe Mother Teresa's goodness only after having adopted the principle of goodness (PG) or something like it. This of course is correct, but it is equally correct that I can observe at dusk the rotation of the earth only after having accepted the heliocentric viewpoint (Hanson 1965). We have already seen that most observation claims are mixtures of direct experience and inferred elements. The inferred elements give meaning to the direct experiences and derive from some more general framework of belief commitments. The observation claim, "I saw a black Buick driving slowly up my street," makes sense only within a general framework of tacit knowledge about what a car is, that people drive them, that they drive on roads, that some roads are public, that cars are made by companies, that there are different cars made by different companies, and so on. All of this must be assumed before you can make sense of and publicly test the observation claim about the Buick. It should not be surprising, then, that before we can test the observation claim about the goodness of Mother Teresa's actions we would need to make assumptions such as PG.

You have been a subjectivist since high school days when you were forced to gobble up false subjectivist doctrines in the name of toleration. So you persist, arguing that we can prove the heliocentric hypothesis which forms the basis of observing the rotation of the earth, but we cannot prove PG. But note that you cannot argue that the reason PG is unprovable is because it is a value judgment, since that is the very issue we are discussing. You would be arguing in circles. The hard thinker points out that the question of whether PG is a good principle is the same type of question as whether Mother Teresa is a good person, except at a more abstract level.

The fact is that we have very good reasons to believe that (A) Mother Teresa is a good person, namely that (B) she devotes her life to caring for others, and (C) PG. We have good reasons to think that she devotes her life to caring for others, because (D) we have numerous reports to that effect. Do we have any arguments for accepting PG? Here is one: (E) Human beings have a right to receive the basic things that they need to survive. (F) To enhance a person's receiving of his basic rights is a good thing. Thus, (G) to care for the poor and sick is a good thing. And so (C) people who do good things consistently are good people. So our argument has the following shape:

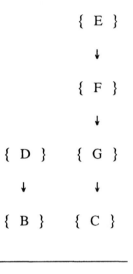

But this could go on forever, you may argue. For example, someone could doubt (E), that human beings have the right to the things necessary for their basic survival, and in that case the argument would have to continue. Since the argument could always continue, you may argue, there is no resolution, no right answer. But your reasoning assumes that no issue gets resolved unless the reasoning stops at a place where no one could think up an objection. This is the foundational fallacy that reasoning must rest on some indubitable, privileged source. Of course someone could doubt (E), but this only means that an argument must start somewhere, and the place that it starts is *not* going to be a self-evident principle. But in fact, since you mentioned it, there are good reasons to accept (E). For example, (H) it's clear that nations that have incorporated some form of (E) into their fabric are preferred as places to live over those that have not. (H) could be supported by citing (I) immigration trends, and so forth. Could the argument go on forever?

Yes. But then again, every argument, whether ethical or scientific, *could* go on forever if there is someone with nothing better to do than to sit around pretending to doubt the premises of arguments. The fact that we have not rested our claim that Mother Teresa is a good person upon some indubitable foundation cannot be a good reason to claim that it is not objective. But subjectivists are a stubborn breed; they have further objections.

Here is another wrong approach of the subjectivist.

Are value judgments matters of taste?

Value judgments concern individual tastes. Since on matters of taste there is no disputing, then there is no way to objectively dispute value judgments.

This is another idea that has absolutely nothing to recommend it. An *expression of taste* is a statement about, or an expression of, what I enjoy or do not enjoy, what pleases me or does not please me, or about the level of enjoyment that one thing provides in comparison to another. To say my value judgments are matters of taste is to say that what I find pleasing or not is what must determine my judgments of good, bad, better, or worse. In this case values would be subjective, since they would be revealing only about my pleasures and so there would be no point in rationally discussing them. We have numerous cliches to describe this: *"A chacun son gout"* (To each his tastes), *"De gustibus non disputandum est"* (On matters of taste there is no disputing), "Beauty is in the eye of the beholder," etc.

Here is why this is a bad idea. The fact that tastes are subjective does not imply that value judgments are subjective. Value judgments based solely upon tastes are in fact very rare, and the more experience a person has with reasoning, the more rare they become. The person who does not know about wines sips a glass, proclaims that he likes it, and so judges it a good wine. His value judgment that it is a good wine is based solely upon his enjoying the taste. The wine expert samples the wine and declares it a poor vintage. He justifies that judgment based upon some specific failing characteristics of the wine. The expert, while declaring the wine a bust, could very well have enjoyed his drink experience. Perhaps he had not drunk any wine for a month. Perhaps he was an alcoholic. Perhaps he was already drunk when he sampled it, and so he was enjoying everything. Perhaps he was with his lover and so the entire world seemed strangely wonderful, even this flat Bordeaux. For one who knows about wine, the fact that its taste is enjoyable on some occasion is not what determines whether it is a good or bad wine.

The same is true of the film critic. She could very well proclaim a movie to be very good despite the fact that it was torture to watch it. Perhaps it was about autism and her son was autistic. Perhaps she was bored because she had already judged four films that day. Perhaps she was tired because she had stayed up the whole night before.

Most value judgments are made on the basis of multiple criteria. The value judgment is a report concerning the degree to which the criteria are fulfilled. This is entirely separate from deciding if something was enjoyed or not. If we say that a Ford Escort is not as good a car as a Toyota Camry, we base that on how the two cars fulfill several criteria such as cost, comfort, repair records, handling, etc. It may be that on one criterion or another the Escort wins, but overall and by some scheme for putting the criteria together the Camry is better. This is also how we could show rather easily that Michael Jordan was a better basketball player than Danny Ainge (shooting percentage, points per game, steals per game, team leadership, assists, etc.).

The subjectivist could argue that although value judgments are not *immediate* expressions of taste, as when we judge a film to be great even though we did not enjoy watching it, they *ultimately* rest upon matters of taste. To claim this is to say that in every dispute about values the participants will always reach a point where there is nothing more to say, and will just fold their arms and proclaim what they enjoy. But while this sometimes happens, and generally to people with little experience on the issues, there is no reason to think that it *must* happen. So there is no reason to think that value judgments must ultimately rest upon tastes, or indeed upon anything else.

Arguments do not need to *ultimately* rest upon anything, as we found out in the discussion of foundationalism. Some very complicated value issues, like whether capitalism or socialism is more fair, just continue on. This is similar to complicated empirical issues, for example, whether reducing capital gains tax rates will increase or decrease tax revenues. Other value issues get easily settled, like whether Monet was a better painter than my four-year-old niece. Just as there is no reason to think that all value claims are just immediate expressions of tastes, so there is no reason to think that value claims lead in some ultimate way to individual tastes. But the skeptic persists, by pointing out that value issues often remain unresolved in the sense that people maintain different viewpoints even after the arguments have been presented.

Do value disagreements indicate that values are subjective?

After even the most sophisticated argument about values, some people will still not accept the argument. This is no doubt true, but it is also irrelevant. Whether a claim is well-reasoned or not does not depend upon how many people accept it. For any claim that you can think up, whether a value claim or an empirical claim, there will always be people who will not accept it. There are thousands of people in the U.S. who believe that four million Americans have been sexually abused by aliens from outer space. For any belief, no matter how outrageous, there will be people who will believe it. As a matter of fact, however, most value issues do result in near unanimous agreement. The reason that this may be surprising is that the value issues about which we hear are those that are still unresolved. Here are some principles that seem to have achieved consensus:

1. I should defend the life of my child before that of my hamster.

2. It is wrong to torture human infants purely for fun.

3. It is good to treat illness in otherwise healthy persons.

The list of value questions about which there have been generally agreed upon answers is at least as great as the list of similar agreed upon empirical answers. But the point still needs to be emphasized that numbers are not what count; arguments count.

In conclusion, most value claims are based upon logically developed criteria that have nothing to do with what the judger enjoys or does not enjoy. When values are based solely on tastes, it is due to two conditions. One is that the judger is ignorant about the issues and so does not know what criteria to use (e.g., one gymnast is judged better on the rings than another because he has a nicer haircut). The other condition is when no logical criteria exist because the value judgment does not arise within some well-defined human practice (e.g., judgments of which babies are cuter). Properly made and well-reasoned value judgments are independent of individual tastes.

The supposed relativity of value judgments

There is such suspicion about the ability of reason to decide value issues that even if the above has put to rest the bad idea of the subjectivity of values, it will not have rescued value judgments from the charge of *cultural relativity*. It was argued in the previous section that value judgments can be argued objectively, are not merely subjective, and that in most cases clear enough criteria exist to accomplish this. It was also claimed that the question of which criteria ought to be used is just another value issue that should be answered in the same fashion.

The cultural relativist attacks this latter claim, insisting instead that the only criteria available for making value judgments are the accepted beliefs of the culture. Once again we find the power of human reason called into question. In this case it is claimed that human reason is powerless to step outside of the culture of the particular reasoner, powerless to establish objective criteria that could be used to evaluate the ethical practices of different cultures.

The ethical cultural relativist would deny reason the power to show that society X (which loves and protects its infant daughters) is superior in the manner of treatment of infant girls to society Y (which accepts the practice of systematic female infanticide in one location by forcing sticks into the infant's mouth). To place such a restriction upon reasoning is preposterous and dangerous, as will be argued below. But where did such a view come from?

The colonialist routes of ethical cultural relativism

The history of European colonialism is replete with the destruction of legitimate, well-functioning cultures. These wars of destruction were at first justified religiously by claiming to bring the true God to believers in false Gods. Later during the beginnings of cultural anthropology, Darwinian frameworks were used to rank cultures on scales of civilization, with the top of the scale occupied by the Europeans.

Anthropology became a rationalization for colonialism (Wong 1991). It did not take long, however, for anthropologists to reject such a stance, adopting for their work a position of nonjudgmental (value free) investigation of cultural practices different from those of their own societies. And there is no doubt that if one is to practice cultural anthropology, attempting a profound understanding of radically different cultures, nonjudgmental investigation is a scientifically superior stance (Benedict 1934). It is also true that anthropologists were at the forefront of protecting non-Western societies from the cultural destruction that often occurs as a result of westernization. But neither the evils of colonialization nor the temporary complicity of anthropology imply that human reason is limited in the way claimed by the relativist.

What is wrong with ethical cultural relativism?

Let's return to society X (which demands love and protection of infant daughters) and society Y (which accepts the practice of killing them). The relativist would be sympathetic with my horror at society Y's practice but would make the following four points that will serve as our description of *ethical cultural relativism:* (1) that in my disapproval I am merely expressing the values of my own culture, (2) that it is literally impossible for me to find a basis in reason, rather than merely the expression of some culture's values, to condemn the practice, (3) that I should not condescend to or insult culture Y by judging, even privately, that its practice is morally wrong (the requirement of judgmental tolerance), and (4) that it would be cultural imperialism (perhaps even "cultural genocide") for me to intervene in an attempt to protect the victims of the practice (the requirement of interventionist tolerance).

The above position is certainly what is taught in public schools to try to get children to avoid the evils of ethnocentrism. It is also the position taken at present by those arguing against including "female circumcision" on the United Nations' list of human rights abuses. And one occasionally finds this position used to argue against the U.S.'s pressuring of China to expand human rights within its borders. But ethical cultural relativism is a morass of illogic and false assumptions. Below are some reasons to reject it.

1. Some have argued that because what one society *believes* to be right or wrong differs from what some other society *believes* to be right or wrong, then what *is* right or wrong in the first society is different from what *is* right or wrong in the second. But believing something does not make it so, whether on the part of the individual or of the society. If you argue that a practice is morally correct in some society just because that society believes that it is morally correct, then why should you not argue that some scientific principle is correct in that society just because the society believes it? This would mean that if there were a society that still believed that the sun orbits the earth every twenty-four hours, then in that society the sun would orbit the earth every twenty-four hours. But this is an absurdity. The relativist might deny proposing the social relativity of scientific claims, along with value claims, since scientific claims can be proven and value claims cannot. But we have already shown that there is no good reason to believe that scientific claims can be proven to any degree greater than value claims. Having established this, then any argument in favor of the relativity of value claims is also an argument in favor of the relativity of scientific claims, which is an absurdity.

2. Ethical cultural relativism is internally contradictory. It argues on the one hand that the only legitimate standards of morality are the accepted practices of each culture, and on the other hand that no one, no matter what culture she belongs to, should practice judgmental or interventionist intolerance toward another culture. It denies that there can be moral principles that apply to all cultures and then proposes two such principles, its two principles of tolerance (Williams 1972).

3. The two principles of tolerance are sometimes defended by the claim that another society's seemingly objectionable practices must be necessary for that society's survival, or to sustain one of its wider practices, and so should not be condemned. There are two things wrong with this "functionalist" argument. First, it assumes that all socially accepted practices are functionally positive, that is, contribute to a society's survival and well-being. This is surely false. No one could argue that the current U.S. system of the prolongation of elderly lives through institutionalization is culturally adaptive. This warehousing of human beings long past their ability to experience quality lives is beneficial neither to them nor to the society at large. Yet it persists and will no doubt continue for decades. Not every socially accepted practice need be socially adaptive (McElroy and Townsend 1989). And so it's very possible that some morally objectionable practices in other societies are in fact socially dysfunctional.

The second objection to this defense of the two principles of tolerance is that even if some seemingly immoral practice A is shown to be necessary to maintain the viability of some wider cultural system B, it could very well be that maintenance of B does not justify A. If one could show that the practice of slavery in the antebellum South was necessary for maintaining some way of life, does that justify slavery? If one could show that the murder of millions in the Stalinist Soviet Union was necessary to continue Soviet-style state socialism, would the murder of millions be morally approved? If one could show that the threat of physical abuse of wives by husbands was necessary to maintain traditional marriage patterns in the contemporary U.S., would such abuse be morally justified? The answer to all of these questions is, of course, no. Then if it could be shown that the liberation of women in Saudi Arabia would destroy the patriarchal and patrilineal social structures as presently existing, this fact would not imply that the continued forced subjection of women to polygamy, segregation, veiling, etc., is morally permissible.

4. It is false to assert that my value claims are always merely reflections of the values of my society(s). This would mean that I am power-

less to be in any way systematically critical of values that are accepted in my own society, which is false when applied to me and when applied to most people. In my own case as just one example, I believe that the American emphasis on the importance of the financial, as opposed to the personal, rewards of work is fundamentally mistaken, and it is a mistake that ruins lives and damages American society. It seems from the polls that the majority of Americans favor the legal right of a woman to seek an abortion, yet a very committed minority opposes this. Within the U.S. there have always been people who have challenged the appropriateness of even the most fundamental American social values, of capitalism, of the nuclear family, of materialism, of institutionalized religion, of education, of integration, of equality, etc. Can it be argued that the holders of these minority views are merely expressing the values of their society? In fact, one of the most important benefits of being educated is to enable a person to escape the parochial values that have been inculcated since early childhood, to empower a person to think his or her own thoughts. Finally, if some person happens to assert a value that is consistent with accepted principles of that person's society, that assertion does not need to be merely an expression of those principles. It could very well be the result of a process of rational deliberation. It follows then that when one person criticizes a practice of another culture, it cannot be assumed that the person is "merely imposing his own society's values onto some other society." This latter claim is another soft thinking slur on the ability of human reason to arrive at well-reasoned conclusions.

5. The idea that right and wrong are determined by each person's society assumes that each of us lives in only one society or only one culture. This is not true. A person may be an American, an Army reservist, a member of the KKK, a Southern Baptist, a Rotarian, and a cross-dressing biker all at the same time. These groups have seriously conflicting values and could themselves be thought of as distinct cultures. Thus the same action, for example an act of anti-Semitism, may be both right and wrong at the same time for that person. This is an absurd consequence of this form of relativism.

6. Ignoring the problems with specifying "culture," if it were true that what is right is whatever a culture says is right, then it would always be morally wrong by definition to oppose or violate any practice that is accepted by one's own society. With this view, the civil rights campaign of Martin Luther King, Jr., was immoral, as were any abolitionist sentiments in the antebellum South, as were any anti-Nazi actions in Hitler's Germany. Reformers would be moral criminals by definition.

This is an absurd consequence of relativism, and ironic as well since relativists often think of themselves as reformers. What we find is that ethical cultural relativism is conservative in the worst extreme. It may defend cultures from intrusion by other cultures, but it also justifies the worst abuses and cruelties that cultures are able to concoct. Anthropologist and medical student Daniel Gordon criticizes the nonjudgmental approach of his colleagues toward female circumcision stating, "... the international women's rights movement has not been far off base in considering anthropologists as perpetuating a cover-up" (Gordon 1991). This is an example of ethical cultural relativism being used to place moral crimes under the shield of noninterventionist tolerance.

Should we, then, condemn ethnocentrism, as is done so vigorously in high school social studies texts? It depends upon how it is defined. If by ethnocentrism we mean believing that some feature of my society is better than the equivalent feature of another society, then there seems to be nothing wrong with it in the abstract. It would have to depend upon whether my belief was well-reasoned. Certainly flush toilets attached to sewage treatment facilities are superior to using the river that is also the source of drinking water. And a society that treats women, children, and people of different races with respect and dignity is better than one in which women are chattel and people of different races are segregated or enslaved. If by ethnocentrism is meant the automatic assumption, without well-reasoned argument, that features of my culture are superior to corresponding features of some other culture, then of course ethnocentrism merits condemnation, as does any form of irrational parochialism. It would be difficult, however, to identify anyone holding this second form of ethnocentrism.

Let's conclude, then, that judgments about values are not subjective in any way that would reduce our ability to rationally argue about them. Let's conclude also that ethical judgments are not relative in any way that would reduce our ability to rationally argue about them. Value judgments are as open to rational debate, dialogue, and argumentation as any other type of judgment that we can make.

How to reason about values

Statements of values, evaluative claims, are judgments about good, bad, better, or worse. We make such statements after we have *graded* something. To grade something is to apply a set of criteria to it and, on the basis of those criteria, give it a rating. The rating may be in words, such as "great," "very good," "good," "fair," etc; in letters such as AAA, AA, A, BB, B, etc.; or in numbers such as, 1st, 2nd, 3rd, etc. When the rating is in numbers, then the numbers constitute a scale. In every evaluation there must be (1) a set of objects, actions, events, or properties to be evaluated; (2) a set of criteria against which they will be evaluated; and (3) a language that reports the outcome of that evaluation.

In order to clearly evaluate something, each of these three items must be clarified with the precision that is necessary given the demands of the evaluation situation. It is one thing to evaluate whether to purchase a Trek or a Fuji bicycle. It is quite another thing to evaluate which gas mask to purchase for the armed services. Given that we want to be clear about our evaluation, we should at least do the following.

Clarify the goal of the evaluation

The goal of the evaluation involves a very general description of what is to be evaluated, for what purpose, and for whose benefit. Thus, if we are evaluating bicycles, the goal would state that we wanted to purchase a bicycle for the purposes of urban commuting and occasional trail riding, that will maximize the benefit of the purchaser/owner of the bike. If we are evaluating candidates for a job, we would state that we wanted a copyeditor for a scientifically oriented publisher, who will maximize the benefit of the publisher. If we are evaluating sites for a nuclear waste disposal, we would state that we want a site for the disposal of waste from nuclear power and weapons manufacturing plants, that will maximize the benefit of the country. A well-stated goal, even though very general, should contain "excluders" that will narrow down considerably the field of options. Thus, for example, by mentioning commuting and occasional trail-riding for the bicycle, the options are limited to some variation of an all terrain bicycle.

Subdivide the goals into objectives

In this step we break down the very general goal into logically separate components. Thus, for example, the goal of the nuclear waste site selection might have as component objectives: human health safety, environmental safety, accessibility by road and rail, and lack of political opposition. These objectives should, then, be prioritized.

Find measures of the degree of satisfaction of the goals

This means to find measurable characteristics of any potential option that will determine its level of satisfaction of each objective. For example, the satisfaction of the objective of human health safety may be in terms of the distance of some site from major population areas. Environmental safety could be measured by the porousness of the earth at the site, the distance from rivers, or the distance from agricultural sites. For any objective that has more than one measure of satisfaction, these measures should be prioritized.

Determine the evaluation language

The assumption is that the criteria can be fulfilled to a greater or lesser degree. A system of reporting needs to be determined that will state the degree to which a candidate fulfills the criteria. It may be just a pass/fail system, such as adequate/inadequate. For example, if there are four criteria prioritized as 1st, 2nd, 3rd, and 4th, we could have the rule that any candidate is adequate that fulfills either the first or two of the three others; otherwise it is inadequate. Or we could have a ''very good,'' ''good,'' ''fair,'' and ''poor'' system such as that used by *Consumer Reports* to evaluate toasters. Or there could be a completely numerical system where each item being evaluated receives a numerically reported evaluation, as is done with the grade point averages in colleges, or the numbers that evaluate competitive platform divers.

Apply the evaluation system

Depending upon how clearly the evaluation system is worked out, the application step will either be routine and mechanical, or require real expertise. While it may seem odd to employ a system such as this in ethical evaluations, this is exactly what is done by human rights groups that evaluate abuses occurring worldwide. In some cases foreign aid and most favored nation trade status depends upon the outcomes of just such evaluation processes.

The creation of an evaluation system is a very complicated matter when a lot is at stake, and quite a simple matter when the issues are trivial. But the hard thinker is one who has taken the time to create such systems for the evaluations that she knows she will have to make. As a result, the hard thinker is able to provide a clear rationale for her evaluations, including her choices. Compare this to the soft thinker who has done none of this, and who is forced as a result to emit some antireason cliche about value judgments being just matters of taste.

6
Mastering Language

What is language for?

Thinking, reasoning, and communication are all carried out in language. The hard thinker will develop a heightened awareness of the nature of this tool that is used for such varied purposes. There are certain features about the nature of language that it is important to understand in order to use language clearly and effectively. These features include the nature of language signs, metamessages, and definitions; the personal and political manipulation of definitions; and the existence of emotive meaning.

Language is a vastly complex and multipurpose human capacity. Think of some of the following uses of language: poetry, singing at religious services, musical scores, drama, descriptions of what is, the making of promises, the issuing of curses, profanity, talking to oneself, obscene gestures, talking to others in private, political speeches, sermons, bicyclists' hand signals, written language, spoken language, and the various forms of signing.

Language is not always used for communication, in the sense of sending an idea from one person to another. What you say when you stub your toe is not intended to convey information. Saying ''I do'' in a marriage ceremony does not transmit an idea as much as it accomplishes a task (getting married), in much the same way as putting your signature on the dotted line effects a contract.

Even when communication is *a* purpose of some use of language, it may not be *the most important* purpose. Like sex, family gatherings, hugging, smiles, winks and having a beer, language is a tool that people use to experience closeness to others. On the other hand, like boxing, debate, outrageous clothing, hair styles, and macho posturing, language is also a way that people set themselves apart from others. When a person whose primary use of language is to establish closeness speaks with someone who is using language to accomplish separateness, both sides are likely to be frustrated. The hard thinker understands the multi-faceted nature of language (Tannen 1986).

When language is used to convey information from one person to another, it is often, though not always, important to be able to do this clearly and well. Clarity is very important in all the various forms of teaching, presenting legal arguments and writing contracts, analyzing problems at work, diplomatic messages, and analyzing personal relationships (for example, with a therapist). It is sometimes important, however, to convey information imprecisely, as for example when you inform someone of the violent death of a loved one, or when you break it gently that you are ending a relationship. Whether you want to communicate clearly or imprecisely, it is necessary to understand the following things about language.

How do words get their meanings?

Language is a system of *signs*. Signs are rather mysterious things that are not by any means completely understood. It is of the nature of a sign to point beyond itself. This pointing is called the intentional feature of signs. Thus with a sign there will exist, in addition to the sign itself, a *denotation*, that to which the sign refers (that which the sign denotes). This relationship between the sign and its denotation can be accomplished in at least three ways, and so there are at least three different sorts of signs.

Icons are signs that denote by virtue of their similarities to their denotations. Maps, photos, some road signs, and diagrams of formations in football are all icons. User-friendly computer systems that make use of pictured menus in which a picture of a file folder indicates a computer file make heavy use of iconic signs. Some ancient languages such as Egyptian hieroglyphics utilize icons.

An *index* is a sign that denotes by being an effect or a cause of its denotation. We often hear that smoke is a sign of fire, the grimace on his face was a sign of pain, footprints were a sign of the presence of the burglar. In these examples the sign is the effect and the denotation is the cause, smoke denotes fire since fire causes smoke. In other instances the sign can be the cause and the denotation can be the effect. We often say that clouds are a sign of rain, the fact that he had a gun was a sign of trouble, and increasing blood pressure was a sign that he would recover from his loss of consciousness.

The most interesting and powerful type of sign is the *symbol*. Symbols are signs that denote by means of the agreements of the users of the symbols. The word "cat" can refer to some furry little animal only because a group of language users agree that this is so. On occasion the same general group will decide to use "cat" to refer to an "earth moving vehicle," or to a young person who is "cool" (1950s) or "hot" (1990s), or to a type of sailboat in which the mast is at the prow and whose beam is half its length, or to a type of sailboat that rests upon two pontoons.

Thus the meanings that exist in a language are entirely the result of human creations. With symbols, the written words and spoken sounds are entirely conventional. The word "cat" could just as well have been "climble," and the word used to denote a young person who is "cool" or "hot" could just as well have been "scrangly." Since symbols get their meanings from social agreements, their character will depend upon the ability of those who make the agreements to keep them.

English is a democratic language

Languages such as the English in which this book is written are made up almost entirely of symbols. So the process of giving meanings to language words, or selecting a language word to express some meaning, is entirely arbitrary. For a word or expression to express some meaning is the same as the word having a use. The ability of a word or expression to carry out and maintain its use (meaning) over time will depend upon the ability of the language users to keep the agreements that defined the meaning in the first place. Groups that are loosely knit and transient will be constantly reshaping their language (for example, teenagers or financial analysts). Groups that are tightly structured and permanent will maintain a rather constant language with stable meanings (for example, doctors and chemists).

Entire societies that are more authoritarian, or less culturally democratic, than the U.S. can institute enforcers of the agreements that make language work. The French Academy was created by Cardinal Richelieu in 1635 partly to oversee the French language, to assure its purity, and to regulate its growth. The Academy is still at work protecting French from intrusions from other languages, particularly from English.

In 1994 the government panel recommended that "jumbo jet" be re-placed by "*gros-porteur*," "databank" by "*banque de donnees*," and "prime time" by "heures de grand ecoute" (times of great impact). The French support such suggestions by laws regulating public communications.

The Hebrew language began to die as an everyday spoken language with the Babylonian exile in 586 B.C. By the time of Jesus and the destruction of the second Temple, Aramaic was the spoken language of the Jews, and Hebrew was preserved as a language of religious ritual only. With the rise of Zionism and its promise of a Jewish homeland, the Hebrew language was painstakingly reconstructed into an everyday language, and it has been the official language of Israel since 1948. In both of these cases, a judgment was made that cultural integrity demanded that language be protected against unplanned change, and official bodies were created to accomplish this.

It is very important to realize that American English reflects the democratic character of American society. As a democratic language, American English has no such enforcer. In most modern languages there is no authority whose job it is to oversee the development of language. As societies go, the U.S. is extremely democratic rather than authoritarian, not only politically but socially. In addition, American society is very heterogeneous, composed of many different subgroups. Most of these groups speak English, of course, but the version of English that they speak will reflect the language agreements that the particular subgroup has, for the time being, made.

The consequence of the socially democratic nature of American society, of its cultural heterogeneity, and of its extreme dynamism is that American English is a fluid and ever-changing, democratically controlled system of meanings. To put it simply, unless you belong to some authoritarian subgroup (lawyers, priests, biologists, police officers, the military, etc.), no one has a legitimate right to tell you how to speak. There is no one in charge of the English language.

There does exist something called "standard English usage" which is defined very loosely by some generally accepted style manuals as well as by some important newspapers and journals. I am trying to write this book more or less in conformity to this usage. And not to have mastered standard English usage can be crippling for anyone with even modest ambitions. But this standard usage is still an arbitrarily agreed-upon set of meanings and grammatical structures, in this case agreed upon by people with various sorts of power.

Metamessages

The picture that has been drawn so far is that language gets its ability to refer beyond itself (in other words to describe the world) by words and phrases that have agreed-upon (standard) denotations. We would expect that when people wish to use language descriptively they would call upon these standard words and phrases. The fact is, however, that conversational practice is immensely more complicated than this. Even though each of us uses language in these more complicated ways, it is still useful to focus upon the fact that this is done.

Here is a simple example of what is being referred to. Occasionally people say what they mean by using phrases that have exactly the opposite standard denotation from what the person intended to say. You walk into a room in which there is a gourmet spread of food and say to your host, "I see you've prepared a little snack." This is *ironic* speech. When it is understood and appreciated, it is taken to mean something like (1) I recognize that the food is something special, and (2) you and I are familiar enough for me to use this form of expression. The first of these points says something about what you think about your host's preparation of the food, and the second says something about your understanding of the relationship between yourself and the host. The rules governing when it is or is not appropriate to use ironic speech are quite subtle, and it would be easy in the wrong context to have irony mistaken for sarcasm or impudence.

When we use language we have an immense variety of ways of expressing the informational message. Which of these ways we select will communicate other messages about what we understand our relationship with the other person to be, or what we believe we are doing by conveying the message. In relaying a specific piece of information, or asking a question with a specific content, we may be at the same time praising, criticizing, trying to hurt, establishing our dominance, signaling our submission, asserting our closeness, establishing distance, and much more.

For example, a wife states to her husband, "We haven't made love in a long time." The informational message of this piece of speech is clear and is called by some linguists simply "the message." But what the wife is doing by relaying this piece of information, data that she knows the husband already has, is another communication entirely. This latter communication about the status of the relationship between speaker and listener, or about what the speaker is doing by asserting the informational content of the speech, is called "the metamessage" (Tannen 1986). The metamessage of the wife's remark may be: "What's wrong?," "I want to make love," or "You have been derelict in your attentions." Since the husband is already in possession of the message, it is the metamessage that he is likely to respond to, as in, "It's not my fault!" This latter response indicates that he took the wife's statement to be a charge (the metamessage), while ignoring the message. Here is a short exchange with possible metamessages in brackets.

Fifth dialogue

Pat (Jamie's boss): "Have you not been feeling well these past few weeks?"   [Why has your work been substandard?]

Jamie: "I don't know why you'd ask *me* that."   [There are others whose work is worse.]

Pat: "There's no need to be defensive."   [Your response was not appropriate.]

Jamie: "It's not *me* who's defensive."   [You are the defensive one.]

Pat: "Perhaps you should think about taking some time off?"   [I wish you'd quit.]

Jamie: "I've really got a lot of work to do."   [Leave me alone.]

First exercises

Directions: In the following situations, distinguish between the message and the metamessage.

1. Child says to parent, "Are we having that meatloaf again tonight?"

2. On his first date with Martha, Harry describes the intimate details of his relationshp with his first wife.

3. Terry says to Fran, "Would you like to see a film tonight?"

4. Mabel says the following statement with the four emphases in italics.
   a. *He* is a good writer.
   b. He *is* a good writer.
   c. He is a *good* writer.
   d. He is a good *writer.*

5. Connie says to her mother who has just recently sold the childhood house, "Did you sell the rolltop desk too?"

6. Cynthia says to her husband Frank, "Have you been working out at the health club lately?"

7. On her first appointment with Dr. Robert Hughes, Ms. Jeannine Miller says, "But Bob, I'm not sure that I can quit smoking." Dr. Hughes replies, "Well, Mrs. Miller, they're your lungs."

8. Mary says to her son, Ricky, "Richard, I'd like to speak with you if you please."

9. Terry: "Why are *you* angry?"
Fran: "*I'm* not angry!"
Terry: "Well then why are you sitting there so quiet and rigid?"
Fran: "Why are you always criticizing me?"

10. Jack says to his younger sister, "Dad's taking *me* to the movies tonight."

The existence of metamessages should alert us to the need to be very conscious not only of exactly what the meaning contents of our words are, but also of what our listener is likely to think that we are doing, in addition, by stating these words. Will the listener conclude that we are being too familiar, being condescending, mocking, expressing impatience, flirting, suggesting romance, rejecting romance, or trying to dominate? This means that we must attend very carefully to the use of language, and to the very subtle ways that different people and different groups communicate their metamessages. We must always be alert to the tremendous complexity of the ways of communicating that language provides.

The explicit messages of language

Focusing upon the metamessages of speech, as well as upon such things as "body language" and "unconscious intentions," has its dangers. It can lead to a breakdown of communication with one party constantly speculating upon what another "really" means, while ignoring the specific message content of what someone is saying. It should be part of the ethics of communication that a person be given the benefit of the doubt that what he or she is explicitly saying is what is intended to be communicated. Let's focus now on the ability to state unambiguous content messages; that is, to speak clearly.

Because American English is so fluid, and because it is used by so many different subgroups, to speak clearly to a broad spectrum of listeners is rather like trying to do precision mechanics with rubber tools in a room with constantly changing temperature. American English is very elastic. It is at its best when there is a premium on ambiguity, as in cases of poetry, dirty jokes, advertising, and political speech. But when clarity is desired, this elasticity creates a need for definition. One of the purposes of definitions is to nail down a set of words for a specific time, audience, and purpose. After such a process, clarity is possible within this set of words, time, and audience. For this process to work, the audience or subgroup must have some sort of authoritarian structure. As examples, think of legal language, medical language, and military language.

To get some idea of what is being discussed, think of some of the uses of language for which clarity is not desired, and some for which it is desired. Think of words whose meanings have changed over time at least twice. Think of how social subgroups affect the language by creating and altering its meanings in a more or less unorganized way (e.g., teenagers, ethnic groups, computer developers). Think of some authoritarian subgroups that nail down American English words for their own uses and enforce that set of definitions through some set of rewards and punishments.

The hard thinker is acutely aware of the fact that how she uses words or phrases may be significantly different from the meanings given to them by others. The differences may be significant without being immediately noticeable. It is necessary in conversations where clarity is important to always be thinking of possible ways in which one's explicit message may be misunderstood, and of ways in which one could be misunderstanding others. When there is a suspicion of misunderstanding, then it is necessary to nail down the meanings of the key terms in the conversation.

Definitions

People often get confused and bogged down in argumentation by the process of definition. Two people, let us say, are arguing about whether Republicans or Democrats are more adept at managing the economy. In the middle of the debate one asks the other, "Well, define what you mean by 'economic progress'." This demand for definition often sidetracks the argument (occasionally what the demander is seeking) and functions as a red herring. The arguers debate irrelevant points of common usage rather than the issues at stake. When you suspect that a demand for a definition is motivated by the attempt to sidetrack the conversation, it need not be responded to, other than: ''What type of definition would you like?'' or ''Define what you mean by 'definition.' ''

When there is reason to believe that a difference in the meaning of a phrase is hampering discussion, then the demand should be respected. But what should you do now? How do you give a good definition?

How not to define terms

The chapter has emphasized the fluid nature of ordinary English. Because of this fluidity there is a certain type of definition that is almost never possible for the terms of this language, and yet is too often attempted. The definer often believes that he or she must name a set of characteristics (a) that all cases referred to by the term have, and (b) that no cases not referred to by the term have. This is sometimes called an *essential* or *real* or *genus/specific-difference* definition. It is associated with the definitional theories of that great biologist-philosopher, Aristotle. Unfortunately, while such definitions are possible in authoritarian subgroups (e.g., chemists, botanists, archaeologists), they are not possible in the democratic, uncontrolled realm of ordinary language. An attempt to provide such a definition in these contexts is doomed to failure. Even Aristotle's famous example:

''Human being means animal (genus) that is rational (difference).''

fails to capture ordinary speech. Are all humans rational? Are only humans rational? To avoid such failure it is necessary to master the art of definition.

Types of definitions classified by purpose

There are at least three distinct purposes served by definitions. We could think of these as types of definitions, *stipulative*, *reportive*, and *explicative*.

Creating new meanings through stipulative definitions

Some definitions create entirely new meanings, by redefining old words and by making up new words, or they refer to an old meaning by using a new word or by using an old word in a new way. These are stipulative definitions. *Stipulative definitions* do any of the following four things:

a. Use a new word or phrase to refer to a new phenomenon.

b. Use an old word in a new way to refer to a new phenomenon.

c. Use a new word to refer to an old phenomenon.

d. Use an old word in a new way to refer to an old phenomenon.

While anyone is free to create new meanings, stipulative definitions are generally accepted into the language only when there is a situation that creates a need for them and conveys a kind of language-making authority on the person wanting to create a new meaning or a new word. The reasons include the discovery of new things, the creation of new ideas, the creation of meanings for the purposes of social coherence, or the altering of language for the purposes of obfuscation, or its opposite, clarity.

At some point the terms "RAM" and "ROM" were introduced to refer to different types of computer "memory." This introduction was a stipulative definition. At some point Sigmund Freud introduced the term "id," the Latin for "it," to refer to the source of human motivation or drive. That was a stipulative definition. At some point the term "black hole" was introduced to refer to a star in the final phases of gravitational collapse. This introduction of the term "black hole" was a stipulative definition. Finally, at some point the term "fork ball" was introduced to refer to a particular type of pitch in baseball. This too was a stipulative definition.

Describing meaning through reportive definitions

Some definitions seek only to report on the existing meanings or uses of words. These are called *reportive definitions*. They are the definitions that you find in American dictionaries. It is important to note that these are merely descriptions of how particular words or phrases are used at the present time. When an American dictionary defines "terminal" as a characteristic of diseases (indicating that they will result inevitably in death) or of academic degrees (indicating that they are the highest degrees expected in their fields), as a workstation in a network of computers, or as a place where passengers can board and depart mass transportation, these are all reportive definitions. Since American English changes so rapidly, dictionaries are often seriously out of date.

Checking the dictionary

People often waste time arguing about what a word's "true" meaning is. This often occurs when they are trying to be precise with an imprecise language, or to make an interesting or controversial point.

> Terry: "I think of pride as the happiness that a person naturally gets when he or she has accomplished something great, like when I was so proud of my last performance report."
>
> Fran: "That was certainly a boost to your sagging ego. You were in the clouds for weeks."
>
> Terry: "Why, then, do we think it's alright for parents to be proud when their children do something great? Aren't they trying to grab credit for themselves?"
>
> Fran: "Why can't you be proud of your own children? That's ridiculous!"
>
> Terry: "As you said, pride is an ego boost. We should only boost our egos on the basis of our own achievements. Anything else is false pride. My pride should only come from my accomplishments."
>
> Fran: "Let's see what the dictionary says that pride is."

In this conversation the dictionary will not help. The claim that Terry is making is that parents should not try to increase their own self-esteem by means of their children's accomplishments. The English word "pride" ("proud") is used ambiguously. In some contexts, it means "conceit" and is negative. In some contexts it means reasonable self-esteem and is not negative. In some contexts it simply means "having admiration for," as when the mayor says to the city's championship team, "We're all very proud of you."

A parent sometimes says to the child, "I'm proud of you," in the sense of simply having admiration. Other times a parents brags about the child, expressing the pride that builds up the parent's own ego. The validity of Terry's objection to this latter practice cannot be decided by the dictionary. It must be decided by well-reasoned argument. What Terry and Fran should do, if they want to continue the discussion, is to agree on some definitions and then get started. Since English does not grow by central planning, they would not be breaking any rules.

Manipulating language for improved communication

If Terry and Fran were to take my suggestion, they could agree to define "pride" as "a person's pleasant feeling of self-esteem, reasonably deriving from his or her achievement(s).'' This would allow them to define ''false pride'' as ''a person's pleasant feeling of self-esteem, unreasonably deriving from someone's achievements (his own or others).'' This would allow them to discuss clearly the question of whether parental pride is false or not. It would not be false pride if it could be shown that some of the responsibility (credit) for a person's achievements belonged to that person's parent(s).

Improving meanings through explicative definitions

Some definitions seek to shave, alter, or slightly change the meanings of terms so that they more effectively carry out one of their existing functions. These are called *explicative definitions* (also called an explication). Explicative definitions are similar to stipulative definitions in that the definer is attempting to alter the language. The difference is that in an explicative definition the job that the word is to do remains the same. The word is altered to make it more effective at doing that job.

To be in a position to have an explicative definition accepted, one must be in some sort of position of authority or get the agreement of the others who will use the expression. Think of the IRS definition of the word ''income,'' the psycho-medical definition of ''paranoid,'' the logician's definition of ''valid,'' a judge's explication to a jury of ''probable cause,'' the kennel club's definition of ''pure bred,'' the computer textbook's definition of ''input device,'' and the definitions of ''pride'' and ''false pride'' in the exchange just above. These are all cases of taking ordinary words and preserving some piece of the standard use, while excluding other aspects of that use.

Operational definitions

When doing research in the natural or social sciences, it is almost always necessary to quantify the results in order to test hypotheses. This means that it is necessary to take measurements through some form of close observation in which something gets counted. Many of the social sciences share the same terms with ordinary language (for example, power, anxiety, aggression, shy, poor, disadvantaged, disabled, narcissistic, and abuse). When doing research the investigator needs to provide definitions of these terms that will make possible the measurement process as well as the testing process. Such definitions are often called operational definitions.

The term ''operational definition'' first appeared in the writings of the physicist Percy Bridgeman (1939), although the idea behind the proposal reaches back to the early British empiricist philosophers of the 17th and 18th centuries. Bridgeman was worried about the fact that his discipline of physics was making reference to phenomena that seemed to be far beyond the reach of any possible observations by ordinary human sense capacities. Examples of these phenomena are not only subatomic particles, but also ordinary forces such as electromagnetism and gravitation.

Bridgeman believed that such a practice would place the hypotheses of science beyond the reach of observational testing. He proposed a technique of definition whereby all such terms should be defined only and completely by the "operations" that were used to detect what the terms referred to. Thus, for example, a simple operation to detect magnetic force in an object is to place iron filings near it and observe whether they move toward it. Bridgeman proposed the following definition:

"X is magnetic" means "If iron filings are placed near X, then they will move towards X."

There are many technical and logical objections to the proposal that operational definitions supply the complete meaning of the terms of any science. But the concern of Bridgeman is a real one, namely that terms be used in science (and elsewhere) in such a way that the hypotheses that incorporate them can be empirically tested. Thus we can define an *operational definition* as an explicative definition whose purpose is to increase the measurability and testability of the claims using the term. In this sense operational definitions are crucial to science, especially to the social sciences.

Suppose, then, that you were interested in researching the relationship between anxiety and eating pickiness in children. Your hypothesis, let us say, was that anxious home environments will increase eating pickiness. You will first need to define "levels of anxiety" for the purposes of your study. You could do this on the basis of some standardized test administered to the child, or on the basis of a questionnaire to teachers, etc. Then you would have to define eating pickiness. Perhaps you could do it by creating a list of foods and having the parent check off the foods that the child is reluctant to eat. This is very complex due to ethnic differences in eating patterns, for example.

Some behavioral researchers and clinicians work with parents of autistic and other developmentally disabled children to try to eliminate troublesome, often very aggressive, behaviors. In the course of the research they may define, for a particular child, "aggressive behavior" as "any instance of hitting, biting, pinching, head banging, throwing objects, slamming hinged objects, inappropriate tearing, and putting objects in the mouth." Such an operational definition (by enumeration— see below in this chapter) allows the researcher and the parent to record specific instances of aggression to be later quantified and correlated with environmental variables such as withdrawal of social attention (Mullen 1994).

Manipulating language for rhetorical advantage

When the meaning of a word is altered in the course of a debate or argument just to enhance a person's rhetorical position in the argument, it is called a persuasive definition. Recall that the rhetorical goal of argumentation is the goal of persuading some audience. So a *persuasive definition* is an explicative definition that is provided only for the purposes of rhetorical advantage. If you are arguing that anyone who disobeys an order from his government cannot be a "patriot," it would be useful to define "patriot" as one who is willing to give even one's life for one's *government*. In the definition you have used the term "government" rather than "country," or "fellow citizens," etc. This use enhances the rhetorical position of your side in the argument just by altering the meaning of "patriot."

In the great popular culture debates of our time (foreign policy, racism, poverty, sexism, the status of homosexuals), there is a constant struggle over the language in which the debate is framed. This struggle can be seen as attempts to create persuasive definitions and have them widely accepted. Here is an example from foreign policy.

The U.S. State Department has an official definition of terrorism. This definition was not taken out of the dictionary, but was constructed in order to serve the interests of U.S. foreign policy. It is, in other words, an explicative definition. It is in the interests of U.S. foreign policy to be able to condemn the Libyan and Syrian supported groups of Lebanese and Palestinians who hijack airplanes, bomb airports, and the like. It is useful to be able to put the immense negative power of the word "terrorist" to work against such groups.

On the other hand, the U.S. does not want to be in the position of using that word, even by implication, against those who are its allies. When French agents blow up the Greenpeace ship, the Israeli secret police assassinate the PLO leader, the U.S. sponsored Contra rebels kill

American aid workers, or government soldiers in El Salvador kill Jesuit priests, the U.S. does not want to be forced to give any of these actions the label of "terrorism." To do so would weaken the force that the word has to condemn those whom the U.S. government determines are our enemies. After all, if the friends of the U.S. are terrorists, how bad can terrorism really be? So the definition of terrorism needs to be crafted very carefully, and it may need to change over time. If one of the important allies of the U.S. engages in repeated actions that fit the definition, it may be necessary to change the definition in order to avoid calling friends "terrorists."

According to the U.S. Department of State, an act is a terrorist act if all of the following are true:

1. It is a violent or threatening act.
2. It is deliberately directed against noncombatants.
3. It is done for some political motive.
4. It is carried out by non-military agents.

For one who wants to call only his enemies "terrorists," there is a lot of room for maneuvering in this definition. Who is a noncombatant? When Israeli agents assassinated a PLO political operative, the State Department after a long debate declared it not to be terrorism, claiming that the political operative had organized PLO raids and was thus a military target. When U.S. planes attempted to assassinate Mu'ammar Khadafi, it was not terrorism since it was carried out by the military. Of course, when someone shoots up a store because he has just been fired from his job there, it is not terrorism since there is no political motive. It is a universal practice to attempt to control language to assist your side of an issue. You either master language by understanding its potential for manipulation, or it controls you.

Suppose that a social researcher wants to measure the level of racism in American society. A difficult preliminary will be to define "racism." This is a necessary step in the procedure of constructing a measure of racism. We cannot measure what we cannot define. Should "racist" be defined in terms of attitudes, and if so which attitudes? Perhaps a person is not a racist unless she has *acted* upon some sort of racially defined belief or attitude.

What sort of actions should count as racist? Surely hate crimes, even verbal displays of hatred based only upon race are examples of racism. But if a white person refuses to sell a next door property to a nonwhite just because she believes that the value of her other property will decrease, is that racist? If a black person refuses to rent to a white because he is afraid of gentrification, is that racist? If a person opposes mandatory busing or affirmative action, is he or she racist? Some claim that the very definition of "racist" prevents the term from applying to members of recently discriminated against groups. This implies that, by definition, only white Anglo-Saxon protestants (WASPs) can be racists.

These are very difficult issues for a social scientist who is studying racism to confront. If the social scientist's politics leads him to emphasize the negative effects of white domination of American institutions, then he is likely to define "racism" very broadly, and so he will find it very prevalent. More politically conservative social scientists will be likely to define "racism" narrowly in terms of some specific set of behaviors, and so will find less racism in American society. In this case it is almost impossible for the researcher to investigate racism without making a political stand in the way that it is defined.

The point to note is how much room for maneuvering the social researcher has in defining his or her key terms. This means that when you see a media report that eating pickiness is caused by anxious home environments, or that racist acts on college campuses are on the increase, one of the things that you need to know is how these terms are defined operationally (that is, for the purposes of quantification in the study).

Effective techniques for defining terms

There are three basic techniques that can be used to define words or phrases, whether the definitions are stipulative, reportive, or explicative.

(1) The first is to make a complete list, an enumeration, of what it is that the word denotes. *Definition by enumeration* is unusual, but useful in contexts where the denotation is composed of a limited number of types of things arbitrarily classified together. Think of how one would define "sunbelt," "rustbelt," "Scandinavian," "common market countries," or "peripherals." In all these cases the easiest technique would be to list the types of things that the phrase denotes.

(2) The second technique is to give an example of the kind of thing to which the word refers, *definition by example*. Not knowing the French word for "car," how would you explain the meaning to a French speaker? You could mention Peugeot (risking confusion with a bicycle), Ford, Cadillac, etc. One variation of definition by example is when you actually point out an example, without or in addition to using

words to describe or name the example. This is *ostensive definition*, and is the most common sort for the teaching of language to young children. To teach a young child the meaning of ''ball'' it would be unhelpful to say, ''circular object intended for the purpose of recreation.'' A much more effective method would be putting a ball in the child's line of sight while saying ''ball'' several times.

(3) The third technique is to produce a series of words that are (or are intended to become) synonymous with the word being defined. This is *definition by synonym*. Because of the fluidity of our language and the fact that no one is in charge, it is not easy in everyday contexts to produce precisely accurate reportive definitions using synonyms, but dictionaries make strenuous efforts. In more authoritarian sublanguages, such as legal or medical languages, definition by synonym is a good deal easier. A definition is a success if it allows those using the defined term to communicate more effectively. It follows, then, that definitions should:

Avoid circularity: Do not use a version of the word you are defining in the definition.

Avoid vague or unfamiliar words: Do not use words in the definition that are less clear or less familiar to the intended audience of the definition than the phrase being defined.

Avoid being either too narrow or too broad: The definition should not encompass either more or fewer cases than the word being defined, or what is intended to be the term's denotation.

The following are examples of some bad definitions:

An ''infinite series'' is a sequence of numbers which has an isomorphic proper subset. [unfamiliar language—isomorphic proper subset]

A ''human being'' is any living being born of a human female. [circular—''human'' used to define ''human'']

''Friendly fire'' is the threat of termination of services either permanent or temporary impacted from supportive missioning. [vague and unfamiliar language—supportive missioning]

A ''communist'' is a person committed to using violent means to achieve his or her goals. [too broad—fits George Washington]

A country is ''democratic'' if all the voters can cast ballots for the country's chief executive. [too narrow—England is democratic]

Second exercises

What are the purposes for and techniques used in the following definitions? Are there any criticisms of them?

1. A brother is a male sibling.

2. A religious person is one who believes in God.

3. A movie star is someone like Gene Hackman or Glenn Close.

4. A religious person is someone who practices a religion like Judaism, Buddhism, etc.

5. A terrorist is a person who injures civilians in pursuing his or her political objectives.

6. I will use the term "discults" in the following pages to refer to the rural poor and the urban ghetto dwellers, and to no one else.

7. A neoconservative is a liberal who just got mugged.

8. A liberal is a conservative who just got laid off.

9. An obscene gesture is something like this . . . (She raises the appropriate single finger.)

10. For the purposes of this investigation we will mean by "unemployed person" anyone who has been seeking a job unsuccessfully for more that two months.

11. Democracy means political systems such as the U.S., Canada, etc.

12. Democracy is the social decision procedure implemented through an aggregation rule that defines a social utility function out of some set of individual preferences.

13. A critical person is a person with well-developed metalogical and cognitive skills, as well as the appropriate dispositions concerning reasoning and dialogue.

14. An input device is either a keyboard, a tape, a disk, or a mouse.

15. An input device is anything used to input information.

The emotive power of language

Some phrases have an interesting and somewhat mysterious power to create strong positive or negative responses in their audience, independent of the responses that the audience would be expected to have to the denotations of the words. You would expect, for example, parents of murder victims to be horrified by the news of their children's death. The death itself (that is, the denotation of the words used to describe it) would provoke this response.

But words themselves have the power to heighten or lessen the feelings that normally accompany recognition of some fact. The way the murder is described, the words that are used, will affect the degree of immediate response from the parent. Using "hacked to death" will produce a greater emotional response than "caused to die by a wood-chopping instrument."

This emotive power is useful when it is appropriate to heighten feelings (as when a commander prepares the troops for battle) or lessen feelings (as when bad news is reported). In both cases there is an intent at some deception, but perhaps to good purpose.

It is even possible to reverse the normal emotional response, to create positive feelings when negative ones would be expected and to create negative feelings when positive ones would be expected. We may expect negative feelings associated with "cemetery," "nuclear waste," or "garbage dump," but we are able to create positive or neutral responses with "memorial park," "spent fuel," or "landfill." We may expect neutral or positive feelings associated with "Democrats" or "young professional," but we can poison the waters just by using "Kennedy liberals" or "yuppie." The *emotive meaning* of words is their ability to create positive or negative feelings that are independent of the feeling towards their denotations. The word or expression "X" is a *euphemism* for "Y" if "X" and "Y" have the same denotation and "X" is substituted for "Y" in order to create a more positive feeling than a clear understanding of the denotation of "Y" would evoke. "X" is a *dysphemism* for "Y" if "X" and "Y" have the same denotation and "X" is substituted for "Y" in order to create a more negative feeling than a clear understanding of the denotation of "Y" would evoke. The use of euphemism and dysphemism is an attempt to manipulate an audience to make a value judgment, rather than to argue that the value judgment is correct.

Euphemisms and slurs

Words that denote unpleasant things seem to have a history, in the sense that it takes time for their full emotional impact to catch up to the word. The word "park," when denoting a place, has a pleasant, peaceful, and "green" association. If there is a place that normally would create negative feelings when thought about, these negative feelings can be smoothed over by calling it a "park." So "memorial park" replaces "cemetery." There was a time, no doubt, when "cemetery," (coming from the Latin "*coemeterium*" meaning "sleeping chamber") replaced "graveyard." And "graveyard," with its nice association with our "backyard" had replace the too descriptive "burial ground." In regard to the ever-handy "park," think of the use of "industrial park". Can we expect "landfill" to become a "refuse park" in the near future?

Great attention is paid in contemporary times to the proper words used to describe groups that have been or continue to be discriminated against. These groups include racial, ethnic, gender, and handicapped persons. There are some words used to describe members of these groups that never had any function other than to insult and wound. These are *slurs*. There are other terms that at one time were legitimate, carrying no intent to wound, but were later replaced. Words like "colored people," "blind," "orientals," "cripples," "deaf," have been rejected at least by some users in favor of "Black" or "African American", "Asians", "handicapped" or "physically challenged," and "hearing impaired." We have emphasized the uncontrolled, democratic nature of the English language. In this sense no one is in charge of these words, so each person has a right to use the words that he or she deems appropriate. Slurs, of course, have no use but to wound people and, since we do not have the right to wound people, we have no right to use slurs.

Terms like "Black" or "African American," "Oriental" or "Asian," "handicapped" or "physically challenged" or "differentially abled" were never intended as slurs, and so it would seem to be consistent with the democratic nature of the language that each person has the right to decide which to use. Another alternative would be to allow each group member or each group to decide how he or she or the group is to be denoted. This goes against the grain of the democratic nature of language and is likely therefore to meet with resistance and resentment (for example, "Who are you to tell me how to talk?"). It would be likely also to lead to confusion on the part of users as to which is the correct term to use. This is a situation that exists to some extent today, where great importance is placed by some upon whether, for example, "Hispanic" or "Latino" is used. The traditionally democratic nature of language would seem to call for tolerance in word selection.

Third exercises

1. Are the following euphemisms or dysphemisms? What are the appropriate neutral equivalents?

nuclear exchange
cripple
revenue enhancements
vertical transport corps
landfill
air support
negative economic growth
development officer
holistic grading (of essays)
juvenile delinquents

bureaucrat
smart bomb
Dept. of Human Kinetics
industrial park
garbage man
friendly fire
Office of Human Resources
incontinent ordnance
young hoodlums
Office of Intellectual Capital

7

Everyday Fallacies of Reasoning

Introduction: The Nature of Informal Fallacies

An *informal fallacy* is a common pattern of argument in everyday reasoning that is logically inadequate but tends to be rhetorically effective. That is, it is a pattern that fails to prove its point but is likely to succeed nonetheless in convincing audiences. By everyday reasoning is meant the kinds of arguments that take place in political campaigns, between parents and children, by lawyers in courtrooms and at bargaining tables, between friends in a bar about baseball, and in all the various contexts in which people argue without reasoning techniques specific to some discipline of knowledge.

Everyday reasoning is that core of reasoning patterns that all human beings use in their daily lives. This core is also used by specialists and experts of all types when they are not employing the special reasoning patterns of their disciplines. There is a set of very common logical mistakes that people make in their everyday reasoning. This set of mistakes has been the subject of philosophers' interests since (you guessed it!) Aristotle, who was the first to write about it. Let's look at a hypothetical but realistic piece of reasoning.

Sixth dialogue: parents and child in conversation

Jean and Harry have two children. The first, Marjorie, will be graduating this year from a very selective college on the East Coast with a degree in economics. She has accepted a job in a large securities firm for the time being until she decides whether to proceed to an M.B.A. or

137

a Ph.D. in economics. The younger, Lucie, will graduate this year from high school. She too is an excellent student, but she is not anxious to go directly to college, or at least not to some high pressure college such as Marjorie's. The fact is that Lucie loves tennis, is very good at it, and has been offered a job as assistant instructional pro at her local club. Jean and Harry are apoplectic at the thought of her not going to college. Some of the fallacious patterns of reasoning have been indicated in italics. After you get through the list of fallacies in this chapter, you can go back and identify these fallacies.

Jean: "You could play tennis on the college team, you're plenty good enough for that, and you could continue to teach during the summers. Don't throw this chance away, it could ruin your whole life."

Lucie: "I could take courses at night at the local community college. I don't need to go away to college."

Jean: "*You know how dangerous that place is! Jennie Turner went there and was mugged one night, right in the parking lot.* And besides, do you know how long it would take to get a degree by taking a course or two a year at night? You'd be a grandmother by that time!"

Lucie: "*I can't be the superstar daughter like Marjorie.* Isn't one enough for you? *The only reason that you want me to go to school is to get me out of town and away from Randy.* You think he's not good enough for me."

Harry: "Randy's not part of this. We're thinking about your future. This is one of those times in life when you are forced to make decisions that will affect you for the rest of your life. *Students who go to college earn much more in their lifetimes than those with only high school diplomas*; that's a proven fact. And you know that *your guidance counselor recommended against not going immediately to college.* And think of what a good time you would have at Marjorie's school; she loved her four years there. *Going to college is what young people like you do after graduation.* How many of your fellow graduates will be seen *hanging around some tennis court playing pick-up games with the members*? I just can't see it."

Lucie: "*Whenever I make a decision that isn't just exactly what you want, you always criticize me and make me feel like I can't think for myself.* Why can't you respect me as a person?"

Jean: "That's not true, and you know it. You wanted to go to tennis camp, and we agreed. You wanted to quit your flute lessons, and we respected that decision. How can you say something like that! And remember the time . . ."

Lucie: "That was third grade, Mother. I'm talking about now. Every guy I ever brought home got the cold shoulder from Dad. Randy won't even come to the door."

Harry: "That's a break!"

And so it went. Let's agree that Lucie caved in, went away to college, became a brain surgeon, quit her residency, and now teaches tennis. It serves Jean and Harry right.

As an argument in the ordinary sense of a heated disagreement, this is fairly typical. From a logical perspective it is a series of arguments that contains quite a few informal fallacies of reasoning. The following is a list of some of the most common of these fallacious argument patterns. Perhaps you can find some of these fallacies in the arguments of Harry, Jean, and Lucie.

Fallacies of authority

From the logical standpoint it is not fallacious to argue that something is true or ought to be accepted on the basis that someone else believes it. We cannot be experts about everything and so must rely upon the judgment of others. But it is legitimate to argue that a conclusion should be accepted because some expert accepts it, only provided that the expert fulfill two conditions, (a) the expert is in fact an authority in a relevant area of expertise, and (b) there does not exist significant contrary belief by equally competent experts. The first of these conditions is obvious, but the second is often overlooked. The principle here is that *experts cancel each other out*. If you are a juror in a trial where the defense presents a pathologist to testify that the blood on the scene is not that of the accused and the prosecution's expert testifies that it is, then you must either ignore both or have a good reason to prefer one expert's testimony over the other's. Logic does not allow you to argue simply that it must be the accused's blood because pathologist X said that it was.

Inadequate expert

Arguing that "P" is true since person X says that "P" is true, where either X is not an expert about "P" or there are significant numbers of other experts who do not believe that "P" is true.

Ad populum (appeal to popularity, momentum)

Arguing that "P" is true because either large numbers of people be-lieve that "P" is true or more and more people are coming to believe that "P" is true.

Ad populum is a fallacy since numbers do not confer wisdom. The fact that many people believe something is not a reason for you to believe it. This is a common fallacy in advertising, as in, "The coun-try's number one selling . . . (whatever) . . ." It is rampant in political campaigns, where candidates are always anxious to make favorable polls public, especially polls showing the candidate gaining ("momen-tum" is called "the big Mo" in politics). The insulting message of all this poll reporting is that you should vote for my candidate because more and more people are deciding to vote for my candidate. "Don't *waste* your vote!" they say. (Take one third of a second to think of the only way in which you can *waste* your vote.) Beware of "it's the wave of the future," always recalling that waves of the future soon become the ebb tides of the past. Finally, the *ad populum* fallacy works both ways, ruling out not only appeals to large numbers but also appeals that something is false or bad based upon small numbers.

There is an exception to *ad populum*'s being a fallacy. That is, there is a circumstance in which it is a legitimate pattern of argument. This is in questions of what should or should not be law in a democracy. Here "the people" are assumed to be the legitimate experts, and so what they say should be law is what should be law.

Traditional wisdom

Arguing that "P" is true because the belief in "P" is part of a cher-ished tradition.

Since traditions conflict in radical ways, believing that traditions con-fer truth would lead to the absurd conclusion that radically conflicting beliefs are all true. The same holds for practices that are traditional. A moment's thought will indicate that some traditional practices ought to be continued and some ought to be scrapped. The point here is that *none* ought to be continued for the reason that they are traditions.

Here are some simple examples of fallacies of authority:

a. Buy Pepsi and be part of the "Pepsi Generation."

b. To understand Ford quality, think of the Model T.

c. There must be a God; how could all those peoples from every culture believe in something that wasn't true?

d. Albert Einstein believed in God, so that's good enough for little old me.

e. As Conservatives have said over and over again, the market will take care of our needs, we don't need big government.

f. You still believe in relativism? That's a postmodernist idea; no one believes that stuff anymore.

Ad hominem arguments

The Latin phrase *ad hominem* means "to the person." It is logically legitimate to investigate the characteristics of the person stating something for your belief if the person asks you to believe it just because he or she said it. However, if the person presents an argument to justify the conclusion, logic requires that you focus on the argument itself in evaluating that argument. The principle here is simple; arguments should be evaluated on their own merits. The character or motives of the person making the arguments are irrelevant to the proper evaluation of the argument.

Abusive

Trying to discredit another's argument by calling attention to undesirable characteristics of the person making the argument.

Circumstantial (by motivation)

Trying to discredit another's argument by calling attention to the motives or circumstances that led the person to make that argument or fail to make some other argument.

A person's motivations for presenting a case, or making an argument, are relevant to the understanding of why he or she is doing what he or she is doing. But these motivations are totally irrelevant to the question of whether the argument adequately supports the conclusion. Only the latter question is of logical concern. The same is true for why someone is not or would not present some argument, as in, "You wouldn't be saying that if you were in his shoes!'' Whether these statements about motive or circumstance are true or false is not the issue. Claims about why a person is arguing the way she is, are logically irrelevant to the evaluation of the argument, whether the claims are true or false.

Examples

Here are some simple examples.

a. I know you have argued that I should stop smoking, but you're just concerned with the smoke smell on your clothes.

b. Despite all your reasons, the bottom line is that you wouldn't have voted to cut Medicare if your parents were dependent upon it for their health care.

c. You accepted the proposal that Jones presented to you? Jones isn't anything but a politician!

d. So you think that I should settle the suit at this point, accept this offer? I've heard all your arguments, but really, isn't it just that you need your 30% of the settlement right now?

e. I saw that you were reading Herrington's work on the distribution of world wealth. I suppose that you know that he's an avowed communist. Why don't you chuck that trash.

f. Smith has a lot of facts and arguments, but the bottom line is that Smith is an (. . .) and only a (***) can understand the needs of the (***).

Fallacies of distortion

Logic demands that you stick to the point in criticizing another's argument. This is a basic tenet of honesty in dialogue. It is also a logical truism that you cannot successfully criticize an argument except by talking about it as it is. It is often necessary or desirable to restate another's argument in your own words. The principles of logic and of conversational honesty demand that in so doing, you reproduce the original as faithfully as possible. When in doubt about what exactly the argument is that you want to evaluate, you should construct the *strongest* possible version of it, not the weakest.

This "principle of charity" follows from the fact that the point of argumentation is to arrive at the truth, not to defeat or humiliate some other person. The fact is, however, that distorting the views of a perceived opponent is the most common fallacy of reasoning. One lesson from this is that you should not allow others to restate your views or arguments. Whenever you hear another say, "What you're saying is . . . ," my recommendation is to deny it even before the person finishes the sentence. It will never be what you are saying. "I would prefer to formulate my views in my own words, if you don't mind," is a polite way to cut off a budding young distortion.

Straw person fallacy

Restating another's argument in such a manner as to weaken the original and proceeding to criticize the weakened version (the straw person), hoping that others will think that the weakened version is the argument of your opponent.

Because of the fluidity of our American English language, it is not easy to restate an argument in a manner that preserves the original. If dialogue is seen as a way of discovering the truth rather than as a contest to the death, the rule of translation should be, *when in doubt, strengthen the other's argument.* A panacea is a cure-all, proposed to cure all of the ills of some problem. Except for the "snake oil" salespersons of the legendary West, almost no one proposes panaceas, especially for complicated social and personal problems.

One common form of straw person is the "no panacea argument." Arguing against the death penalty, Terry claims, "I just don't think that capital punishment is the answer to the rising murder rate! Let's get rid of the guns in our society." The gun control lobbyist argues, "Taking away a person's right to firearms will not eliminate crime." Of course, no one proposed that the death penalty was *the* answer, and who would say that hand gun control would *eliminate crime*?

Red herring fallacy

When in danger of "losing" an argument, raising an irrelevant issue in an effort to trick the opponent into changing the topic of the argument.

During the training of tracking hounds it was common to test the tracking ability of the hound by dragging a red (smoked) herring across the trail and off in a different direction. If the hound was not well trained it would follow the "false trail" rather than the original.

Examples

Here are some examples of fallacies of distortion.

a. So you think I should see a doctor for this swelling in my arm? I'm really not the kind of person who runs to doctors every time I get an itch.

b. I know that she argued that capital punishment is wrong, but to me coddling criminals just creates more crime.

c. Sure, I read in the paper that my candidate was with some prostitute last night, but tell me, do you think it's proper for reporters to be hiding in the front bushes of politicians just to get a story? Don't people have a right to privacy?

d. All right! I don't need any more reasons why I shouldn't quit this job. You're right as usual! The real issue though is that you're just jealous that because I'm not married like you, I'm free to do what I want. That's why you criticize every move I make. Why can't you either accept your own situation, or get out of it?

e. Requiring people on welfare to work is not going to get rid of poverty!

Fallacies of circularity

Premises should lend credibility to conclusions. They can do this only if they are in some sense more credible than the conclusions. Premises cannot be more credible if they include as a necessary element the conclusion itself. To use the conclusion as a premise to prove that very same conclusion in no way increases the credibility of what you are arguing for. To do so brings your argument around in circles. This is perhaps the most inadvertent of fallacies, but still very common.

Circular reasoning (begging the question) by restatement

Arguing that "P" is true because "Q" is true, where "Q" = "P". That is, merely restating in different words in the premises the conclusion that those premises are intended to support.

Circular reasoning (begging the question) by expanding the circle

Arguing that "P" is true since "Q" is true, and "Q" is true since "R" is true, and "R" is true since "S" is true, and "S" is true since "P" is true. The argument comes down to "P" is true since "P" is true.

· **Examples**

Here are some examples.

a. You ought not tell lies, because you should avoid being mendacious.

b. California is the best state to live in since no other state is as good as a place to reside.

c. You can believe what Henry tells you. I know that because I have spoken to his boss, who raves about him. It did occur to me of course that his boss was just saying that in the hopes that I would hire Henry, but that can't be because Henry tells me that his boss is a real straight arrow.

Fallacies of cause and effect

Many arguments attempt to justify a conclusion that one thing caused another to happen. There are two kinds of cause and effect claims. A *singular causal claim* asserts that some specific event or condition, or some effort or condition of a person, existing at some time and place, caused another event or condition to occur. Examples of such claims are: that a blocked fuel valve caused my car to break down yesterday, that her sneezing in my face caused me to get a cold, that spilling the hot water on my hand caused the blister, and that his deliberate firing of the gun at the burglar caused the death of the burglar.

The second kind of cause and effect claim asserts that one type of thing is a factor in causing another type of thing to occur. This is called a *general causal claim*. It does not refer to specific events that happened at specific times and places. Examples include the claims that smoking causes cancer, that poverty causes crime, that repression causes aggressive behavior, and that unprotected sex causes AIDS. We will deal with general causal claims in chapter 8. One point to remember always is how very difficult it is to adequately justify claims that one thing *caused* another. If you keep this difficulty in mind, then you will carry with you a healthy skepticism to such claims when you hear them, and you won't rush into making causal claims without sufficient evidence.

Post hoc, ergo propter hoc (the *Post Hoc* fallacy)

The Latin expression above means, "after which, therefore because of which." It is the claim that since Y occurred after X occurred, then X must have caused Y to occur.

It is the pattern:

X happened and after that Y happened

---

so, X caused Y to happen

It does not matter in this fallacy whether the conclusion is true or not. The point is that the premise refers only to a sequence in *time*, while the conclusion refers to a *cause and effect* sequence. The latter does not receive anything like adequate support from the former.

One misunderstanding that leads us to the *post hoc* fallacy is *misperception of regression to the mean*. Billy Hero was in his thirteenth year as shortstop for the Boston Red Sox, with a consistently distributed batting average of .327 (meaning that the fraction created by hits over hits-or-outs was slightly less than 1/3). In January of that year Billy had become a vegetarian for health reasons, and two months into the season he was batting only .213. Billy changed back to his traditional diet of burgers and fries, and by mid-August he was batting at .319. He swore that he would never tamper with his cuisine again.

Daniel Kahneman and Amos Tversky report that flight instructors would criticize a pilot whose landing was below expectations and praise the pilot if his landing was better than expected. But they found that the better than expected landings were usually followed by landings not as good, and the really bad landings were usually followed by better landings. The instructors concluded that criticism is a better motivator than praise (Kahneman and Tversky 1972). Can you figure out where the reasoning of both Billy Hero and the flight instructors went wrong?

If we consider the idea of performances, we can say that people or things have "expected" or "mean" levels of performance at any particular time. It may be a bowling average, a particular level of accomplishment in piano, distance from the bull's-eye in archery, percentile standing on standardized verbal/math exams, or average gross sales per day in the deli business. By definition, these expected levels are the levels that it is most probable that the performer will achieve.

The probability is always highest that these mean performance levels, rather than any other particular level, will be accomplished. Thus when one of these levels is deviated from significantly, when the performance is way above or way below expectation, the probability is highest that the *next* performance will be closer to expectation than the previously observed deviation. This means that if you have an extraordinarily good day on the firing range, scoring way above your mean performance level, it is more likely that you will do worse (closer to your mean) on your next outing than that you will stay the same or get better. Your performance will tend to regress to its normal mean.

Beware! We are not saying that the deviation affects the next performance in any way. That would be the *gambler's fallacy*. The reason that you can expect the deviation to be followed by a more normal performance is that it is ALWAYS most probable that the normal performance is achieved. That is why it is the normal performance. This tendency of an abnormal performance to be followed by a more normal performance is called *regression to the mean*. Billy Hero's performance was way below his mean. Assuming that his abilities were not deteriorating, we would expect him to regress to his mean and thus to experience an increase in batting average. It is very likely that diet was irrelevant. In like manner when the pilot landed way below or above expectation, the probability is that the next landing would be closer to the pilot's mean level of achievement. Thus neither the praise nor the criticism need have had any effect.

Misperception of the various phenomena of regression to the mean leads people into the *post hoc* fallacy. It is the *post hoc* fallacy when the real explanation of the phenomenon is the fact of regression to the mean, and so no special circumstances need to be cited to explain the phenomenon. When searching for the causes of changes in performance, be sure that the change cannot be understood as the tendency to perform at one's normal level of accomplishment. That is, always consider regression to the mean as a possible explanation for changes in performance.

False denial of a cause

> *Arguing that since Y did not change after X occurred, therefore X had no effect upon Y.*

In the *post hoc* fallacy, the conclusion is a claim that one thing caused another, while the premise contains only a statement that one thing came before another in time. The conclusion in the fallacy of false denial is a *denial* of a causal relation, again based only upon a relationship in time. Thus the pattern is:

X happened and after that Y did not change

---

so, X had no effect upon Y

It may have been that X kept Y from becoming greater or less. The fact that Y did not change is no reason to conclude that X had no effect on Y. It is as fallacious to conclude the absence of a causal claim merely from a time relation as it is to conclude the presence of a causal claim merely from a time relation.

Examples

Here are some examples.

a. Janet went to the therapist, Dr. Worthington, when she became depressed after the death of her husband. Six or seven months later she was back to her old self. Worthington's approach really seemed to work with her.

b. Leroy was treated with AZT for AIDS. Now it's three years later and he still has AIDS, so I don't see why they are still giving him this worthless medicine.

c. Rabb was elected governor when the unemployment rate was 9%. She's coming to the end of her four years and it is virtually the same. I think we need to elect someone whose policies will have some effect.

d. When I got the flu my mother gave me heaping portions of chicken soup for six straight days. By that time she had me just about cured.

e. I borrowed my father's expensive pen for my final in Calc II. I got a 93. That was two years ago, and I've been using it only for emergencies ever since.

Fallacies of sampling

Bridget and Tom went to the romantic city of Paris for a week on their honeymoon. It was their first European excursion and their last to France. They found the cab drivers that they met to be gruff, the concierge at their hotel was perturbed that they came in after his closing time of 11:00 P.M. (he had to open the door for them), and the waiters seemed snooty. In the eleven years since this unhappy trip, they have never tired of informing all who would listen about the nastiness of the French people.

We often hear the charge, "That's a generalization!" It seems to imply that there is something wrong with drawing conclusions about groups from samples of those groups. If there were something wrong with generalizing, human knowledge, including all of science, would be impossible. In fact, to say that generalizations are bad is itself to make a generalization (about generalizations), and thus to be condemning your own claim. The issue is not with generalizations themselves, but with whether there are well-reasoned arguments to support the generalizations that you make. Bridget and Tom may have met twenty or thirty French people, of whom four or five may have been nasty (and of course the nasty ones are the ones that they remembered). From this "sample" of French people, Bridget and Tom drew their illogical conclusions about the French.

In the spring of 1994 *The New York Times* and CBS News did a poll to determine some attitudes of teens (13 to 17 years old) in the U.S. They discovered, for example, that 19 percent considered crime to be ". . . the biggest problem where you go to school . . . ," 36 percent worry about being a victim of crime "a lot or some of the time," and 22 percent feel "a lot" of pressure from their parents. *The New York Times* reported that the results were based upon a sample of 1,055 teens. "In theory, in 19 cases out of 20, the poll results will differ by no more than three percentage points, up or down from the results that would have been obtained from polling all American teenagers" (July 10, 1994). Another way of stating the results of the first question is that 95 percent of the time (19 out of 20) that a similar question is asked of a similar sample, the answers will be within the range of ±3 percent of the proportion of actual attitudes of the entire population of American teenagers. The 95 percent is the *reliability* or *confidence level*, and the ±3 percent is the *confidence interval* or *degree of sampling error*.

To understand the difference between a confidence interval (sampling error) and confidence level (reliability), suppose you are purchasing a missile system for the government. The manufacturer tells you that they can develop a design that will hit exactly on the target for $20 million per copy, or within one mile of the target in any direction for $17 million, or within five miles of the target for $12 million. These ranges are like the confidence intervals or degrees of sampling error. Then you ask, "If I go with the $17 million missile, what percentage of the times will it impact within the range of one mile of the target?" The manufacturer tells you that 85 percent of missile firings will land within this range. For an extra $2 million per missile, that figure can be raised to 95 percent. These latter figures are the reliability or confidence levels of the missile. Note how both confidence intervals and levels are tied to cost, and in research to time and effort.

In July 1994 the Field Organization, California's leading pollster, found that 38 percent of the Black Californians surveyed believed that the football great O. J. Simpson was guilty of the murder of his former wife and her companion. (This was after he had been charged, but before any trial.) The poll's confidence interval was ±13 percent, meaning that we are allowed to conclude only that the percentage of black Californians who believed then that Mr. Simpson was guilty was between 25 percent and 51 percent (*The New York Times*, July 22, 1994). This is rather like designing a rocket that, when pointed at Moscow, will land anywhere between Paris and Hong Kong.

The conclusions of Bridget and Tom and the poll of the teenagers are both statistical generalizations, claims that the members of some group or population (P) have some characteristic (C). When we want to know about group characteristics, we could examine every member of P (the population). But there are many reasons why using a sample is preferable. Samples are easier to work with, significantly cheaper to examine since they are smaller, and for the same reason they take less time to examine. What is often overlooked is that in many cases the results will be more accurate if samples are used than if one tries to examine the entire population. If you have a fixed amount of time and/or money to spend trying to learn about some population, it is often much better to do a very thorough job of sampling than a sloppy job of trying to examine the entire population.

A good example is the U.S. census. It attempts to collect information about the class of U.S. citizens by examining every household. In so doing, it undercounts the poor and the urban dwellers due to the fact that they are more difficult to contact, their families are less easily identifiable, their homes are more difficult to reach, and some have no permanent residence at all. The results affect the federal aid going to cities and the number of Congressional seats going to states with large urban and poor populations. In the 1980 U.S. census, the Census Bureau had good evidence that it undercounted Black Americans by 5.9 percent. It was unable to add that undercounted group back into the population, however, since it had no way to determine the specific areas from which the undercounted came. In 1990 the problem surfaced again, with statisticians urging that counts be based upon statistical adjustments. The Census Bureau has still refused.

The basic logic of the sampling procedure, including what can go wrong, is indicated below.

a. Clearly identify the population that you want to collect information about. If the question is what percentage of brooms coming off a particular assembly line is defective, there is no problem with the identification of P. But if you want to research the percentage of women who have been battered that suffer lasting psychological effects, there will be a problem. If you define "battered" in terms of very serious consequences (in terms of, e.g., "injury that required attention by a medical professional in a hospital") then the percentage of women who had lasting psychological effects would be greater than if you defined "battered" to include less serious abuses. Where there is a problem at this stage, it is likely to be with a *persuasive definition* of P (that is, a definition of P that alters the ordinary meaning in a particular way in order to achieve some rhetorical advantage).

b. Clearly identify the characteristic (C) that you are interested in measuring in P. This requires an operational definition of C as discussed in chapter 6, in order that the presence of C be measurable. The danger is once again with persuasive definition. If you are interested in finding a large percentage of "lasting psychological effects" (C), then you can define that phrase to include less serious conditions.

c. Decide how accurate your results need to be (a confidence interval of $\pm e\%$), as well as how confident you need to be that the results fall within that interval (degree of reliability, $r = n\%$).

d. Draw a sample (S) from P.

e. Test S to determine the level of C ($m\%$ of S has C).

f. Infer from the fact that S has C to $m\%$, that P has C to $m\%$ ($\pm e\%$) with a confidence $= n\%$.

From a technical standpoint, step d is often the most difficult. When information about a population is based on a sample, the sample must be truly representative of the population; that is, the characteristics of the sample must accurately reflect the characteristics that are of interest in the population. There are two fallacies associated with step d that would result in step f being unjustified.

The fallacy of small sample

Drawing a conclusion about a population based upon a sample that is too small.

Assuming an unbiased sample, the rule is that the larger the sample, the more likely it is that the properties of the sample will reflect the properties of the parent population. More precisely, as the size of a properly selected sample gets larger, so does the probability that the sample will reflect the parent population. This is a version of what is called "the law of large numbers." Ten thousand coin tosses is more likely to be within ±3 percent of 50 percent than one thousand coin tosses.

Three things need to be noted about sample size. The first is that for properly chosen samples, as more members are added to the sample the size of the *additional increments* of reliability will decrease. Additional sample members will always provide additional increments of reliability, but at decreasing rates. Thus it is much more costly in time and money to go from 90 percent to 95 percent reliability than to go an equal 5 percent jump from 70 percent to 75 percent. Second, it is obviously not possible to say how large a sample should be in terms of some percentage of the population. Adequate sample size will depend upon the confidence interval and reliability that you can live with, as well as the homogeneity of the population that you are sampling. The third point is that properly selected samples can be amazingly small. The sample of 1,055 teenagers can faithfully represent millions of teens if properly chosen. Typical national political polls use samples of about the same size to represent over a hundred million potential voters.

The fallacy of small sample is rarely committed by professional samplers, and when it is the low confidence levels and wide intervals tell the story. On the other hand, it is almost always committed when we as individuals generalize about our own experiences, and make claims about large populations. Listen to men talking about women and women about men, to straights talking about gays and vice versa, and to races talking about each other. It is these types of contexts that give generalizations a bad name.

This fallacy is also a pervasive feature of journalism. During a presidential election a reporter roams the country to "take the pulse of America." Each night for a week he or she interviews four or five people from the area visited that day. This so-called man on the street interview must inevitably commit this fallacy. Why should the views of one or two people walking on a particular street at a particular time be of any news interest, if not because these views were meant to represent the views of others? The reporter will sometimes refer to the poll as a "personal poll" or as "unscientific," as if these admissions absolve it of disseminating false information. Such samples, no matter how they are chosen, are always too small to represent any group.

The second fallacy of sampling concerns sample *fairness*. The intuitive idea of a fair sample is one that is similar to, or representative of, the population from which it was drawn, or at least similar enough to allow for inferences from the sample to the population. In actual practice, the fairness of a sample is defined by the process by which it was selected. The key to a fair selection process is a random selection process. A *random sample* of some parent population is defined as a sample in which every member of the population has an equal chance of being included in the sample.

If you wanted to decide what percentage of adults in the U.S. considered themselves Democrats, you would not want to take your sample only from adults in Chicago, even if you sampled the entire city. This is because adults in Chicago are more likely to be Democrats than adults nationwide. If you wanted to determine the percentage of defective Hansui VCRs you would not want to take the sample only from the morning's production. It may be that this shift is particularly sloppy or that workers are more efficient in the morning.

For a sample to be truly random does not mean that the sample is selected haphazardly. To the contrary, it is often quite difficult to assure that a sample has been selected randomly. Television news programs have begun to "sample" the views of Americans by asking talk show hosts what their viewers think about some issue. This sample is anything but random. Think of all the built-in biases. The talk show is likely to have a particular type of audience, liberal or conservative, Black or white or otherwise, urban or rural, male or female. In other words, the sample that we get from the talk show will be much more homogeneous than the population (and the show's host may tend to remember certain types of callers and not others).

Some parent populations are very homogeneous in the sense that there is not a wide range of divergence among their members, while other populations are very heterogeneous. Consider for example a women's Roman Catholic college of full-time, day, residential students, compared to an urban, nonsectarian, coed college with day and evening divisions, of full- and part-time students of all ages. Clearly for obtaining an opinion poll, one population is more homogeneous than the other; and just as clearly it is easier to sample a homogeneous population than one that is more heterogeneous.

To sample the opinions of the students at the Catholic college we could give each student a number and then have a computer select a random sample from the collection of numbers. We could then give a questionnaire or interview to the sample members. This is a purely random selection process. In the case of the other college we would want to be sure that we got the opinions of commuters and residential students, the young recent high school graduates and the older students, the day and the evening students, and the men and the women. To assure this, we would need a larger sample to protect against some subgroup being underrepresented in the sample. We could also divide up the student population into relevant subgroups and randomly sample each subgroup. In this case, the size of each subgroup in the sample would vary depending upon the size of that subgroup in the population, although it is always necessary that the subgroup samples be large enough to be representative. This is called a *stratified sampling procedure*. It is this procedure that TV networks use to predict the outcomes of elections on election night. The more heterogeneous a population is, the greater the need for care in the sample selection process and the larger the sample must be.

The fallacy of biased sample

Drawing a conclusion about a population based upon a sample that is not chosen according to a legitimate random procedure.

Almost all "self-selected" samples will be biased unless they are treated very carefully by professionals. Thus telephone polls where viewers call a 900 number to register an opinion or vote on some issue or candidate are invariably biased samples of the population. In politics self-selected telephone polls are biased in favor of groups that watch a lot of TV, in favor of groups willing to pay the phone charge, in favor of groups with a strong commitment on an issue as opposed to a mild preference, etc. In cases where questionnaires are mailed to purchasers to determine attitudes toward some product they purchased, the returns are likely to be biased in favor of those who had bad experiences with the product. The point to remember is that it is a very complicated matter to get an unbiased sample of a population, and so we should be careful when generalizing about a population from a sample.

Step e in the sampling procedure calls for the testing of S to determine the level of C. Suppose you are interested in the percentage of defective rebuilt carburetors for 1982 Chevrolet S10 pickup trucks, and that your sample is large and well selected. Would you simply visually inspect the units in the sample? Would you install them in trucks and then determine if the trucks started? Would you install them and drive the trucks for fifty thousand miles? Clearly, a visual inspection of an uninstalled carburetor is an invalid sample test. Suppose you are interested in the attitudes of the workers at the carburetor rebuilding plant toward their managers. You select a perfectly constructed stratified sample and assign the manager of each subgroup to interview the workers in that group. This too is not a valid test of the sample.

Since opinion polls are such a pervasive part of our lives, the question of validity in the construction of the test is tremendously important. If, shortly after a dangerous foreign policy incident, you happen to be asked by a pollster to evaluate the overall job of the U.S. president during his entire term in office, the chances are that your response will be more a measure of your wish to be a good and supportive American than a true reflection of your opinion of the president's job. If we want to find out the percentage of liberals among U.S. voters, it is not sufficient to ask a well-chosen sample whether they are liberal or conservative. From this question we could only conclude that a certain percentage of people are willing to classify themselves as liberals. Given that "liberal" is now a bad word in U.S. politics, the percentage of voters that would call themselves liberal would be less than the percentage that would be liberal, based upon the positions they would take issue by issue.

The fallacy of invalid sample test

Drawing a conclusion about P on the basis of an examination of S that did not adequately test for C.

This brings us to the end of the fallacies of everyday reasoning. In the next chapter we will look at some common fallacies in more technical contexts involving probabilities and cause/effect reasoning.

Fallacy Check

Situations and rules

1. Are you asked to believe something because of someone else's word?

CHECK: *Inadequate expert*—Is the person an expert in the right area? Are there other experts who disagree?

2. Are you asked to believe something because of the beliefs of many people, or a longstanding tradition?

CHECK: *Ad populum* and *traditional wisdom.*

3. Does the arguer talk about the person of his or her opponent? Is the arguer explaining the motives of the opponent?

CHECK: *Ad hominem—circumstantial.*
Is the arguer saying abusive things about the opponent?
CHECK: *Ad hominem—abusive.*

4. Does the arguer describe, reword, or imply the argument or position of his or her opponent? Is the arguer distorting the opponent's position?

CHECK: *Straw person*

5. Does the arguer change the topic of the argument or discussion?

CHECK: *Red herring*—Has the prior topic been settled?

6. Does the argument seem to be going in circles?

CHECK: *Circular reasoning*

7. Does the conclusion of the argument claim that some specific event is the cause of some other event?

CHECK: *Post hoc*

8. Does the conclusion of the argument deny that something had an effect on something else?

CHECK: *False denial of a cause*

9. Does the argument conclude that some group has a characteristic based upon the fact that a sample of the group has the characteristic?

CHECK: *Small sample*—Is the sample large enough for the desired accuracy? How heterogeneous was the population? Should a stratified sample have been used?
CHECK: *Biased sample*—Did the selection of the sample insure that every member of the population had an equal chance to be in the sample?
CHECK: *Invalid measure*—Was the test performed on the sample a valid measure of the presence of the characteristic?

Exercises

A. Find the fallacies in each of the following. The letters ''A'' and ''B'' refer to people.

1. A: ''Jack's proposal to upgrade the zoning was impressively argued.''
    B: Hey, of course he's going to argue that. He's got land there.''

2. A: "It's time we started to do something about the homeless in America."

B: "It's not government's job to care for us from cradle to grave."

3. A: "I say that it was the best movie of the year. You don't have to look any further than the lines that are two blocks long."

4. A: "Some people say that American products are not well-made, but I'll tell you that I've had this here Westinghouse refrigerator for going on 12 years now, and I fully expect to have her ten years from now. I don't know what they're complaining about."

5. A: "John K. Galbraith, who is one of the world's leading economists, says that we ought to insure that inflation does not return by imposing price controls now. That's enough proof for me."

6. A: "One of the values of a college degree is that it helps you to be a more well rounded individual. This is true because the education provided by one's four years as an undergraduate expands your knowledge and skills in a myriad of different directions."

7. A: "Here we are, folks, at old Dowling College in Oakdale, New York, a school of over 4,000 students. We came to determine what today's college students think about skiing. Surprisingly, we've found that skiing has significantly decreased in popularity since our last survey three years ago at the University of Denver, in Colorado."

8. A: "The union wants us to consult with them when we intend to change any of the workers' conditions of employment, but I say that once management begins to turn its decision-making prerogatives over to the unions, American capitalism is dead in the water."

9. A: "We have to maintain a strong nuclear deterrent since the world is such a dangerous place. This danger is seen by terrorism in the Middle East, Communist expansionism throughout the world, and the Communist nuclear threat. If you need any proof of the dangers of the Communist nuclear threat, just look at the what weapons we have had to build by way of deterrent to counter it.

10. Jack had a kidney stone attack on the day that he had earlier bragged about never having had to go to a hospital. He made sure that he never bragged about his health again.

11. A: "As Aristotle himself once said, the essence of tragedy as an art form rests in the catharsis experienced by the audience."

12. A: "The Alsatian shepherd is absolutely the greatest of all breeds, because no example of the canine types meets so completely the standards that one should adopt to judge the worth of a dog."

13. A: "Why should the rich get tax breaks by deducting the interest on their second homes, when I can't deduct the interest on my first and only car?"

B: "You wouldn't be singing that tune if you had a summer place in the wealthy Hamptons."

14. A: "If public school teachers in New York are to be professionals, they shouldn't break the law by going out onto the picket line."

B: "Being a professional does not mean giving up all control over your own conditions of employment."

15. B: "Teaching children and administering schools are activities that call for training and expertise. It's time then that we did away with the antiquated system of layperson interference in the carrying out of these important functions. School boards must go."

A: "The education of young people is too important for parents and citizens to leave entirely to a group of unaccountable professionals. And besides, you're still angry because the school board turned down your request for paid leave last year."

16. Jim was a student pilot in Dowling's Aero program. Every time he made a really terrible landing, his flight instructor would shout at him. Every time he made an absolutely unbelievable landing he got praised. But he found that it occurred more often that the shout was followed by an improvement, than that the praise was followed by improvement. In fact, the praise was usually followed by a worse landing. So Jim only shouts at his own kids and never praises them.

17. A: "It's clear from all the polls that the Shoreham nuclear power plant is too dangerous and costly to put on-line."

18. Jack saw that the place where he was intending to build his house had once been struck by lightning. This clinched it for him. He would definitely build here since at least he would be safe from lightning.

19. A: "I have a medical practice that specializes in headaches. Not one patient of mine that I have ever treated with aspirin has ever experienced relief, and I can tell you that the number is in the tens of thousands. I think that it's time that the American public was told of the ineffectiveness of aspirin for headaches. There should be labeling to that effect."

20. In tests that were performed to determine how levels of aggression were influenced by violent TV, the aggression levels of the youngsters were measured by the number of times a child would strike a life-sized stuffed doll of a man when told by a researcher to "Punish that doll for hurting your friend."

21. The electric company wanted to find out what the people of the county thought about the safety of nuclear power. It reassigned the duties of 24

day-shift linemen to do in-depth phone interviews during the times that they would normally be on the lines from a very large and randomly selected number of Long Island homes. Since 99.8 percent of all Long Island homes have a phone, it was not concerned with a biased sample.

22. A: "In an effort to find out in depth what the American people think of the latest scandal hearings in Congress, I'm here with the Phelps family in Waukegan, Ohio. There are fully three generations represented here, so let's see first whether the President still has the kind of credibility problem that polls have indicated he has . . ."

23. A: "*Jaws III* was in 3-D, and so was *Friday the Thirteenth III*. So every time they do the third version of a movie, they make it in 3-D."

24. A company sent out 7,000 questionnaires to the buyers of a new product to gauge customer satisfaction. One thousand people responded of whom 70 percent said they were dissatisfied. The company concluded that 70 percent of its customers are dissatisfied with the product.

B. In each of the following three essays some fallacies, euphemisms, dysphemisms, and persuasive definitions have been placed in italics and enclosed by brackets. Identify these. You may also want to construct a tree diagram of the essays.

25. A TIME TO LICENSE?

With cases of child neglect and abuse piling up in the press, there have been many calls to license parents before permitting them to care for their children in the home. The proposals generally call for the passage of some basic test of safety, nutritional, and medical knowledge before being given custody of the child. My feeling is that [*depriving parents of the right to love their own children*] is contrary to human nature and to God's law. Sure some say that we require licenses to drive cars so why not require licenses to raise children since both would exist for safety reasons. But [*even though we have been requiring drivers' licenses since the beginning of the automobile, the highways of the world are still a scene of slaughter and mayhem, so this is a case where licenses have had no good effect*]. But there's much more to my argument. The fact is that [*my grandfather drove for 45 years with no license and no accidents, whereas my brother has had a license and three accidents in the two years since he's been sixteen. This is further proof that people with licenses are not necessarily better drivers than people without licenses*]. [*To be a good parent means to love your child*], and this love is not something that can be taught in a course. I could rest my case on that alone, but there's more. [*Resorting to this solution to the problems of child abuse and neglect is wrong because it is wrong for the State to have the power to decide when a parent should have his or her child removed from the parent's custody*]. On these points my case stands or falls.

26.   RAMPANT MATERIALISM

In years past there were traditional meeting places for Americans to go to be with their fellow citizens. The churches, village squares, the grange meetings, and even the saloons served this purpose. Today the meeting place is the MALL. On any hot summer afternoon you can find hundreds of thousands of [*mercenary compulsives*] buying their way into bankruptcy, all the while sharing this frantic experience with their compatriots in greed. I have seen this with my own eyes. [*That Americans are compulsive shoppers was proven recently by a poll taken in shopping malls the country over, and representing a sample of over seventy-five thousand! In the poll the American people chose the mall over their places of worship as a preferred way to spend a weekend afternoon*]. [*There is no question that this compulsion that has gripped America has weakened its moral fabric. Since the mall has come to be the center of U.S. social life, the institution of the family has declined*]. This decline is measured by both the divorce rate and the lower rate of families eating Sunday meals together. Something is the meaning of life if it constitutes the primary goal of one's existence. It is clear from the above that THE MALL IS THE MEANING OF LIFE to the American people. [*Even Miss Manners stated recently that the mall has become the center of American social life*]. Sure there are those who say that too much has been made of this compulsive shopping phenomenon. But [*I don't think that putting our heads in the sand every time a social problem arises is effective as a problem solving principle.*] Malls should be closed on our days of worship.

27.   ACADEMIC QUESTIONS

It has become increasingly the practice of college teachers to use multiple-choice and true/false exams. They argue that these are valid measures of student learning when in fact they measure only memorization of facts, [*and the real reason that teachers argue this is because these exams are so easy to grade*]. [*Statistics will show that since "multiple-guess" exams have become widely used students' reasoning skills as measured by LSAT exams have declined. It's ironic that colleges have joined the public schools in the attack against reason*]. Another reason why multiple-choice tests are not valid as measures of learning is that they give the same score to the student who selects the "wrong, but almost right" answer as to the student who selects the absurd answer when their level of learning is very different. Some faculty argue that they don't have time to grade essay exams because they are teaching seven or eight courses, but no faculty member can ever adequately teach more than five courses. [*I know this because I once tried to teach six courses and failed miserably.*] [*In some colleges they have tried to encourage non-multiple-choice testing and yet it continued, so informal measures are of no use];* only a formal ban on true–false and multiple-choice tests will solve the problem. Some argue for such exams on the basis that students like them. But the only reason that students like true–false exams is that [*they have an even chance of getting a correct answer (true or false)],* and that's not a very intelligent reason.

C. Read the following argument. Do a tree diagram, exhibiting all of the logical relationships (premises, counterpremises, etc.) among the sentences. Then find the fallacies in the argument.

28. Atreus (speaking to his grandson, Orestes): "Look, you want to get a good job when you grow up. College grads get all the good jobs. Your uncle's friend Paris never went to college, and he ended up a bum. That's not what you want. And besides that, college will make you a more educated person because college will teach you a lot of things that you don't already know. Did you know that statistics show that people who complete college make more money in their lives than those who don't? So the investment is certainly worth it. I know that your father, Agamemnon, says that you should join him in his carpet business since you'd make more money that way, but if he had your brains, he would never have been a rug salesman in the first place, and then he'd be singing another tune. I know that those who argue against going to college say that going to college and studying all those liberal arts will turn you away from God, but they are just being bigots. What is a bigot, after all, but a person who is against learning. Studying the liberal arts is the core of what has made Western civilization the greatest in history. I say, go for it."

D. In each of the following brief arguments, continuing the topic begun by our friend Atreus, define, find, and explain the fallacies.

29. Electra (Orestes' sister): "Look, whether he goes to college or not, he is going to get either a good job, a bad job, or some mediocre job, so the odds are always going to be one in three."

30. Clytemnestra (Electra's mother): "Don't listen to that little %#@*&! The point is that this family has had so many losers—Menelaus who can't hold onto his own wife, Agamemnon (my *dear* husband), Atreus the chef of humans, and Electra who won't give me the slightest respect—that we're due for a winner. It's the law of averages."

31. Atreus: "Oh, I forgot, the average yearly salary of graduates of Growling College (to name just one) is $37,000. So not only do I recommend that Orestes go to college, but that he go to Growling College, be-

cause I think that it's great if an almost-ex-con like Orestes (having been justly found innocent of the murder of Uncle Aegisthus) can make $37,000 per year.''

D. Read the following argument. Do a tree diagram, exhibiting all of the logical relationships (premises, counterpremises, etc.) among the sentences. Then find the fallacies in the argument and in the continuing dialogue.

32.   WHY NOT THE TRUTH?

HORACE: ''It is clear from every way of looking at the matter that it is false to say that all people are equal. Some people are smarter, stronger, more beautiful, and nicer than others. Those who say that every person is better at something than all others in the world are ignoring the fact that there are some people that are just pure losers. Some people are good at nothing at all and are mean and nasty in addition. Those who keep harping on equality are the very ones who experience *ressentiment*, the envy that the mediocre and the losers feel in the face of those who are their betters. I learned this one day when I heard the biggest loser in the world, my eighth grade teacher, talking about how those who thought that they were better were just conceited. Besides, as Oprah likes to say, 'To each his or her own, baby.' In other words, if you're better, you're better, and Oprah is one of the best. It used to be recognized at the time of the ancient Greeks up through the Middle Ages that some people were just better than others. It was after we lost that idea that all this business about socialism and communism and the rest of that lefty nonsense began to drag us down. Haven't we had enough evidence of the bad effects of equality? So what's the point? It is that democracy, the rule of the people, is ridiculous.''

33. MATILDE: ''You wouldn't be saying all those things if you hadn't been born with a golden spoon in your mouth—with a rich Mommy and Daddy.''

34. HORACE: ''Look, a study was done that showed that the vast number of successful entrepreneurs believe that the idea that all people are equal is false. This shows how a simple idea—that some are better than others—can even have a good effect on your career.''

35. MATILDE: ''To say as you do that we should not care about people just because they may not be born to greatness violates the golden rule. That shows that this idea leads to immoral behavior, even if it leads to business success.''

36. MATILDE: ''Besides, I think that it's more likely that successful entrepreneurs are immoral persons than moral persons; just look at all those

guys lately that have gone to jail for stock fraud, BCCI scandals, and the Savings and Loan rip-off.''

E. Find the fallacies, euphemisms, dysphemisms, and persuasive definitions in the following.

OUTLAW BOXING?

37. YES: "It is my position that the sport of boxing is a violation of the most basic codes of human civilized behavior because to be a boxer is to engage in an activity that any person who was not morally backward would condemn. For this reason, it should be illegal."

38. NO: "To say that an activity should be outlawed just because it violates someone's code of social niceties implies that I should be arrested if I serve a burgundy in a chardonnay glass."

39. YES: "I think that my opponent, who by the way makes a good living by owning a gym where fighters train, is not entirely unbiased. The fact is that boxing damages the brains of 48.6 percent of all professional fighters."

40. NO: "I have trained eight fighters in my time and not one shows signs of brain damage, so your statistics are a lot of bull . . . ! They tried to outlaw boxing once before and people still fought and went to fights, so laws are of no use. Joe Louis said it best, 'If a man wants to see a fight, he'll find two fighters willing to put on the gloves.' Joe put on the gloves enough times that he ought to know."

41. YES: "We ought to get to work to end the slaughter that occurs when two fighters set out to create concussions, subdural hematoma, and trauma in the brain of the other. What is a boxer but a person who is licensed to engage in assault with a deadly weapon. It's time we took the license away."

ARE EXTRAMARITAL AFFAIRS OK?

42. YES: "Since the beginning of time, moral teachers and clergy have tried everything they could think of to get married people to practice sexual exclusivity. Extramarital affairs still continue, showing that no amount of moral persuasion is going to have any influence. The simple fact is that the practice of utilizing the benefits of supplemental relationships is gaining wider and wider acceptance. Those who try to oppose this phenomenon are just acting out their repressed sexuality that stems no doubt from having reached sexual maturity in an uptight culture. I didn't see this until I myself underwent analysis and finally got in touch with my true feelings."

43. NO: "We are no doubt living in a time of great moral decay. To advocate sexual promiscuity in such a time is irresponsible. Since it is wrong, as everyone knows, to break one's promises of sexual faithfulness to the one to whom one has pledged such faithfulness, then extramarital sexual relationships ought to be condemned on moral grounds. Besides, the 1920s were a time of great moral and sexual decay and were followed by a great depression and a world war. I don't think that we want that repeated.

F. Do a tree diagram of the following argument. After that, identify, define, and explain the distinct rhetorical devices (fallacies, persuasive definitions, euphemisms, etc.) that are found in the arguments.

BACK TO BASICS

44. Since the 1960s when the practice of requiring the study of logic for all students was discontinued, the reasoning abilities of students as measured by LSAT, GMATS, and other tests have significantly declined. While the practice of requiring college students to take specific courses is not popular, the damage that eliminating the logic requirement has done is justification enough to reinstate it. It goes without saying that a logic requirement has been one of the touchstones of higher education in the West since Plato created his academy in 380 B.C. Should we tamper with this? You should have heard what I heard in the cafeteria last week; two students were discussing politics in a very serious way. I noticed one of my former logic students as one of the two, and she was easily trouncing the other in the discussion, so there's no doubt in my mind that those who study logic are better arguers. Sure some will say that students should be taking more courses in their own specific areas of study and not be burdened with outside requirements, but they're the very persons who never studied logic and so they don't have an appreciation for its benefits. The bottom line is that to be educated is to be able to reason effectively and persuasively, and so we can't claim that our students are educated unless they have the basic skills of logic. Finally, a recent report in the *Chronicle of Higher Education* noted that there is in fact a trend at colleges to return to the past systems of requirements. So I think now's the time to get on board or be left at the station. Isn't that logical?

FOOLISH TALK

45. It has been in the last ten years that daytime TV talk shows have sprouted like weeds into our living rooms. Does anyone know the damage that is being done to the minds of our country by this parade of misfits that passes for entertainment? There is no question that absenteeism from school has risen since their popularity blossomed, and even though some school districts have added more truant officers, the children still stay

home in droves, showing that more enforcement of education laws is useless. What child would rather go to geometry class than stay home and watch a studio audience harass the mother of some serial killer who says that he's really a good little boy? The only solution seems to be a total ban on talk shows during school hours. Sure the civil libertarians will claim that the principles of free speech allow anything to be shown on TV, but they're making a good living off of saying these things just as the talk show hosts are raking in their filthy lucre. To be a responsible entertainer means to abide by the moral standards of the community. It certainly follows from this that these shows are grossly irresponsible, and so there is no violation of free speech in my proposal.

THE PLAIN TRUTH

46. Ever since the beginning of our great Judeo-Christian-Islamic tradition of monotheism there have always been those who have refused to accept the reality of the One Deity. I think it's safe to say that there is a part of each of us that wants foolishly to be the complete master of our own destiny, even at the expense of all the evidence that we aren't. It is those who can't resist this self-centeredness, the refusers, who are the unbelievers. And so they refuse to accept the One Deity. It's also true that since the beginning of the scientific revolution in the sixteenth century there have been those who have tried to say that human reason, especially science, can answer all questions worth asking. They believed and taught that we cannot know the One Deity with the same certainty that we can know the results of science. But people still flock to the churches, temples, and mosques of their choice, proving that this line of thought has not had any effect. Do the atheistic refusers, these people who say that human life is a worthless flicker of consciousness in the vast expanse of the universe, really believe what they profess? If they really did believe it, why would they bother to try to get us to agree with them? Why would they do anything? The answer is that if the atheists were right that life is worthless, there would be no reason for ever doing anything. So it seems that atheism is a belief that can't be lived. On the other hand, believers are able to face life's inevitable hardships with acceptance and peace. How do I know this? I learned this at the knee of my grandmother who was as devout a person as you could imagine, and her faith allowed her never to despair despite great hardship. When the atheist lives out his or her belief it is just a life of continuous striving for pleasure, a search that is never fulfilled. For those who are still skeptical, they will have to admit that the probability of the existence of the One Deity is at least fifty/fifty, since there either is or isn't such a being. And besides, it was after people began to turn their backs on the acceptance of the One Deity that talk of alienation, dread, and despair began to fill the pages of literature. This alone, the fact that the rejection has had such negative effects, is enough to refute the views of the refusers.

8

Fallacies in Technical Reasoning

What Is probability?

Chapter 1 made the point that argumentation and its logical rules are necessary only because the human brain is not an automatic truth tracker. As great as the brain is, the complexities of life require that we achieve truth after clarifying, searching, arguing, conjecturing, and testing. And we must do this while maintaining the ironic sense that our most firmly held convictions could some day turn out to be wrong. But not all our beliefs are firmly held. In fact, it is a characteristic of beliefs that they vary greatly in the degree of conviction that we give them. It is for this reason that we so often find ourselves stating, comparing, relying upon, and in general grappling with probabilities. *Probabilities* are a device that allows us to measure the degree of certainty or conviction that a belief deserves to be given, relative to the information that we have available. Where "PROB (B)" means "the probability that belief B is true (or that event B will occur)" and "e" means "the available evidence that "B is true (or that B will occur)," we can say:

PROB (B) given e means the degree of confidence that we should have, given e, that "B" is true or B will occur.

This definition allows probability judgments to qualify beliefs or judgments or the occurrence of events. There are several philosophically respectable ways of interpreting exactly what we mean when we make the statement, for example, that there is a 40 percent probability of rain. For our purposes it is most useful to think of probability as a measure-

167

ment of the degree of confidence that we ought to have in the truth of some belief or the occurrence of some event.

If I show you a normal coin toss and then say, "I believe that it will come up heads," you say that there is a fifty-fifty chance that my belief is true (belief) or that it will come up heads (event). The "fifty-fifty" or the "0.5" is a measure of the confidence that you as a rational person should have in my prediction. If you are wondering what the probability is that your newly married friend will still be married (to the same person) in seven years, the divorce statistics tell us that it is only slightly greater than 50 percent. That 50 percent (or 0.5 or ½) is the degree of confidence that you ought to have, given that your friend falls into the appropriate class from which you took the statistic.

The fundamental principle of probability

The first rule of the hard thinker concerning probabilities is that we should base our beliefs, where possible, upon probabilities and forget about possibilities. There is an advertisement for the New York State lottery, describing all the wonderful things that you can do with your winnings and ending with, "Hey, ya never know!" This often-heard expression means nothing other than the claim that it is *possible* that you would win if you played. The problem is that, with the exception of logical contradictions being true, anything is possible! Since anything is possible, something's being possible is not a reason to do or believe anything. Thus, the possibility of winning is not a good reason to play the lottery. It's also possible that you could die of Legionnaire's disease contracted from the lottery ticket. That possibility is not a good reason to refrain from playing.

The fundamental principle of probability: When deciding what to believe or what actions to take, probabilities are relevant, possibilities are not.

Sandra is responsible for the medical care of her aged father, who is suffering from dementia and from painful bone cancer. He has contracted pneumonia and she must decide whether to send him to the hospital, where he will be intubated, given intravenous antibiotics, and probably cured of the pneumonia. If he remains at home he will most likely die of pneumonia. (In a previous era it was called "the old person's friend.") She argues with her brother.

Sandra: "It would be better for him to die in peace than to go through more procedures, more pain, and more indignity."

Hank: "They could save his life!"

Sandra: "For what? More pain? More confusion? He doesn't even know who we are any more! Let him go."

Hank: "And what if they find a cure for his cancer the next week?"

Sandra: " What's the likelihood of that? Come on!"

Hank: "It's possible! And maybe the cancer is what's making him demented. Who's to say? It could happen; ya never know!"

Hank is arguing possibilities; Sandra is arguing probabilities. Hank's possibilities are bad reasons for making choices.

Estimating initial probabilities

Assuming that we are to make our judgments on the basis of probabilities, how do we know what the probability of some event is? Suppose that I have found an obviously ancient coin while walking the countryside of Greece. Having identified a "heads" and a "tails" on this ancient coin, how would I determine the probability that it will come up heads on a toss? Do not answer that since the coin must come up either heads or tails, the probability is 50/50. That would be a logical error. When I drive to work tomorrow I will either have a car accident or not. Does that mean that each time I drive to work I have a 50/50 chance of an accident? This would imply that in my last 5000 commutes I should have had about 2500 accidents. Not quite!

How should we determine what the probability of some event is? Here we must distinguish between the initial determination of the probabilities and the calculation of combinations of previously determined probabilities. The determinations of initial probabilities are most often, and most reliably, based upon evidence of the frequency with which some event or property has occurred in the past. This also carries the implication that this frequency will continue in the future under similar circumstances.

With this in mind, the way to determine the probability of the ancient coin's flip coming up a head is to flip it a number times and calculate the percentage of heads. Perhaps, for example, the coin is crudely made so that the tails side is heavier than the heads side. In this case the coin will have a bias toward coming up heads (the tails side will tend to face down). It may be, then, that PROB (H) = 70% for this particular coin. In like manner, the best way for me to determine the probability of my being in a car accident on the way to work is to locate accident rates for those roads at those times on those days.

The main point here is that a probability statement is a measure of the confidence that we should have in the truth of a statement or the occurrence of an event. The premises that give reasons for the truth of the probability statement are most often statements about the relative frequency of some type of occurrence in the past, implying that the frequency will continue under similar conditions. *Where past frequencies do exist, and have been studied, and are available to us without undo effort, they should be used to justify our probability estimates.* This will insure the maximum accuracy of those estimates. This may seem obvious. But as we shall soon see, people make probability estimates on the basis of reasoning that is often quite biased and inaccurate.

Suppose that, having determined for our ancient coin that PROB (H) = 70%, you wonder what the probability would be that two flips will yield two straight heads, PROB (H & H). In this case you could treat the question the same way that you treated the problem of one heads— that is, perform two flips many times and calculate the percentage of (H & H).

A quicker way would be to use the information that you already have, that PROB (H) = 70%, and employ a rule for calculating probabilities to arrive at PROB (H & H). The rules for calculating the probabilities of combinations of events based upon prior probabilities are known as the calculus of probabilities, or the mathematics of probabilities. In this case the rule would tell us to multiply the probabilities of heads on each of the two flips (70% $\times$ 70%), arriving at PROB (H & H) = 49%.

Whichever way you determine the PROB (H & H), the results should be approximately the same. We will be concentrating in this chapter on common mistakes that people make in arriving at judgments of initial probabilities. The calculus of probabilities is most commonly treated in mathematics courses.

Fallacies Involving probabilities

There are some rather standard or common ways that people go wrong in reasoning about probabilities. We think of these as fallacies since they are patterns of reasoning that lead us astray. Below are some of these fallacies.

The gambler's fallacy

Treating probabilistically independent events as if they were not independent.

In probability theory two events are said to be *independent* if the occurrence of one does not affect the probability of the other. Thus A and B are independent when PROB (B) = PROB (B given A). In the film *The World According to Garp*, Garp is looking at a house with the idea that he might purchase it. Suddenly a small plane crashes into the front of the house. "I'll take it!" says Garp. "It's been predisasterized." Does the fact that a plane has crashed into the house affect the probability that some future disaster will happen to the (reconstructed) house?

Where the ball rested on past spins of a purely random roulette wheel does not affect the probability of it resting at any future place on the wheel. Spins of a roulette wheel are probabilistically independent. In Monte Carlo in 1913 a roulette wheel came up red an incredible 26 straight times. By the 14th straight red the gamblers where heaping great amounts of money upon black, acting upon the assumption that the wheel was "due" to come up black to "correct itself." But roulette wheels have no memories, and so cannot act on the principle of "compensation." On the other hand, two occurrences of chicken pox are not independent. Having chicken pox once greatly reduces the probability of having it again.

He's due for a hit!

Wade Boggs is a baseball player and a great hitter. It is late August; Boggs's batting average is .329, meaning that his ratio of "hits" to "hits or outs" is slightly less than $1/3$. This average is close to his lifetime average, based upon many thousands of times at bat. Boggs has batted twice already today and made outs each time. Is it *MORE, LESS,* or *EQUALLY* likely that Boggs will make a hit during his third time batting?

Here are two wrong answers based upon fallacious reasoning: First wrong answer—a hit is MORE likely because he is due for a hit. Individual hits over long strings of batting appearances are distributed relatively randomly. No doubt Boggs will "bear down" a little more after two failed appearances at the plate, but not enough to raise the probability to greater than 50 percent. You could test this by checking all the times in Boggs's career that he came up at bat with two previous outs. His average in such circumstances is not likely to deviate very much from his normal batting average.

Second wrong answer—there is a 50/50 chance, and thus it is EQUALLY likely for a hit, since he will either get a hit or not. If this were good reasoning, then Boggs (and every other player) would have an average of .500, something no player has ever accomplished in the major leagues over a season. The right answer—it is LESS likely since performances during times at bat are relatively independent, and so the probability of a hit should be based upon past frequencies, indicating an approximately .329 chance of a hit, and thus a .671 chance of an out.

The event at the roulette wheel in Monte Carlo is so famous in the history of probability theory that this fallacy is often called the "Monte Carlo Fallacy." Jack just came through a painful and dangerous attack of kidney stones. He feels a sense of relief, since he figures that he's had his bad health episode for the year. Mim was miserable last winter during all that incredibly bad weather. She takes comfort in the idea that it's very unlikely to have two such winters back to back. Louise wins the lottery against great odds, so her husband, Alex, decides that it is futile for him to play next week since wives and husbands almost never win in successive weeks. All these are cases of the gambler's fallacy.

Specific sequences vs. frequency

One reason that people commit the gambler's fallacy seems to be that they confuse *frequencies in some set* of events with *specific sequences* of events. Alex's reasoning was as follows:

Prem: It is much more likely that unmarried people would win the lottery in successive weeks than married people.

Prem: My wife Louise won the lottery last week.

_____

Concl: My chance of winning the lottery has been decreased.

To illustrate where Alex went wrong, let's look at a four-person society: Louise, Alex (Louise's spouse), Kim, and Pat (both unmarried). Below are listed all the sixteen ways that the lottery in this four-person society could come out in two successive weeks.

Week #1	Week #2
Louise	Louise
Louise	Alex
Louise	Kim
Louise	Pat
Alex	Alex
Alex	Louise
Alex	Kim
Alex	Pat
Kim	Kim
Kim	Louise
Kim	Alex
Kim	Pat
Pat	Pat
Pat	Louise
Pat	Alex
Pat	Kim

There are three things to consider about this list. First, since lottery drawings are independent, the probability of winning the lottery in this four-person society each time that the lottery is run is one in four for every person. Thus every person has an equal chance of winning every time the lottery is played. Second, the probability of each of the *pairs* winning for each successive two weeks is equal, and is $(1/4 \times 1/4) = 1/16$. Third, out of the sixteen possible successive results, only two are of married people winning. So the PROB (marrieds winning) = $1/8$, and PROB (unmarrieds winning) = $7/8$. The first premise of Alex's reasoning, that it's more likely that unmarrieds will win in successive weeks than marrieds, is correct. But Alex confuses two different questions.

Frequency in a set question: What's more likely, that unmarrieds or that marrieds will win? Answer: unmarrieds.

Specific sequence question: What's more likely, that Louise and then husband Alex will win, or that Pat and then stranger Kim will win? Answer: equally likely.

Alex's mistake, which led him to the gambler's fallacy, was that he answered a specific sequence question based upon a (correct) answer to a frequency in a set question. The moral of the story is that if you win the lottery one week, then you can be happier but no more surprised if your spouse wins it the next.

The remedy for our tendency to commit the gambler's fallacy is that when calculating how probable something is, we should use the principles of the mathematics of probability rather than intuitive judgments about ideas of chance or randomness. More specifically, ask yourself when thinking about the probability of sequences of events whether the events are or are not independent, and whether the question is about frequencies in some set or specific sequences. Be aware that it is very common for people to have incorrect ideas about how chance operates.

The fallacy of equiprobability

Arguing from the premise that there are "n" possible outcomes to the conclusion that the probability of each is 1/n, while ignoring the question of whether each of the "n" outcomes is equally likely.

Let's return to the question of the probability of Boggs getting a hit, after two outs, during his third at bat. One wrong answer was that, since he will either get a hit or not, it was 50/50. The bad reasoning was as follows:

Prem: He must either get a hit or not.

Prem: There are only these two outcomes.

Concl: The probability of each is one over two.

We say correctly that the probability of a die coming up even is .5. This is because first it must come up either even or odd; second, the number of ways for it to come up even is equal to the number of ways that it can come up odd; and finally, each of the ways that it can come up are equally likely. It is common for people to neglect the second and/or third of these reasons (Shaughnessy 1981; Dawes 1988). Thus someone might argue that the probability that a thrown die will come up a three is .5, since it will either come up three or not. While it is true to say that a thrown die will either come up three or not, there is only one way for it to come up three and five ways for it to *not* come up three, and each of the six ways that it can come up is equally likely.

What is the probability that a family of three children will have children of all the same sex, assuming there is an equal probability of boys and girls? Someone might argue that you could have (a) all girls, or (b) all boys, or (c) two girls and a boy, or (d) two boys and a girl. Since two of these four are all the same sex, the probability is ½. What is wrong with this reasoning? The problem is that although it indeed must be either (a) or (b) or (c) or (d), there are only two ways to get all the same sex (GGG or BBB). There are six ways to get children of different sexes (GGB, GBG, GBB, BGG, BGB, BBG). Since PROB (boy) = PROB (girl) = ½ (approximately), and since the production of gender at any successive births is independent, each of these eight possible results is equally likely. So the probability of three children with the same sex is two out of eight or one quarter.

To avoid the fallacy of equiprobability when calculating probabilities, be sure that the options that you identify are in fact equiprobable. One check is to see if there are more ways to achieve one of the options than the other. If so, then they are not likely to be equiprobable.

The fallacy of availability

Basing a judgment that one event is more likely than another on which event it is more easy to think of examples for, or upon some imagined scenario of events.

We have emphasized that in estimating the probability of some event's happening, the most reliable information upon which to base the estimate is knowledge of past frequencies. There are some very common rules of thumb or heuristics that people use when estimating probabilities that it would be better to avoid. Since it would be better to avoid them, and since they are likely to lead us astray, we call them fallacies.

There is a "law of memory" that states that repetition increases memory strength. Kahneman and Tversky point out that the availability fallacy is the inverse of this law in that it assumes that memory strength is evidence for frequency (1972). The fact that people commit this fallacy has been shown in an interesting set of experiments by Amos Tversky and Daniel Kahneman (1972), and by Lichtenstein et al. (1978). Subjects were asked questions such as, "What is more likely, lung cancer or stomach cancer?" and "Is it more likely that an English word will begin with "r" or have an "r" as its third letter?" It was found that subjects overestimated the probabilities of events that they could more easily think up (e.g., words beginning with "r") as well as diseases that had recently received publicity (for example, lung cancer as opposed to cancer of the stomach) (Wright 1984). Find a person who for some reason knows few people who are divorced. Find another whose friends seem all to have been divorced. Who is more likely to underestimate the frequency of divorce? Find someone who has just driven past a particularly gruesome traffic accident, and ask him or her a question about the probability of traffic accidents. How do you think that his or her response would be different from a response to the same question had it been asked the day before?

The fact is that there are many factors that influence what most readily can be brought to mind. These factors would include the frequency of occurrence, which *is* relevant to probability, but would also include how recent is the experience, the vividness of the experience, our own preferences in the matter, etc. None of these latter factors are relevant to the probability of the event. When estimating initial probabilities, therefore, be suspicious of the first things that come to mind. Ask yourself, do I think this is more probable because it is easy to recall or has recently been discussed? If so, search for other possibilities and, if you have time, research the statistics.

Ignoring comparative population sizes

Making a judgment that one thing is more likely to have some characteristic than something else of a different type, based only upon the different stereotypes, while ignoring the comparative sizes of the populations.

For the next common error, suppose that you knew that in a particular section of a company there worked 30 engineers and 70 lawyers, and no one else. As you might expect, 70 percent of the engineers liked to do math puzzles in their spare time, while only 30 percent of the lawyers displayed this odd proclivity. Suppose that I randomly select someone from that section, describing the person only as an inveterate math puzzle solver. Do you think its more likely that it's an engineer or a lawyer? If you are anything like Tversky and Kahneman's subjects you will guess that the puzzle solver is an engineer (Kahneman et al. 1982). This tendency is to focus in upon the description (inveterate math puzzle solver), associate that with the characteristics of engineers, and ignore entirely the population sizes of 70 lawyers and 30 engineers. If you think about it, there are exactly 30% of 70 = 21 lawyers who like math puzzles, and exactly 70% of 30 = 21 engineers who like math puzzles, so the probability is equal that either would be selected. When the population sizes (the base rates, as they are sometimes called) were reversed so that there were 70 engineers and 30 lawyers, the subjects did not change their estimates.

That's a stereotype!

There is confusion about what a stereotype is and whether it is a bad thing to think in terms of stereotypes. The word "stereotype" has two different meanings that I can discern from how people use it. In one sense "to stereotype" means to treat something in terms of its *general* characteristics, ignoring what is unique about it. You encounter two dogs on the street that you've never seen before. You are more nervous about the pit bull than about the St. Bernard (Cujo notwithstanding). Your extra nervousness stems not from any specific knowledge of these particular dogs, but from the general characteristics of the breeds. A class of things, or a type, has a characteristic when its members have that characteristic to some significant degree. You have *stereotyped* each of the dogs, attributed to them characteristics that you believe to belong to their type (category, class) without stopping to get to learn about them individually.

If we could not stereotype in this manner, we could not live our lives. We don't eat a wild mushroom of unknown variety, because mushrooms are often dangerous; we teach our children not to get into strangers' cars; we give a beggar money because we assume that he or she is not wealthy; and we believe that if we purchase a new Toyota then it is likely to be reliable. Clearly this form of stereotyping is an appropriate form of reasoning.

The second sense of "stereotype" is equivalent to "false stereotype," that is, attributing to members of a type characteristics that you *falsely* believe to belong to the type. Some forms of racial prejudice are likely to stem from this false stereotyping.

There is also an expression, "negative stereotyping," and it is sometimes claimed that we should not do it. But it is a mistake to think that we should never negatively stereotype another thing or person. We are correct to stay clear of rattlesnakes as a matter of policy, without checking each individual rattlesnake to determine if it's friendly. A man who hangs around elementary school-yards offering candy and free rides home to the children ought to be judged dangerous until proven otherwise. We ought to be more careful about a convicted murderer who has served his time than about a law-abiding pharmacist. The relevant point is not whether the stereotype-based judgment is positive or negative, but whether it is based upon actual group characteristics or is a false stereotype.

Estimation of probabilities

The percentage of great danes who have hip dysplasia is far greater than the percentage of retrievers with the disease. If a veterinarian told you that he had operated upon a dog with hip dysplasia, would you think it more probable that it was a retriever or a great dane? The answer should be retriever. Since there are so many more retrievers than great danes, there are many more retrievers with hip dysplasia than great danes with the problem.

Comparative population sizes are important pieces of information when estimating initial probabilities. The evidence is that the only time that people utilize this information is when it is the only information available (Kahneman et al. 1982). Jean is a serious young woman who loves to read literature. Do you think that it is more likely that Jean is a librarian or a waitress? Most would say librarian, but since there are so many more waitresses than librarians, there are likely to be more serious waitresses who read literature than serious librarians who read literature (Taylor 1982). This is not necessarily to deny the accuracy of the stereo-type of the librarian or of the waitress (whatever the latter may be); it is only to take into account the relative sizes of the two groups when estimating p.robabilities.

The answer to this error is not to stop using stereotypical clusters in the estimation of probabilities. They are too useful to give up, especially when the clusters themselves are based upon frequency data, as when we know that the rate of hip dysplasia among great danes is very high. The remedy is to be sure that the stereotype is accurate and to be very careful about the application of the stereotype to individual cases until the population sizes are considered.

The fallacy of raw mean

Assuming that the mean of a group of numbers is the most frequently occurring number, confusing mean with mode.

It is often the case that we base probability estimates on data about averages or means. For example, if you find that the mean combined SAT score of students at Midwest University is 1,050, and if your son's score was 1,065, then you may conclude that it is most probable that he will find students at Midwest that are about at his level. This can be a mistake. There are some public colleges that are popular with out-of-state students, and which reserve a certain percentage of student places for in-state students. At such places it is easier to gain admission as an in-state student than as an out-of-state student. As a result, the average SAT score of the out-of-state student will be significantly greater than that of the in-state student. The average SAT score of *all* the students may well be a figure that very few students actually have.

The *mean* number is an average, calculated by summing all the numbers and dividing by the number of numbers. The *mode (or modal number)* is the most frequently occurring number. And the *median* is the middle number, where half are greater and half are less. Only in rather unusual groups of numbers with "normal distributions" or "bell shaped curves" do these three measures (mean, mode, and median) coincide.

Frequently, for example, numbers are distributed bi-modally, that is, there are two different clusters of frequently occurring numbers. In the first exam that I give in my course in logic there are frequently a good number of very high grades and a good number of very low grades, with few in between. This is a bi-modal distribution caused by the fact that on this test, the student either gets it all or misses most of it. Very few students would have the mean or average score.

Life expectancy numbers are most often means. Low life expectancies that occur in ancient or underdeveloped societies include very high rates of infant mortality. Thus if the life expectancy is forty-seven, we should not conclude that this age is a frequent time of life for people to die. Most would die very young or a good deal older than forty-seven.

Since it is rarely the case that mean, median, and mode coincide, we should look not only at the "average," but also at the distribution. That is, we have to determine first the high and low figures. This will give us the *range* of values, that is, the difference between the highest and lowest values. We then have to determine how many figures are at various places along this range. That is the *distribution*, telling you how much deviation from the mean that there is. When seeking information about groups of numbers or statistics, beware of the ambiguous term "average." Determine if the report intends to stipulate mean, median, or mode. Be aware that it is almost always necessary to have information about range and distribution, in addition to average, in order to infer probabilities from means.

The nature of general causal claims

In chapter 7 we discussed fallacies involving singular causal claims. Examples of such claims are:

The weakness in the garage's beams was caused by termites.

He was unhappy because he failed to get the promotion.

My sore back this morning was relieved by the aspirin.

These are claims that some specific event or condition (weakness, unhappiness, relief) at some time and place was produced by some other specific condition (termite damage, failure, taking aspirin). These singular causal claims were distinguished from general causal claims. Examples of these are:

The presence of termites causes beams to weaken.

Failure at work causes unhappiness.

Aspirin relieves back pain.

Fatty diets cause colon cancer.

Poverty is a cause of teen pregnancy.

Note that there is a reciprocal relationship between singular and general causal claims, in that each can be evidence for the other. One of the ways that we know that aspirin relieves backaches is that in the past when many people have taken aspirin their backaches have been relieved. Repetitions of (true) singular causal claims, properly controlled, can be evidence for general causal claims. On the other hand, if I know that the general causal claim ''Aspirin relieves back pain'' is true, and if I notice that my back pain is better now than this morning, then I have reason to conclude that the aspirin that I took relieved my pain. I will have argued:

Prem: Aspirin relieves backaches.

Prem: I took two aspirins and later my back felt better.

———————————

Concl: The aspirins that I took caused the relief.

Without the first premise I would be guilty of the post hoc fallacy. General causal claims can be evidence for the truth of singular causal claims.

The question that we face now is, what do general causal claims mean, and how do we determine if they are true? What does the general causal claim "A is a cause of B" actually assert? Such claims do NOT mean, "in every case." Not every aspirin relieves back pain; not every person with a fatty diet gets colon cancer; not every person who fails to get promoted becomes unhappy. These claims do not even mean "in most cases." Although smoking is a cause of lung cancer, most smokers never get cancer. Most teens in poverty do not get pregnant. The above statements of causation in fact state two things. The first is a correlation, and the second is a counterfactual. Since these two things are what general causal claims assert, each must be shown to be true if the causal claim is to be shown to be true.

Correlation—the first condition of causation

The question that faces us now is the following: When do I have good reason to believe a claim that some kind of thing A is a cause of some other kind of thing B? What needs to be shown before I have a right to claim that aspirin (A) is a cause of backache relief (B); or that poverty (A) is a cause of teen pregnancy (B); or that fatty diets (A) are a cause of colon cancer (B)? Before I have a right to claim that these causal relationships exist, I must be able to show that there is a correlation between A and B. To say that there is a correlation between A and B means (Giere 1979):

A correlates with B means: The percentage of B in the class of A is greater than the percentage of B in the class of non-A.

We are going to use the term "correlation" to mean "positive correlation." We know that fatty diet (A) correlates with colon cancer (B). This means that the percentage of colon cancer (B) among the class of people with fatty diets (A) is greater than the percentage of colon cancer (B) among the class of people without fatty diets (non-A). Let's ask the question of whether there is a correlation between cars with rock music playing on the radio (A) and cars that get into accidents (B). This means that we will ask if the following statement is likely to be true: The percentage of accidents (B) among the class of cars playing rock music (A) is greater than the percentage of accidents (B) among cars not playing rock music on the radio (non-A). In fact this is likely to be true, so there is a correlation. (Question: Why do you think that this claim to a correlation is likely to be true?) Remember that if A correlates with B, this does not mean that all A are B, or even that most A are B. Not all cars playing rock music have accidents, not even most rock music cars have accidents. In fact, the percentage of rock music cars having accidents is very small.

In some cases when A correlates with B, something either is an A or it is not. For example, being a male correlates with having heart disease. Being pregnant correlates with diabetes in young women. This means, as we know, that the percentage of males having heart disease is greater than the percentage of nonmales (females) having heart disease, and the percentage of pregnant young women with diabetes is greater than the percentage of nonpregnant young women with diabetes.

In this case, a person either is a male or not, is pregnant or not. In the case of the correlation between fatty diet and colon cancer, the fattiness admits of degrees. Thus the correlation is not between simple fat in the diet and cancer, but between levels of fattiness (grams per day) and colon cancer. We could say that being a male is a qualitative property (like being married, pregnant) and having a fatty diet is a quantitative property (like being heavy, educated, intoxicated). Correlations involving quantities can be represented with more or less smooth curves, which is not the case with qualitative properties. But the distinction between the two is not crucial.

Quantities can always be treated as qualitative properties. For example, instead of one correlation between weight and life expectancy, we could break it up into many correlations between selected weight intervals and life expectancy. How it is done will depend upon the needs of the situation. We are also going to ignore for simplicity the fact that some correlations are stronger than others. If 5 percent of those with fatty diets get colon cancer and only 2 percent of those with nonfatty diets get colon cancer, the difference is 3 percent. If 9 percent of smokers and only 2 percent of nonsmokers get lung cancer, the difference is 7 percent. In this case, the correlation between fat and colon cancer would be weaker than the smoking and lung cancer correlation (Giere 1979). The measurement of the strength of correlations is a good deal more complicated than this, but we won't deal with it here. The important principle to remember for now is that CORRELATION DOES NOT PROVE CAUSATION.

If A correlates with B, you should *not* simply conclude that A causes B. What you should do is ask yourself why A correlates with B. The following possibilities are all consistent with there being a correlation between A and B. In fact, if any of the five conditions below are true, A will correlate with B. They are patterns that could provide the explanation for why A correlates with B.

1. B causes A.

2. A and B mutually cause each other.

3. A and B are both caused by C (no cause between A and B).

4. A and B correlate as a result of accidental factors.

5. A causes B.

The following claims to correlation are all likely to be true. Use your general knowledge and your imagination to guess at which of the above patterns would be most likely to provide the explanation for the correlation.

Pattern #	A	correlates with	B
{ }	Dense ear hair (men)		heart disease
{ }	Spanked child		aggressive behavior
{ }	Below poverty line		high school drop-out
{ }	Moderate alcohol drinking		healthy heart

Assuming that high levels of ear hair correlates with heart disease (which is true!), it is probably because both result from a third factor (pattern #3), perhaps hormone levels. Thus the removal of ear hair (electrolysis, perhaps?) would leave the probability of heart disease unchanged. Unlike many these days, I am not opposed to parents using judicious spanking to control their children's behavior. Reports showing that spanked children tend to be more aggressive do not convince me that it was the spanking that caused the added aggression. I would guess instead that the fact that the child was aggressive caused the child to be spanked (pattern #1), and judicious spanking would reduce levels of aggression.

Counterfactual—the second condition of causation

The problem that faces us then is how to decide if the correlation between A and B is also a case of A causing B. We know that if A causes B, then there must be a correlation between A and B. What else must be shown? The answer is that the counterfactual condition must also be fulfilled. This is as follows:

"A causes B" means:

(1) (correlation condition) The percentage of B in A is greater than the percentage of B in non-A, and (2) (counterfactual condition) had the members of the class of A not been members of A, and all other things remained the same, then the percentage of B in A would have been less.

There are two parts to condition (2). The first states a counterfactual conditional. We make such statements all the time. Having failed a test, Jan states accurately, "If I had studied, I would have passed." The statement is probably true, even though the first part, "I had studied," is not true (counter to the facts). My mother claims that eggnog is good for the flu on the basis that every time she has given me eggnog when I've had the flu, the flu went away in just a few days. One day it occurred to me to ask the following counterfactual question (to myself, of course): "What would the flu have done had I not had the eggnog?" Since the flu probably would still have gone away, I conclude that the eggnog was not a causal factor in the cure. *All causal claims imply a counterfactual claim.*

In the statement of the counterfactual condition it is always necessary to include the qualification, "and all other things remained the same." This qualification is called the *ceteris paribus* condition. Suppose that we think of all those men who walk around with bits of tobacco in their shirt pockets. Is there a correlation between cigarette bits in a man's shirt pocket and a man's having lung cancer? The answer is, clearly, yes. (Why is the answer yes?) Yet if we took all the members of that class, changed the course of their lives so that they never had carried bits in their pockets, would the percentage of lung cancer among them decrease? It would decrease if the way that the bits were prevented was by their never having been smokers. But this would not satisfy the "all other things being equal" clause, and so we would not say that carrying cigarette bits in a man's shirt pocket causes him to have lung cancer. If we had changed nothing about these men's lives except for the cigarette bits, if they had still smoked the same as before, then the percentage of cancer would not change. This is enough to conclude that having cigarette bits in your pocket is not a cause of cancer, even though it correlates with cancer. *In order to show that a counterfactual claim is true, we need to meet the ceteris paribus condition.*

Statistical controls in experimental research

To show that a causal relationship exists, for example that aspirin relieves backaches, is to show that the counterfactual condition is true, including the *ceteris paribus* clause. Clearly, we can't do this by bringing the groups back in time to undo what has been done. We can't take present backache sufferers into the past and give them aspirin to determine what would have happened had they taken aspirin. How is one to know when a correlation between A and B does in fact result from the fact that A causes B? How can you tell if the difference in percentage of B between A's and non-A's would not have existed had all the A's not been A's?

This is an exceedingly difficult question to answer in actual concrete cases. The general answer is easy. You have to have controls. A control means that you hold all factors the same except for one, the one that you suspect to be the cause, and then see if the correlation still exists to the same degree. This is like waiting until your next flu, not taking eggnog, and doing everything else exactly the same (*ceteris paribus*), and seeing how long the flu lasts. If it takes a month to get rid of the flu, give your mother a kiss. In research settings the most common case of controls is that of statistical controls. There are two forms of research that use statistical controls, experimental research and nonexperimental survey research.

Let's say that we are interested in whether aspirin relieves backaches. This means, remember, that a greater percentage of aspirin takers get relief than those who take nothing, and had those relieved people not taken aspirin, *ceteris paribus,* a smaller percentage would have gotten relief. To have *statistical controls in experimental research* involves the following elements.

POPULATION (P) = A pool of potential experimental subjects.

EXPERIMENTAL GROUP (G) = A sample (G) randomly selected from P.

CONTROL GROUP (C) = A sample (C) randomly selected from (P).

A CONDITION OR EFFECT (E) = A change or difference in the level of some condition to be explained.

A PRESUMED CAUSAL FACTOR (F) = A potential cause of (E).

A CONFIDENCE INTERVAL $\pm e$ = The range within (E) that is targeted.

A CONFIDENCE LEVEL $n\%$ = The probability that the (E) will fall outside of $\pm e$, given that (F) is a cause of (E).

The intuitive idea is to subject the experimental group to the presumed causal factor (for example, aspirin as a potential reliever of back pain), and then to compare level of (E) (for example, change in back pain) in the experimental group to the level of (E) in the control group that has not been subjected to the presumed causal factor. If the difference in (E) between the experimental group and the control group is greater than $\pm e$ (for example, a difference of ± 5 percent of those reporting "some pain relief"), then there is an n percent or greater chance that (F) is a cause of (E). If the difference reported between the experimental and control group is within the ± 5 percent range, then the probability that (F) is a cause of (E) is less than n percent, and the results are said to lack statistical significance. Schematically it looks like this:

Step #1:

Establish confidence interval $\pm e$ and level $n\%$.

Step #2:

PRE-TEST	APPLY FACTOR	POST-TEST
level L_a of E in G	F	level L_g of E in G
level L_b of E in C	none	level L_c of E in C

Step #3:

Measure the difference between L_a and $L_g = D_g$.
Measure the difference between L_b and $L_c = D_c$.

Step #4:

Measure the difference D between D_g and D_c.

Conclusion

If D is greater than $\pm e$, then the results are *statistically significant*, which means that there is an $n\%$ or greater probability that D is caused by F.

If D is equal to or less than $\pm e$, then the results are *not statistically significant*, which means that there is an unacceptably high probability that sampling error (chance) caused D (a too-low probability that D is caused by F).

If 36 percent of the experimental group while 34 percent of the control group report relief of back pain after aspirin and a placebo respectively, then the difference of 2 percent is not likely to be statistically significant. The 2 percent difference would be attributed to *sampling error.* In trying to see if the presumed causal factor will be followed by results that are outside of the confidence interval or range of sampling error, the experimenter is trying to disprove the *null hypothesis.*

It is very important to keep in mind that to say that results are significant in the statistical sense does not mean that they are important or worth being concerned about. If the confidence level is set very low, then it is simple to achieve significance, but the probability that (F) caused (D) is still low. Even if confidence levels are set high, statistically significant results could be very unimportant (except to the researcher). If studies show that pesticide use has had a significant effect upon a bird species' reproduction, that only means that there is an *n* percent or greater probability (the confidence level) that pesticides affected that reproduction in some detectable way. It does not mean that the effects were serious or important.

If we are able to show, using the method described above, that there is an *n* percent chance that aspirin causes back pain relief, there is still a 100 minus *n* percent chance, even in a perfectly-carried-out experiment, that aspirin had no effect, that the detected difference (D) was due to *sampling error.* Even though we call this error, it is not the result of any imperfection in the experiment. Rather it is a trick played by chance.

On the other hand, not all experiments are perfectly designed in the sense of meeting the strict *ceteris paribus* condition. In this case some other factor different from the presumed cause may have caused the detected difference (D). Such a factor is called a *confounding factor*, or simply *a confound.*

The fallacy of inadequate controls

Designing a study in such a way that the results can be explained by a confound.

There are three very famous potential confounds, famous enough at least to have names. The first is called the *Hawthorne effect.* It seems to be true that people's performance on many tasks improves just as a result of interest being shown in them. For example, you may devise an elaborate intervention technique for reducing "acting-out" behaviors in children, apply the technique, and get good results. Yet, if the Hawthorne effect was not prevented, then the change in behavior could be attributed merely to the attention given the group rather than to the elaborate intervention that was being tested for. To avoid the Hawthorne Effect it is necessary to tell the subjects as little as possible about what the study is about, and about what its expected outcome is. Most importantly, it is necessary to treat the experimental and control groups as identically as possible. Problems with Hawthorne effect are problems of inadequate controls.

The second famous confound is the *placebo effect*. It is also true that human performance can be changed or improved simply because people believe that it will change or improve. We are all familiar with the doctor who gives the patient a placebo pill telling him that it will cure his headaches. The belief that the headaches will be cured will go a long way toward cure in some cases. In order to eliminate the placebo effect in our aspirin case, it would be necessary to do something with the control group, for example, give them some sort of inert pill so that the frame of mind of the two groups is the same. If there is going to be an expectation of improvement, it should be the same for both groups.

The third famous confound is *subject mortality*. Suppose that a college were to claim that it could dramatically improve its students' IQ. It claims to demonstrate this by showing that entering freshmen had mean IQ scores of 110, whereas graduating seniors had mean scores of 130. Forget about all the problems with controls, and with the fact that test scores increase upon retaking due to test experience. The college failed to mention that the freshman class had 300 students and the senior class had 175 students. Clearly, the students with the lower IQ's were more likely to be the ones who dropped out, so that the mean score will increase without anyone's IQ improving.

The fallacy of no controls

The attempt to establish a general causal claim without using a control group.

For example, a psychiatrist may look back over his practice of the past five years to discover that 70 percent of his depressed patients left his care no longer depressed. He concludes that his treatment is 70 percent effective. This would be fallacious since he had not ruled out the possibility that the patients would have gotten better without his treatment, or even that they got better *despite* his treatment. A school system may introduce a new math textbook to see if scores rise. When the test scores rise, the school attributes the difference to the new text. But without controls, this attribution is unjustified. The improvement could have resulted from new teachers, better students, the newness of the text rather than its actual content, more teacher enthusiasm from knowing they were part of a study, etc.

Nonexperimental survey research

A great deal of the everyday reporting of social science research in the popular media deals with survey data providing descriptive statistics such as unemployment rates, school dropout rates, etc. Often these data simply report trends, as for example, the cost of living rose 0.4 percent last month. Equally often correlations are noted and causes are inferred. This is when the trouble begins.

Survey research is a legitimate alternative to experimental research, using statistical controls. In experimental research the researcher actually introduces the test condition into the group. The researcher changes the world in order to study the effects of the change. Where this is impractical, for example in studying the existence and effects of sexual discrimination, then the researcher studies data that is collected by various sources and tries to "tease out" the causal explanations for trends. This is a very difficult thing to do, and so we should always avoid jumping to conclusions.

This is especially true when the issues are hot, and where we may already have some partialities to which we are committed. For example, it is often reported that women in the U.S. earn on average about two-thirds of what men earn. There is then a correlation between womanhood and lower paychecks. But it takes a great deal more study before we can conclude that this is a consequence of sexual discrimination, that is, that the correlation should be explained by the claim that womanhood causes low pay.

A common social science enterprise is to take interesting classes of people, such as men vs. women, or Jews vs. Protestants vs. Catholics, and attempt to determine if they as classes differ in some common measure such as liberalism, income, or football watching. The dangers of jumping to unwarranted conclusions about cause and effect in research like this are manifold.

The most general reason for the difficulties is the fact that any person belongs to literally an infinite number of classes, religious, ethnic, economic, geographic, educational, cultural, occupational, sexual, physical, sports preference, leisure preferences, age group, IQ, and on and on. So if we find that German Americans as a class have a higher income than Irish Americans as a class, do we conclude that "Germanness" causes income at one level, and "Irishness" causes income at another level? That is, do we conclude that one person's Germanic genetic heritage will make it likely that he will make more money than someone of Irish genetic heritage? If we could be assured that German Americans *differed in no other relevant ways* (the *ceteris paribus* condition) from Irish Americans than the income difference, then we would have some evidence for that conclusion.

But think about how difficult this question is. We would have to rule out such possible other differences as when each group arrived as immigrants, occupational preferences (farmers earn less than merchants), economic development of nations from which the emigration took place, religious differences (some religions encourage economic advancement in ways that others do not), preferences for schooling, educational levels of each group at the time of immigration, family size of each group, divorce rates, mean age of each group, and on it goes. The initial correlation explains nothing. Correlation does not prove causation. *Much of what is pure prejudice about ethnic groups could be accounted for by errors of this sort.*

When the researcher attempts to explain why it is that women earn less than men, as an example, he or she will attempt to break up or "decompose" the groups into smaller groups in which the *ceteris paribus* condition more nearly applies. For instance, the groups of men and women would be further broken down into groups:

A: Men, age X, occupation Y, mean years of service Z

B: Women, age X, occupation Y, mean years of service Z

If the difference still exists, then it is more likely that gender is an explanation. But this is still not the end of the question. What exactly is it about gender that causes the difference? Some possibilities would include the outright exclusionary discrimination of others on the basis of gender, differing expectations of others on the basis of gender, different attitudes toward career and family among men and women, different levels of achievement motive between the sexes, etc.

In all of this, beware of your political inclinations. If they are of antifeminist varieties, then the income discrepancy may lead you to the conclusion that "women can't hack it in a man's world." If they are of the feminist varieties, then the same fact will lead to the conclusion that men are reluctant to give women a chance to compete on an equal footing. Each claim contains an implied causal explanation of the income discrepancy. Both claims would be jumping to hasty conclusions if the only data available were the income differences between the two groups. Consider the following as examples of *very tentative* analyses:

(a) Asians with doctoral degrees make more money than Hispanics with doctoral degrees. Why? For one thing, Asians study in the sciences and technological areas far more than Hispanics, who concentrate upon areas such as education, social sciences, and social work, which pay considerably less.

(b) Crime began to rise in the mid 1960s and continued to rise until about 1980. Why is that? Before blaming Dr. Spock and the permissiveness of the 1960s think about demographics, the study of population trends. The huge postwar baby boom began to come of age in the 1960s, and began to mature in the 1980s. Statistics will show that the 15–24 age group is disproportionately crime prone in comparison to other age groups. Any demographic trend that increases the number of this group in a population will result in an increase in crime.

(c) American Jews as a group earn more than Puerto Rican Americans as a group. Before jumping to hasty conclusions that will reinforce dangerous false stereotypes, think again of demographics. The average age of American Jews is about forty, almost twice that of Puerto Rican Americans. This is the result of trends in birth rates, family size, average age of mothers giving birth, immigration trends, etc. Any group whose average age is twice that of another group will earn more on average. The one steady factor that determines salary is years on the job.

(d) Family income of Japanese Americans is very high in comparison to other ethnic groups. Why? One factor to consider with family income is how many of the family members are working. The more working, the larger the income. As it happens, the average workers per family of the Japanese American family is almost three, while other groups have two or fewer (Sowell 1984). This fact could by itself explain the family income discrepancy.

(e) Infant mortality among the poor is high in comparison to that among the middle class. While there are no doubt differences in prenatal care among the two groups, as well as nutritional differences, we should also consider age. Poor mothers are significantly younger (often teenagers) when they give birth, in comparison to middle class mothers.

(f) Death from cancer and heart attack has grown steadily during this century. Should we look at pollution rates and changed eating habits?

Certainly, but we should again consider demographics. More people live longer now than in 1900, and so the rate of older person's diseases (cancer and heart failure) will increase as the average age of the population increases.

The fallacy of inadequate decomposition

Occurs in nonexperimental survey research when the ceteris paribus *condition has not been adequately met due to the fact that classes have not been adequately decomposed.*

When this fallacy is committed, the groups that are being compared differ in other relevant ways in addition to the purported cause. This is the result of the fact that the groups that are being compared have not been adequately decomposed into smaller groups to "tease out" these other relevant differences. It has been shown that Black Americans who kill whites get the death penalty at a higher rate than Black Americans who kill Blacks. The most common explanation for this is that jurors, or prosecutors, or judges give greater value to the lives of white victims. This may be the explanation. But other possibilities need to be ruled out. For example, if it were shown that the murders of whites took place in rural settings (where the death penalty is more frequently applied) to a greater degree than murders of blacks, then the explanation would be location rather than racial bias.

Perhaps all of this has caused you to be skeptical that we are ever able to determine what causes what. While it is right to receive general causal claims with a critical eye, the plain fact is that researchers have been tremendously successful in the use of both experimental and non-experimental controlled research. Just consider the discoveries concerning smoking's contribution to various diseases, high cholesterol as a cause of arteriosclerosis, the role of AZT to retard the development of AIDS, and the benefits of moderate exercise. In purely social science research the problems are more difficult because the phenomena are so much more complex. To inquire as to the cause of the tremendous rise in teen pregnancy is to try to understand a system that is hundreds of times more complex than the biological systems that medical researchers work with.

One of the major benefits of understanding the research principles described in this chapter, as well as the sampling procedures described in chapter 7, is to be a more critical *consumer* of research findings, to be able to ask the right questions about research reports. An understanding of the difficulties of statistically based research should also provide you with an admiration for the skill and the professional dedication of those who engage in it.

Fallacy Check

1. Does the argument estimate the probability of some event?

CHECK: *Availability*—Is the most probable event the easiest to recall? Is frequency data available?

CHECK: *Gambler's fallacy*—Does the estimate assume that independent chance events affect each other's probability?

CHECK: *Equiprobability*—Does the estimate assume that events that have different probabilities are equiprobable?

CHECK: *Ignoring comparative population sizes*—Does the question involve stereotypes? Have you considered the sizes of the groups involved?

CHECK: *Raw mean*—Is range and distributional information included in the data? Would the conclusion be different if different ranges and distributions were the case?

2. Does the conclusion claim that one thing is a cause or causal factor of another based upon experimental research?

CHECK: *No controls*—Is the claim that A causes B based on pre- and posttesting of some group? Was a control group employed?

CHECK: *Inadequate controls*—If a control group was employed, was the *ceteris parabis* condition fulfilled? Were both groups randomly selected? Could the effect be more easily explained by placebo or Hawthorne effects, or by subject mortality?

3. Does the conclusion claim that one thing is a cause or causal factor of another based upon survey nonexperimental research?

CHECK: *Inadequate decomposition*—Were the groups adequately decomposed in order to rule out alternative causal factors?

Exercises

A. Identify the fallacies concerning probabilities and cause effect reasoning in the following.

1. Western University was interested in improving mathematics learning in its introductory courses. It decided to change to three 50-minute periods

rather than the usual two 75-minute periods. To test its change, it took four sections of MATH 001 in the evening and made the change. At the end of the semester it compared the scores in these four sections to those in four day sections of MATH 001 that had stayed with the 75-minute periods. The 50-minute period students did much better on the final exam, so the university decided to make the change throughout its sections.

2. When Jack heard the tragic news of the accidental death of his young nephew, he experienced a secret sense of relief that now it won't happen to his own children. The odds against two such events in the same family would be incredibly large.

3. Mary was a clerical worker in the cardiac ward of Children's Hospital. On Friday her son came home from his first day of high school football practice complaining of pains in his chest. Mary decided not to see their family doctor, going immediately to the very expensive cardiologist.

4. James was beginning a new job for which he was not sure he was qualified. The expert at the employment agency believed that he would be fired in a week. He just didn't have the experience. James was not dismayed, arguing that he had a fifty-fifty chance of success, since after all he was either going to succeed or fail.

5. Franklin had to drive to Washington, D.C., from New York. He was afraid of driving ever since his accident. He could travel the Jersey Pike or Rt. 1. The morning he was to depart he heard of a terrible accident on the Jersey Pike, so he decided to take that route since it's very unlikely that there would be two such accidents on the same day.

6. Jean bought a pit bull terrier (Scrappy) for a pet, and to protect her and her three young children. Sam asked whether she wasn't worried that the dog might injure one or more of the children. Jean thought about Scrappy, about how well he played with the little ones, about the time that her two-year-old stuck a pencil in its eye, and laughed. She answered Sam that she couldn't conceive of Scrappy ever hurting the kids. It just would never happen.

7. My computer dating service here in Dallas has arranged a date for me with an attractive young woman who is well dressed and well educated. Everything seemed great until they told me that she speaks French fluently. I didn't say so, but I was really disappointed, because I had really hoped for a good old American born woman, and this one's probably French.

8. "Well folks, it's come down to this one field goal with 4 seconds left. If Kramer gets it, the Lions win. It's fifty-fifty, he either gets it or he doesn't. A whole game coming down to the flip of a coin."

9. The principal of the school selected the ten students who obtained the lowest grades in a standardized reading test. She assigned them to a special reading instructor. When retested at the end of the year, the group showed marked improvement. She decided to make the position of special reading teacher a permanent item in the budget.

10. Mimi works in the State Court building, which keeps records and statistics on marriage and divorce. She is about to be married, and a lawyer that she works with suggests a prenuptial contract that would protect her assets in the event of a divorce. Mimi has nothing in principle against such an agreement, but thinks about how much in love she and Humberto are; about how they never fight; about how they agree on everything; about how placid Humberto seems to be; and so Mimi decides that such an agreement is unnecessary in their case.

11. Will has had two straights in a row in poker. He now has to decide to go either for a third straight or for a full house. He figures that he would never get three straights in a row, and for that reason decides to go for the full house.

12. Jake was trying to decide where to place his house on the large parcel of land that he had bought. He noticed that there was a tree that had been damaged by lightning. He put his house on that spot, reasoning that at least here it would be safe from lightning.

13. The chairman of the math department in Bayville High School wants to know if changing the textbooks in ninth grade math will increase the students' achievement on the regents exams. There are two math teachers, each of whom teach four sections of ninth grade math. The chairman asks your advice in helping him decide how to find out if the change of textbooks will result in increased student achievement. What would you suggest that he do?

14. Mary is a secretary at the department of health statistics in Washington, D.C. Her mother, who is 53, has recently been very ill with heart disease and Mary seems obsessed with the illness. Her husband has been constantly away on sales trips. Her son was doing a project for his ninth grade health class that was due in three weeks. In answer to his question, Mary told him that it is her understanding that heart disease is the leading killer of women under sixty.

15. When Jake saw the terrible accident along the highway on his way home he breathed a sigh of relief. At least it's not my turn today, he thought, and jammed the accelerator to the floor.

16. Bob was astounded to discover that the average life expectancy in France in 1750 was 37 years old, whereas today it is 70. He felt that he now understood why progress came so slowly in the past. As soon as

someone discovered something, he died with very little opportunity to educate the next generation.

17. In order to test the frequency of police brutality in the nation, Hanna and Fallon, a social research firm, selected a large sample of police officers from around the country. The sample was selected according to the most rigorous statistical standards. Observers from Hanna and Fallon rode with the officers for 30 randomly selected work shifts. They found that police brutality in the U.S. is almost nonexistent.

18. If we ban violence on TV, then the pattern of violence among our young will either increase, decrease, or stay the same. A one-third chance of decreasing youth violence seems to be something worth trying.

19. It was discovered that parents of seriously disturbed children lacked the same sort of physical nurturing and warmth toward the disturbed children as did parents of normal children. Should we institute parent warmth courses to try to decrease the incidence of seriously disturbed children?

20. I didn't do so well in law school, but I'm either going to pass the bar exam or not. So my fifty-fifty chance is as good as anyone else's.

21. Briarmanor University advertises that the mean income of its graduates is $73,000 with surprisingly little deviation. It bases this figure on the returned responses of 30 percent of its graduates to a questionnaire mailed to every graduate. All agree that this was a surprisingly large response rate.

22. Larry Bird can win the game with a foul shot. Since he will either make it or not, the probability that the Celtics (his team) will win is 50–50.

23. While watching the World Cup on the TV Sandra noticed that soccer players tended to be shorter than the average person. She decided that she would encourage her son to play basketball.

24. Carlo's daughter was thinking of attending Eastern University, where in her last three years she would be required to live off campus, in the surrounding area. Carlo checked out the area, he thought of all the ways that his daughter could be harmed, by muggings, rape, murder, theft, etc. He decided that it was too dangerous and insisted that she reject the acceptance.

25. A recent study of TV habits of 10,000 youngsters found that those who watched more than twelve hours of violent TV per week tended to be significantly more aggressive in their social behavior than those who watched less. This is one good reason for preventing children from watching violent TV.

26. It has been found that executives who are more willing to take risks are wealthier and more successful than those who are risk-averse. It is for

this reason that I am planning to open a clinic to help executives overcome risk aversion. I expect significant corporate financing.

27. A recent report by the Association for the Preservation of Natural Childbirth indicated that on a test of self esteem of fifteen-year-olds, those who had been breast fed as youngsters scored significantly higher than those who had been bottle fed. You conclude that it is your obligation to see to it that your child has every possible opportunity, so you will be sure that your child is breast-fed too when he or she arrives.

28. Sam noticed that in a surprisingly large number of auto accidents the radio was playing loudly at the time of the accident. He concluded that loud radio playing must distract drivers, and so started a campaign to limit the decibel level of car radios.

29. It was reported last week in the *Western Journal of Medicine* that a large study of coffee drinking and health has shown that those drinking five or more cups of coffee a day have a much greater likelihood of heart disease than those not drinking coffee at all. Fran decided that coffee was dangerous to the heart.

30. In this problem, check for fallacies of probability, and fallacies of causation. Donna is wondering whether to move herself and her family to Florida. There are so many things to worry about. Fortunately, she's not worried any longer about whether she'll get a good job. It occurred to her that she either will or won't, and that a fifty percent chance of a good job is better than what she has here on good old Long Island. Her family would really like to know what's going on, and where they'll be living, but when they press Donna she always talks about that raise that her boss has been talking about for two years now. She can't help it if her boss can't make a decision. How can she decide where to live if she doesn't know what she'll be leaving? She does know that life in Florida is really good. One of her acquaintances at work moved down there and you should see the letters that she writes home. She was really able to get her life together. Florida, Donna believes, must be good for the soul. Another good thing is the school system that her daughter little Amy would be moving into. The average IQ of the students is exactly 112, which happens to be Amy's IQ, so she'll be with kids at her own ability level. On the other hand Donna is very worried about the crime, drugs, murders, and all that's down in Florida. She thinks about all the ways that Amy could get mixed up in that mess. Is it really fair to take Amy into a situation where more likely than not she will in some way be harmed by their drug problems? While she's at it, Donna worries too about her little poodle, Garcin. Friends of Donna's had a poodle and three months after they moved to a different house it died of heartworm. It's amazing how the stress from changes in environment can cause physical illness. She'd hate to see Garcin get heartworm after all the good care Donna has taken of him. And

she worries too about her own health now that she's past thirty-five. She knows for a fact that the rate of deaths by stroke and heart attack in Florida is one of the highest in the U.S. She wonders if there's something in the environment in Florida. Anyway, she doesn't want that for herself. But alas, one day Amy bugged her until she said, "OK, we're going!" Later she explained to friends how much she loved ocean swimming, but hated the cold water here on good old Long Island.

31. Will a sedentary, overweight male of forty-three years old increase or decrease his chances of getting cancer by going on a doctor-designed program of diet and exercise? Circle one.

32. You find an ancient coin in the heart of China dating back to 500 B.C. You want to know the probability that, when you flip it, it will come up "heads." Jim tells you that it's obviously fifty–fifty since it will be either heads or tails. How's Jim's reasoning, good or bad?

33. In his ten-year career as a football place-kicker, Kramer has made about one-third of his field goals from beyond forty yards, and his average this season is the same. It's the Superbowl and he has missed two so far from that distance. He is about to kick again from the same distance. Is he more, less, or equally likely to make the kick? Circle one.

34. Jane is a rather intellectual person who loves to read Emily Dickinson's poetry and Flannery O'Connor's fiction. The clothes she wears are well-made and neat, but unstylish. Jane has no TV and lives in Sayville, New York. Is it more likely that Jane is a librarian or a waitress?

35. You heard that three weeks ago Jack from Oakdale and his wife Janet both won the lottery. This week Mildred from Albany and (unrelated) George from Rochester won. Which week's outcome was LESS likely if any?

36. A "skin peel" is used to remove precancerous sun spots and also to remove wrinkles from your face. You are thinking of getting one in order to look younger, but then learn that there is a strong correlation between having the "peel" and having skin cancer. Should this make you more or less willing to get the peel done, or should it have no effect?

37. You are depressed and visit a psychiatrist, who informs you that the therapy will be long and costly but that 80 percent of her patients with depression leave treatment symptom-free. Is that a logical reason to begin treatment? Yes or No?

9

Aristotle's Herculean Try

Aristotle's Problem

Aristotle was a Macedonian who came to Athens about 367 B.C. to study at Plato's Academy. Upon the death of Plato, Aristotle began his own school, which was more like a research institute that one would find today. By the time of his death in 322 B.C., Aristotle and his students had created a system of knowledge that included astronomy, physics, biology, psychology, politics, ethics, rhetoric, dramatic criticism, metaphysics, and, of course, logic. It should be emphasized that this body of work was a *system* in the sense that each part fit together with the other and could come to the defense of the other. This powerful system of thought dominated the regions of Europe and the Middle East until the end of the Scientific Revolution. The latter could be symbolically dated as A.D. 1689, the year of the publication of Isaac Newton's *Mathematical Principles of Natural Philosophy*.

In presenting Aristotle's system of logic, we will not attempt to be historically accurate. The system has undergone many changes, additions, and subtractions since his death in 322 B.C. Ours will be an imaginative reconstruction of Aristotle's thinking. So let's first imagine Aristotle during his initial days in Athens marveling at the Greeks as they talked and argued in the Agora, or square of the city. They would, of course, be arguing about politics, the passion of the classical Greeks of every city-state.

Despite the eloquence and rhetorical virtuosity of the speakers, there was something about the scene that bothered Aristotle. The audience would agree or not agree with a speaker, but give very poor reasons why. The closest that he could find to reasons for agreeing were how the speaker, or his arguments, "sounded." "That sounds right," said one man. "No, I prefer the first speaker. His speech sounded better," said another. It was as if each person had a sixth sense, a "logical intuition," that could "see" which arguments were successful and which were not.

But if such a logical intuition existed, thought Aristotle, then there would be broad consensus on which arguments were best, in the same way that there is broad agreement concerning what people see with their eyes. But no such consensus existed, and Aristotle could see that the audience tended to agree for all kinds of poor reasons. Perhaps the hearer had something to gain by the speaker's views being accepted. Perhaps the listener was afraid of the speaker. Perhaps the speaker flattered the audience. There must be a better way. At that time, however, he didn't have a clue as to what the specifics of it would be. But he knew what he sought. He wanted to create a system of logic, of principles, that could decide for any possible argument whether it was a good or a bad argument. It would be like figure 1.

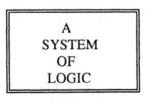

Fig. 1. System of logic

What made this a particularly difficult problem was the fact that the set of all possible arguments is infinite. This is true at least for the reason that the set of all possible sentences, which are the components of arguments, is infinite. You may wonder how there can be an infinite number of distinct sentences when there is only a finite number of words, which are the components of sentences. The answer is easy. Suppose that I had a huge vocabulary of *three and only three* words. I would still have an infinite number of sentences at my disposal. Here is my three-word vocabulary, "walked," "she," and "and." Here are just some of the sentences that I can now form:

She walked.
She walked and walked.
She walked and walked and walked.
She walked and walked and walked and walked.

Do you doubt that I have an infinite number of potential sentences at my disposal? Although we are not trying to be historically accurate about Aristotle, it should still be noted that the Great One did not believe that any collection could be infinite. But we can still conjecture that the set of all possible arguments, for Aristotle, must have seemed immensely large. How can we have a system of logic that will divide an infinite class of arguments into two subclasses, good and bad? Will we need an infinite number of rules? That would not be very useful.

The Idea of Logical Form

As Aristotle approached for the first time the doors to Plato's Academy, he noted over the front door the inscription, "He who knows no mathematics need not enter." Fortunately Aristotle had learned his mathematics, or at least enough to matriculate. While in Plato's school he learned much more, and what he learned gave him the key, the central concept, that would allow him to fulfill the promise of a system of logic. The mathematics that may have given him the clue was geometry.

Geometric form

The name "geometry" indicates what its original purpose was considered to be. "Geo" means "earth," and "metry" refers to the "measurement of." So the function of geometry is to develop ways to measure the earth (for example, to lay out farming plots), as well as to measure the things on the earth (for example, to construct buildings). At the hands of the Greeks, geometry was to become a very abstract discipline, concentrating on the very general formal properties of things. Look at the items in figure 2.

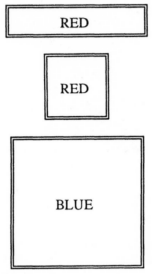

Fig. 2. Geometric forms

How many items do you see? You see three items, of course. Aristotle asks that you put on your geometer's eyeglasses and look again. How many figure do you see now? Here are some possible answers:

a. Two items, red and blue.

b. Three items, two red items and one blue item.

c. Three items, one on the top, one in the middle, one on the bottom.

d. Two items, equilateral right-angled parallelogram (square) and nonequilateral right-angled parallelogram (nonsquare rectangle).

All of these observations would be correct from some perspective, but with your geometer's glasses on, only answer (d) is correct. The geometer is not interested in the color of things, nor in their placement relative to each other. The geometer is interested in the abstract shapes, the geometric forms of things. Given this idea of geometric form, the two items on the right are identical. The fact that one is so much larger than the other is irrelevant, since gross size is irrelevant to geometric form.

With the notion of geometric form, it is not necessary that geometry discover the structural properties of every object in the world. It need only concentrate on the shapes that these objects share. The properties of a right triangle (for example, the Pythagorean property that the square of the longest side will equal the sum of the squares of the other two sides) will hold for *all* right triangles. It won't have to be rediscovered for each one. Thus, by concentrating only upon the form of objects (forgetting about their color, gross size, position relative to each other, or their motion) the geometer vastly simplifies his job of "measuring the earth."

The forms of sentences

Aristotle's problem was that there are so many possible arguments because there are so many possible sentences that could make up arguments. But when he constructed a pair of logician's eyeglasses, modeled after the geometer's glasses with which he was so familiar, something happened. He looked at the sentences below and saw something different from what others without the glasses saw.

All trees are green.
Some trees are green.
All Republicans are conservative.

With his logician's glasses on, how many sentences does he see? Here are some answers:

a. Since there are three periods, there are three sentences.

b. Two sentences, one about green trees, another about conservative Republicans.

c. Two sentences, one stating that All A is B, and another stating that Some A is B.

You are right in thinking that (c) is the correct answer from the point of view of logic. What is described in (c) are two *logical forms* of sentences. Simply put, in Aristotle's logic, the logical form of a sentence is what you get when you replace all the nouns and adjectives with variables.

The four categorical propositions

So now Aristotle's problem is to decide how many logical forms of sentences there are. He ponders this question for three one-hundredths of a second and decides that there are only four. The four logical forms of sentences are generally called the four categorical propositions. This is not a very apt description since they are not really propositions at all. They are logical forms that propositions can take.

THE FOUR CATEGORICAL PROPOSITIONS

A: All A is B
E: No A is B
I: Some A is B
O: Some A is not B

Aristotle did not exactly claim that these are the *only* forms that sentences take. He claimed that any sentence (1) either would have one of these four forms or (2) could be translated into one of these forms with no change of meaning.

Note that the die has already been cast for the outlines of a system of logic. This system will ignore the *content* of arguments in order to concentrate upon their logical forms. If the system of logic ignores the content of arguments, then how will it be able to evaluate the truth of the sentences that make up the premises of the arguments? The answer that Aristotle gives is the following.

It is the job of all the various sciences to determine if sentences are true or not. This can be done only by paying direct attention to the world. It is the job of logic to determine which sentences *must* be true, given that other sentences are true. As an example, it is the job of the ornithologist (bird expert) to determine if the sentence "All crows are black" is true. She does this by observing crows. A system of logic can tell us that the sentence "Some crows are black" is true, once it is established that "All crows are black" is true. In the language of logic it is said that "Some crows are black" can be validly derived from "All crows are black." Logic, as conceived by Aristotle, deals with the question of which sentences can be validly derived from which. It should be noted very clearly that the reason that "Some crows are black" is validly implied by "All crows are black" has nothing to do with crows or blackness. It has to do only with the fact that "Some crows are black" is an example of "Some A is B," and "All crows are black" is an example of "All A is B." And the form "Some A is B" validly follows from the form "All A is B." The correctness of the argument about the crows depends entirely upon the logical forms of the sentences.

Finally, the correctness of the argument "All crows are black, therefore Some crows are black" does not depend upon whether the sentence "All crows are black" is true. From the standpoint of logic conceived as a system of formal relationships, the argument,

All crows are red.

―――――――――

so, Some crows are red.

is equally correct. But let's get rid of the word "correct" and use the proper term, "valid." To say that an argument is valid is to say that it has a structure that guarantees that whenever the premises are all true, then the conclusion will be true.

The argument above has the structure,

All A is B

―――――――

so, Some A is B

which is a valid structure. The fact that the premise "All crows are red" is false does not affect the structure. Put another way, we could say that if "All crows are red" were true (even though it isn't), then "Some crows are red" would necessarily be true.

Let's take a closer look at just what the four categorical forms actually say. The wordy translations are given as follows:

A: *All candidates are honest.* = The class of candidates has at least one member, and every one of them is a member of the class of honest things.

E: *No candidates are honest.* = The class of candidates has at least one member, and not one of them is a member of the class of honest things.

I: *Some candidates are honest.* = The class of candidates has at least one member, and at least one of them is a member of the class of honest things.

O: *Some candidates are not honest.* = The class of candidates has at least one member, and at least one of them is not a member of the class of honest things.

There is some controversy about the translations provided above, with some alternative possibilities, but it need not detain us. Note that the term "some" means only "at least one." Thus when "Some A is B" is true, it could be that All A is B, or it could be that just one A is B. And the truth of "Some A is B" does not imply that Some A is not B, although the latter *could* be the case.

It has become traditional to give the components of the four categorical forms specific names. Let's use as an example the sentence form:

No	A	is	B
↓	↓	↓	↓
quantifier	subject	copula	predicate

The names of the parts are as listed above. The quantifier talks about how many, and will be either "All," "No," or "Some." The subject, what is being talked about in the sentence, comes right after the quantifier. The predicate, what is being said about the subject, comes last in the sentence. The word that links the subject and the predicate will always be a version of the verb "to be," and is called by the Latin name, the "copula." The copula is the linking or coupling word; it comes from the same Latin root as the English term "to copulate."

If we look at the four forms, we will see that two of them are *universal* in the sense that they are talking about all of the class of the subject, and two are *particular* in the sense that they are talking about not necessarily all of the class of the subject. You will also discover that two of the four forms are *affirmative* in the sense that they are referring to what *is* the case, and two are *negative* in the sense that they are referring to what *is not* the case. Finally, the four forms are traditionally named the A, E, I, and O forms, probably taken from the vowels of the Latin words "affirmo" meaning "to affirm" and "nego" meaning "to negate." The affirmative sentences are A and I, and the negative sentences are E and O. To summarize:

A: All A is B   universal affirmative

E: No A is B   universal negative

I: Some A is B   particular affirmative

O: Some A is not B   particular negative

Let's envision Aristotle thinking about all of this at lunch one day, having just written the four categorical forms on his napkin. Into the room dashes his young pupil, Alexander, whom Aristotle tutors privately. It is the same Alexander who was later to be known as "The Great." The master explains to the young man what he is doing, and how these four forms alone can represent any possible sentence. An impish smile forms on Alexander's face as he jots onto the napkin, "Only men are drafted," grabs an olive, and runs out. Aristotle ruminates:

Only men are drafted = All men are drafted? No, that can't be right since it's true that only men are drafted, but some men, for example those who are sickly, are not drafted, and so it's not true that all men are drafted.

Only men are drafted = Some men are drafted? No, since although both are true, there are many cases where "some A is B" is true, while "only A is B" is false. For example, it is true that some men are parents, but it is false that only men are parents.

But wait! He could reverse the subject and predicate.

Only men are drafted = All draftees are men. That works. Aristotle calls Alexander to the table and shows him the solution. "Only A is B" shall become "All B is A." Alexander, seeming slightly interested, grabs the pen and scrawls, "Not all parents are men" onto the napkin, and smiles. Aristotle thinks furiously as his young challenger looks on.

Not all parents are men = Some parents are men. This will be his answer. Alexander shakes his head to the side, grabs the pen, and writes, "Not all mothers are men" is true, but "Some mothers are men" is not true. He's right, thought Aristotle, "Not all A is B" can't be translated as "Some A is B." It must be translated as "Some A is not B." Alexander has grown bored of the exercise, nods his head, and runs out. Aristotle now tries a number of other possible forms such as "No A is not B," "Some A is not non-B," "Not all non-A is not non-B." He convinces himself that the four forms will handle any other possible form.

First exercises

A. Translate the following English sentences into A, E, I, or O form, and circle whether they are universal or particular and affirmative or negative. Circle also, based upon your common knowledge, whether they are true or false. NOTE: There will be absolutely no correspondence between affirmative and true, and negative and false. These are entirely different distinctions.

1. Sailboats are sometimes sloops.

   _____ U or P; A or N; T or F

2. Only Fords are automobiles.

   _____ U or P; A or N; T or F

3. Not all fires are caused by arson.

   _____ U or P; A or N; T or F

4. Fire does not cause heat.

   _____ U or P; A or N; T or F

Immediate inferences

Aristotle is still eating lunch and begins to think about how many types of arguments there are. He has already mentioned arguments of the form:

All A is B

———————

so, Some A is B

He decides to call this an "immediate inference," since one sentence is inferred immediately from another sentence. More formally, an *immediate inference* (or immediate argument) is one with only one premise, and two subject/predicate terms. The two subject/predicate terms above are A and B. The above immediate inference is valid since in every case where "All A is B" is true, then "Some A is B" must be true.

Here are some examples of immediate inferences:

"Some A is not B" is false

———————————

so, "All A is B" must be true

"Only M is L" is true

———————————

so, "No L is M" must be false

The square of opposition

We can try to decide if these are valid by using our logical intuition, that is, by focusing and thinking very hard about it, but Aristotle would rather that we leave the thinking to him. To relieve us of the need ever to think again, he devises the following system of logic for all possible immediate inferences. It begins with a figure called the "Square of Opposition," which looks like figure 3.

A: All A is B   E: No A is B

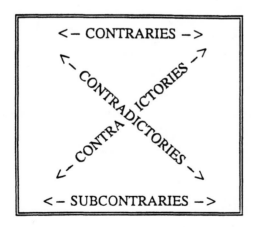

I: Some A is B   O: Some A is not B

Fig. 3. The square of opposition

At each corner of the square is one of the four categorical forms. The problem is to determine what the logical relationships are between the corners. Let's look at the possibilities:

Contraries:
SUMMARY: Two sentences are contraries if they can't both be true.
If "A" is true, then "E" must be false.
If "E" is true, then "A" must be false.
If "A" is false, then "E" could be true or false.
If "E" is false, then "A" could be true or false.

Subcontraries:
SUMMARY: Two sentences are subcontraries if they can't both be false.
If "I" is true, then "O" could be true or false.
If "O" is true, then "I" could be true or false.
If "I" is false, then "O" must be true.
If "O" is false, then "I" must be true.

Contradictories:
SUMMARY: Two sentences are contradictories if they can't both be true and they can't both be false.
If "A" is true, then "O" must be false.
If "O" is true, then "A" must be false.
If "A" is false, then "O" must be true.
If "O" is false, then "A" must be true.
If "E" is true, then "I" must be false.
If "I" is true, then "E" must be false.
If "E" is false, then "I" must be true.
If "I" is false, then "E" must be true.

No-thought solution to the validity of immediate inferences

You can check your logical intuitions about these relationships against Aristotle's if you wish. With the summary statements above, it will be possible for you to decide, without the benefit of your own logical intuitions, whether an immediate inference is valid or not. Let's take an example:

Since it's false that all Californians are surfers, it must be true that some Californians are not surfers.

To decide if this is valid, follow the steps below.

1. Put the argument in exactly the following premise/conclusion form, using the indicator words.

            is
"All Californians are surfers"   ————> false

———————————————

          must be
so, "Some Californians are not surfers" ————> true

2. Check to be sure that it is an immediate inference. It has one premise and two subject/predicate terms ("Californians" and "surfers"), so it is an immediate inference.

3. Decide which of the four forms the premise and the conclusion are. The premise is an "A" sentence, and the conclusion is an "O" sentence.

4. The argument's claim is that since the "A" is false, then the "O" must be true. Put the argument in exactly the following new form, using only the four categorical form letters.

is
A ————> false

————

must be
so, O ————> true

5. Check the square of opposition to see if it agrees that if the "A" sentence is false, then the "O" sentence must be true. Since the "A" and the "O" are contradictories, they cannot have the same true/false value, so if the "A" is true, then the "O" must be false. The argument is valid.

Let's try another example:

> It must be false that some Baptists are not Rotarians, because it's false that no Baptists are Rotarians.

1.

     "No Baptists are Rotarians"   is ————> false

————————————

     so, "Some baptists are not Rotarians" must be ————> false

2. One premise and two subject/predicate terms.

3. The premise is an "E", the conclusion is an "O".

4.

     E   is ————> false

————————

     so, O must be ————> false

5. The square does not mention the relationship between the "E" and the "O" directly. We will need to reason as follows:

> If "E" is false, then "I" is true (contradictories).
> If "I" is true, "O" can be true or false (subcontraries).
> so, If "E" is false, then "O" can be either true or false.

We could also have reasoned differently:

> If "E" is false, "A" could be true or false (contraries).
> If "A" could be true or false, "O" could be false or true (contradictories).
> so, If "E" is false, then "O" could be false or true.

Either way we reason, the argument is not valid. It is not enough that "O" *could* be false; "valid" demands that it *must* be false.

Aristotle has given you a system of logic that relieves you of the need to think ever again in the case of an immediate inference. He has created a logical system, as depicted in figure 4.

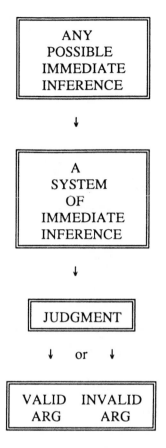

Fig. 4. System of immediate inference

Second exercises

A. Decide, based upon the square, if the following argument schemes are valid or not.

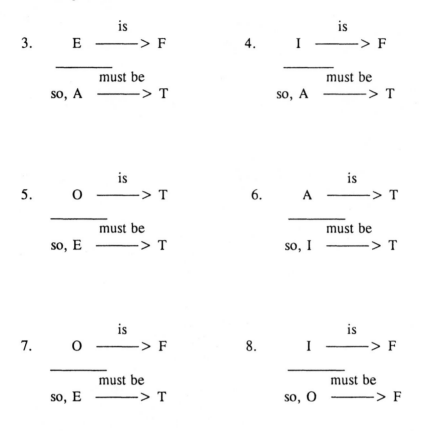

3.
```
        is
E ——————> F
————————
        must be
so, A ——————> T
```

4.
```
        is
I ——————> F
————————
        must be
so, A ——————> T
```

5.
```
        is
O ——————> T
————————
        must be
so, E ——————> T
```

6.
```
        is
A ——————> T
————————
        must be
so, I ——————> T
```

7.
```
        is
O ——————> F
————————
        must be
so, E ——————> T
```

8.
```
        is
I ——————> F
————————
        must be
so, O ——————> F
```

B. Put the following into the proper argument schemas and then decide if they are valid or not.

9. Since it's false that all philosophers are postmodernists, so it's true that some postmodernists are philosophers.

10. Some entomologists are buglovers is false, so it is true that not all entomologists are buglovers.

11. Since only beefeaters love steak is true, then it must be false that not all steak lovers are beef eaters.

12. Since it's false that some elms are diseased, then it must be false that all elms are diseased.

13. Not all books are literature is true, because only literature is books is false.

The question for us now is whether Aristotle can continue his string of successes and create an analogous system for all the other forms of inference. Fortunately for us, Aristotle believes that there is only one other form.

Mediated Inference: The Syllogism

Aristotle has finally reached the main course of his luncheon. He has solved the problem of immediate inference, and now presses on to the other forms of inference (or argument). He sees immediately that the other form of argument is *mediated* inference, the prime example of which is the *syllogism*. *Mediated* inference is any argument that has more than two subject/predicate terms. The *syllogism* is a form of mediated inference in which there are two premises and three subject/predicate terms. An example of a syllogism is as follows:

<blockquote>

All dancers are athletes.   A

Some dancers are unhappy persons.   I

_____   ____

So, some unhappy persons are athletes.   I

</blockquote>

The parts of the syllogism, like all else in Aristotle's system, have names, lots of them. They are as follows.

a. The syllogism has three *subject/predicate terms*, in this case "dancers," "unhappy persons," and "athletes." Each term appears twice.

b. The term that appears as the predicate of the conclusion is called the *major term*.

c. The term that appears as the subject of the conclusion is called the *minor term*.

d. The term that is in each premise, and not in the conclusion, is called the *middle term*, although *mediating term* would be better.

e. The premise that contains the major term is called the *major premise*.

f. The premise that contains the minor term is called the *minor premise*.

g. It is traditional to write the major premise on top of the minor premise.

h. The combination of A, E, I, or O sentences that make up a syllogism is called the *mood* of the syllogism. In our example above, the mood is AII. Since there are four possible sentence forms for the major premise, and the same for the minor premise, and the same for the conclusion, Aristotle rightly concluded that there are $4 \times 4 \times 4 = 64$ possible mood combinations.

Let's recall that the task before Aristotle now is to create the system depicted in figure 5.

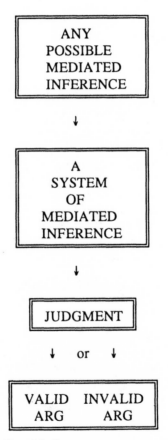

Fig. 5. System of mediated inference

We already saw that when this was done for the simpler immediate inference, it was still necessary to put arguments into a very specific form before the system of immediate inference could work.

The situation is similar to what you need to do with your thoughts if you want a computer to "understand" them. When you program a computer (whether in FORTRAN, BASIC, or PASCAL), it is necessary to put your instructions in a very specific form; otherwise the machine will not produce the desired results. Even putting a comma where a semicolon belongs will ruin a program. The same is true, though to a lesser extent, with Aristotle's system of mediated logic. Before we enter anything into the box in figure 5, we need to be sure that it is in exactly the right format. The first thing we must do is to set up the syllogism properly. Let's try a couple of examples.

> Since no logicians are philosophers, only philosophers are illogical, because some logicians are illogical.

Here are the steps:

a. Use the indicator words to find the conclusion. There are two indicator words and both are premise indicators, so the conclusion must be "Only philosophers are illogical." But this is not an A, E, I, O sentence, so it must be made into one. We agreed that "Only X is Y" should become "All Y is X," so the conclusion is, "All illogical people are philosophers."

b. Find the major term. The major term is defined as the predicate of the conclusion. It is "philosophers."

c. Find the minor term. The minor term is defined as the subject of the conclusion. It is "illogical people."

d. Find the major premise. The major premise is the premise that contains the major term. It is "No logicians are philosophers."

e. Find the minor premise. The minor premise is the one that contains the minor term. It is "Some logicians are illogical people."

f. Construct the syllogism.

No logicians are philosophers.	E
Some logicians are illogical people.	I
———————————————	——
So, All illogical people are philosophers.	A

g. Find the middle term. The middle term is defined as the term that appears in each premise and not in the conclusion. It is "logicians."

Another example:

Not all Q is P since All P is L and since No L is Q.

a. The conclusion is "Not all Q is P" = "Some Q is not P."
b. The major term is "P".
c. The minor term is "Q".
d. The major premise is "All P is L."
e. The minor premise is "No L is Q."
f. The syllogism should be set up as:

All P is L	A
No L is Q	E
——————	——
So, some Q is not P	O

Distribution of terms

What we are heading for is a set of rules that will tell us whether this is a valid syllogism or not. In order to present this set of rules, we need one more piece of terminology. If we look at the four forms of sentences, we see that in some cases the subject/predicate term refers to every member of its class, and in some cases it does not necessarily refer to every member. For example, the sentence "All candidates are liars" surely refers to every candidate, but does not necessarily refer to every liar. This is true for the subject and the predicate of every "A" sentence.

In the language of Aristotle's logic, the subject term of an "A" sentence is *distributed* and the predicate term is not. A subject/predicate term in an A, E, I, or O sentence is *distributed* if it says something about every member of the class to which it refers; otherwise it is not distributed. There are four sentence forms, and each has a subject and a predicate, so there are eight possible distributions that concern us. They are as follows, in which the distributed terms are in brackets:

A: All [A] is B   only subject distributed

E: No [A] is [B]   both terms distributed

I: Some A is B   neither term distributed

O: Some A is not [B]   only predicate distributed

Third exercises

A. Put the following syllogisms into proper form of major premise, minor premise, and conclusion; state the mood, and circle all the distributed terms.

1. Since no logicians are friendly and only friendly people are trustworthy, then some logicians are not trustworthy.

2. No standardized tests are valid, since only essay tests are valid and some standardized tests are not essay tests.

3. Not all police officers are women, since some police officers are men and not all women are men.

4. Some computers are user-friendly, so all computers are easy to use since only easy to use things are user-friendly.

5. Only Freudians believe in the Oedipal stage, since only Freudians believe in the Electra stage and all who believe in the Electra stage also believe in the Oedipal stage.

Rules of validity for syllogisms

With all of this in mind, it is now possible to present a system of rules with which we can determine, for any possible syllogism, whether it is valid or not valid. This is the heart of Aristotle's logic. There are only four rules. If a syllogism breaks one or more rules, then it is not valid; if it breaks none, then it is valid.

RULES 1 - 4

Rule 1: The middle term of a syllogism must be distributed at least once.

Rule 2: If either the major or the minor term is distributed in the conclusion, then that term must be distributed in its premise.

Rule 3: No valid syllogism can have two negative premises.

Rule 4: No valid syllogism can have only one negative sentence (sentence = either premise or conclusion.)

Let's look at some examples; distributed terms are bracketed.

Example #1.   All [Q] is R   A   universal affirmative

Some Z is R   I   particular affirmative
_____   _____

So, some Z is Q   I   particular affirmative

R1: broken—The middle term R is not distributed.
R2: OK—No distributed terms in the conclusion.
R3: OK—No negative premises.
R4: OK—No negative sentences.
NOT VALID!

Example #2.   No [G] is [M]   E   universal negative

Some A is M   I   particular affirmative

_____   _____

So, all [A] is G   A   universal affirmative

R1: OK
R2: broken—The minor term A is distributed in the conclusion but not in the minor premise.
R3: OK
R4: broken—There is only one negative sentence.
NOT VALID!

Example #3.   Not all R is A, so Some Z is A, since No Z is R.

This can be set up only as follows:

Some R is not [A]   O   particular negative

No [Z] is [R]   I   universal negative

_____   ____

So, some Z is A   A   particular affirmative

R1: OK
R2: OK
R3: broken
R4: OK
NOT VALID!

   Does Aristotle now have a system of logic that can handle any possible syllogism? Well, how many possible syllogisms are there? There is an infinite number of syllogisms, but there is a finite number of *logical forms* of syllogisms. So how many forms of syllogisms are there? We have seen that there are sixty-four possible moods. But there are more syllogistic forms than moods because the same mood can at some time be valid and at other times be not valid. Look at the arguments below.

1st	2nd	3rd	4th
All F is P	All P is F	All F is P	All P is F
All L is F	All L is F	All F is L	All F is L
─────────	─────────	─────────	─────────
All L is P	All L is P	All L is P	All L is P
valid	invalid	invalid	invalid
	R,1	R,2	R,2

The arguments above are all the AAA mood. There are four distinct forms, and only the first is valid. The distinction between them can best be seen by focusing upon the placement of the middle term (F in all these four cases) in the major and then the minor premise. The placements are as follows:

1st: subject of major—predicate of minor
2nd: predicate of major—predicate of minor
3rd: subject of major—subject of minor
4th: predicate of major—subject of minor

These four configurations of any mood are called the *four figures* of the syllogism. Separated from any mood, they are as follows.

1st	2nd	3rd	4th
F P	P F	F P	P F
L F	L F	F L	F L
────	────	────	────
L P	L P	L P	L P

Any mood can be configured in these four distinct ways; some of that will be valid, and some will not. This mood/figure combination provides Aristotle with a complete logical description of any syllogism. If a mood/figure combination is valid in one case, then it will be valid in all cases. This also gives Aristotle the number of possible forms of syllogisms that there can be. There are 64 possible moods, and 4 possible figures per mood, giving us 256 possible logical forms of syllogisms. Some of these are valid, and most are not. Is, for example, the AOO mood in the 3rd figure valid? Let's see. The 3rd figure is:

F P

F L

———

L P

If we add the AOO mood to the figure, we get:

All [F] is P   A

Some F is not [L]   O

————————   ——

So, some L is not [P]   O

R1: OK
R2: broken—Q is distributed in the conclusion and not in the premise.
R3: OK
R4: OK
NOT VALID!

Fourth exercises

A. Set the following syllogisms up into proper form, write in the mood, circle the distributed terms, and state whether they are valid or not, using Rules 1–4. Using your general knowledge, state whether the syllogisms are sound. Use the space under the arguments.

1. Since some letters bring bad news, some letters cause sadness because all bad news causes sadness.

2. All poetry is difficult to understand, since anything symbolic is difficult to understand and some poetry is symbolic.

3. Not all novels are interesting, because some novels are didactic and nothing didactic is going to be interesting.

4. Only Labradors are intelligent dogs, since some Labradors are seeing-eye dogs and only intelligent dogs can be seeing-eye dogs.

5. Not all M is P, so Some P is not Y since All Y is M.

The enthymeme

At this point Alexander enters once again and receives a briefing from the Great One concerning the syllogism. Aristotle explains that, excluding immediate inference, every argument either is a syllogism or can be put into the form of a syllogism without change of meaning. Since he can determine the validity of any syllogism, it follows that he can determine the validity of any argument. Alexander looks perplexed for half a second, and then writes,

Example #1.

Some people must be intelligent, since some people are college graduates.

For an instant Aristotle thinks that this is an immediate inference, but it becomes clear that it is not. It does have only one premise, but it has three rather than two subject/predicate terms. What can it be then but an *enthymeme*, which is an argument with one premise and three subject/ predicate terms. As Aristotle thinks about the enthymeme, he is also thinking about what a great meal he just had, and so is in quite a good mood. He decides to apply the "principle of charity" to the en- thymeme. He will assume in cases like this that the arguer has merely neglected to state one of his premises. He will further assume, and this is his charity, that the premise which remains unstated is the very one (or ones) that will make the enthymeme into a valid syllogism. So we have this rule:

The rule of the enthymeme: If there is an A, E, I, or O sentence that will make the enthymeme into a valid syllogism, then the enthymeme is valid. If there is no such sentence, then it is invalid.

Here is what to do in the case of an enthymeme, using our example #1 above.

a. Find the conclusion, and pick out the major and minor terms.

conclusion: Some people are intelligent.
major term: "intelligent"
minor term: "people"

b. Decide if the premise in the enthymeme is the major or minor prem- ise by whether it contains the major or minor term.

premise: minor premise, since it contains "people"

c. Construct the syllogism, leaving room to insert the missing premise.

A,E,I,O [   ]

Some people are college graduates.

_____

So, some people are intelligent.

d. Decide what subject/predicate terms will be in the missing sentence.

"people": will not be in the sentence, since it already appears twice.

"college graduates" and "intelligent" will be the terms; one will be the subject, and the other will be the predicate.

e. Decide which of the A, E, I, or O sentences the missing premise CANNOT be.

E: cannot be E because of rule 4.

I: cannot be I because of rule 1.

O: cannot be O because of rule 4.

A: cannot be "All intelligent people are college graduates" since that would break rule 1.

So, the missing sentence is as follows:

A   [All college graduates are intelligent.]

I   Some people are college graduates.

⎯⎯ ⎯⎯⎯⎯⎯⎯⎯⎯⎯⎯⎯⎯⎯

I   So, some people are intelligent.

RESULT: Since this is a valid syllogism, the enthymeme from which it was made is a valid enthymeme.

Example #2.

Since not all computers have hard drives, it follows that some computers are inexpensive.

Skipping steps, we can set this up as follows:

A,E,I,O [   ]

Some computers are not hard driven.

⎯⎯⎯⎯⎯⎯⎯⎯⎯⎯⎯⎯⎯

So, some computers are inexpensive.

A: missing premise cannot be A, rule 4.

E: missing premise cannot be E, rule 3.

I: missing premise cannot be I, rule 4.

O: missing premise cannot be O, rule 3.

RESULT: The enthymeme is invalid.

Fifth exercises

A. Decide if the following enthymemes are valid or not valid by using the procedure illustrated in the two examples above. Using your general knowledge, state whether the enthymemes are sound. Use the space below each question. NOTE: None of the following is an immediate inference; why not?

1. Since only sailboats are catboats, it follows that not all catboats are pleasure craft.

2. All democracies are prosperous, since only prosperous countries are capitalist.

3. Only rich people are rock stars, since not all popular people are rich people.

4. Since some friendly bankers are successful, not all successful people
are druggists.

5. All cameras use lenses, so some eyeglasses are cameras.

The sorites (pronounced sor-eye'-tees)

Alexander is finally feeling the challenge of Aristotle's ideas. He
grabs a handful of black olives and goes off to meditate. An hour later
he returns and hands Aristotle the following argument.

Example #1.

All P is F, so some R is not S since some R is not F and all S is P.

But the Master has beaten him to it. "Ah ha! a sorites," exclaims Aristotle. "You've discovered the heartbreak of sorites. Here is what we
will do."

Rule of the sorites: A sorites is valid if a sentence or sentences can be
added to it that will make it into an interlocked chain of valid syllogisms.

An interlocked chain of syllogisms is a sequence of two or more
syllogisms in which the conclusion of one is a premise of the other. In
finding this chain, we will ignore the tradition in which the major premise is written on top of the minor premise. The argument above will be
set up as follows.

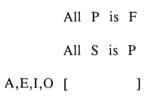

All P is F

All S is P

A,E,I,O [   ]

So, Some R is not S

The missing sentence must contain S and F. Could it be:

E: cannot be E, rule 4, first three sentences.

O: cannot be O, rule 4, first three sentences.

I: cannot be I, rule 2, last three sentences.

A: cannot be "All F is S," rule 2, last three sentences.

must be "All S is F"

RESULT: The sorites is valid, since with the addition of "All S is F" the first three and the last three sentences are interlocked, valid syllogisms.

The sorites is crucial to Aristotle's system, since this is his way of dealing with extended arguments such as one would find in a legal brief. Alexander capitulates, decides to give up logic and philosophy, and joins the army. The rest is history.

The Limitations of Aristotle's Logic

Recall that Aristotle's intention had been to construct a system of logic as described in figure 1 (see page 202). Aristotle was forced to substitute valid for good and invalid for bad. This was a serious reduction in his aspirations for at least two reasons. Since validity is a purely structural property, even for deductive arguments, having this property is only half of what is necessary for an argument to be a good or *sound* argument. The other half is that the premises be true. The most that Aristotle can counter to this is to claim that his system also assures that the premises of arguments are true by providing a way to determine if they too are conclusions from valid arguments. But of course, literally every sentence is a valid conclusion from *some* premises, and so this counter is not too much help. Thus, within the category of valid arguments there will be some very bad arguments, and Aristotle's logic has no way of excluding them.

Modern formal logic

There are also valid arguments that Aristotle's logic is not equipped to evaluate for validity. Modern formal logic is able to analyze and judge the validity of a whole class of arguments that seem out of the reach of Aristotle (see Chapter 10). A very brief example is the following:

> Since if either the knight is taken or the rook retreats then the queen is threatened, and since it is not the case that the queen is threatened, and since if the rook does not retreat then the game is lost, then it follows that the game is lost.

In modern formal logic this argument has the following structure, is valid, and can be proven to be valid.

$$(K \vee R) \to Q$$
$$\sim Q$$
$$\sim R \to L$$
$$\overline{\text{so, } L}$$

Aristotle's logic would have a very difficult time with this argument, to say the very least. In fact Aristotle's logic has a very difficult time with any extended argument of more than three or four premises, although theoretically the sorites is meant to deal with this. In fact, though, most arguments of any use are much longer than this. Thus within the category of valid arguments there are many that Aristotle's logic cannot show to be valid, or at least it has great practical difficulty doing it.

Inductive logic

It is also true that within the category of *invalid* arguments there will be some very good arguments. One feature of Aristotle's logic is that it is an "all or nothing" judgment. However, within the class of formally invalid arguments there are levels of success. Recall that an inductive argument is one that is not intended to be valid, but is intended to establish its conclusion with a high or sufficient degree of probability. It has been a dream of philosophers for centuries to have a logic of inductive arguments that would be as formal and clear-cut as Aristotle's and other logics of deductive arguments. Such a logic would accomplish what is depicted in figure 6.

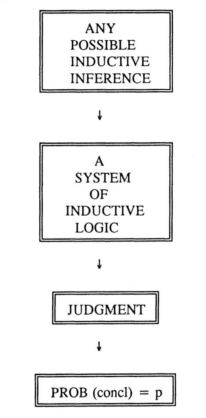

Fig. 6. System of inductive logic

An inductive logic would be able to analyze any inductive argument and succeed in determining the probability that the conclusion is true, given that the premises were true. Unfortunately, the best efforts of philosophers, logicians, and statisticians have succeeded only in finding more reasons why such a logic is practically impossible. Only in the areas of statistical hypotheses establishing correlations, and in sampling, has some progress been made toward a *formal* logic of inductive reasoning.

Aristotle Review Sheet

DIRECTIONS: If you cannot fill in the following answers without guessing, then you are missing some concept. Go back over the Aristotle chapter until you get it.

1. Define:

Contraries _____

Subcontraries _____

Contradictories _____

2. Which of the following are contraries, contradictories, and subcontraries?
a. Lincoln was the best U.S. President ever.
b. He hit the ball for a home run on his third at-bat.
c. Lincoln was not the worst U.S. President ever.
d. Lincoln was not the best U.S. President ever.
e. He struck out on his third at-bat.
f. Lincoln was the worst U.S. President ever.

3. Define:

immediate inference _____

4. Which of the following are valid?
a. It is true that no Z is Q, so it is false that only Q is Z.
b. Only Y is M is false, so some M is Y must be true.
c. It is false that not all dogs are illogical, so "No dogs are illogical" is true.
d. Since "No M is H" is false, "All M is H" is true.
e. If E is a true sentence, what do you know about:

    A:

    I:

    O:

f. If E is a false sentence, what do you know about:

    A:

    I:

    O:

5. Define:
    mediated inference _____
    major term _____
    minor term _____
    middle term _____
    major premise _____
    minor premise _____
    subject/predicate term _____
    universal vs. particular _____
    affirmative vs. negative _____
    distributed term _____
    syllogism _____
    sorites _____
    enthymeme _____

6. Circle the distributed terms:

    A: All   A is B

    E: No   A is B

    I: Some A is B

    O: Some A is not B

7. Are the following valid or not?
a. Only existentialists are phenomenologists, so all socialists are existentialists, because no phenomenologists are socialists.
b. Not all logic students are communists, since some communists are nudists.
c. Not all Z is Q, because all Z is N.
d. No accountants are Republicans because only Republicans are Unitarians.

8. Define:

Valid————————————————————————————————

Sound————————————————————————————————

9. True or False?
a. A valid argument with a false premise must have a false conclusion.
b. A sound argument must not have a false conclusion.
c. A valid argument must have at least one true sentence.
d. A valid argument cannot have only one false sentence.
e. A valid argument must have at least one false premise if its conclusion is false.

10

Modern Formal Logic

Bertrand Russell

It was the night of February 2, 1970, while driving home from having taught an evening class, when I heard of the death that day of Bertrand Russell. The report left me sad in a way that surprised me. Bertrand Russell was a towering figure. He was a brilliant logician, a stylish writer, a committed philosopher whose writings ranged from technical matters of metaphysics to marital advice. And he was a passionate and devoted social critic and activist, a candidate for the British Parliament in 1907 on a women's rights platform. He actively protested war and nuclear weapons until his death at age 98. In logic he wrote, with co-author Alfred North Whitehead, the monumental three-volume *Principia Mathematica* (1910–13), which changed the course of modern logic. This chapter describes a system of formal logic that represents a small portion of that great work of genius.

A formal system of logic is one in which the validity of some types of arguments can be proven rigorously with the use of precise rules. An *argument* is a series of claims, one of which (the conclusion) receives support for its truth from the others (the premises). To say that an argument is *valid* is to say that it has a structure that absolutely guarantees that the conclusion cannot be false whenever all the premises are true. Put in another way, where "=df" means "equals by definition":

Argument "A" is valid =df "A" has a structure such that there is no logically possible world in which all premises of "A" are true while its conclusion is false.

In Aristotle's formal system any argument that is correctly formulated as either an immediate inference, a syllogism, or a sorites can be conclusively evaluated for its validity. There are other systems of formal logic, however, that apply to types of arguments that cannot readily be evaluated within Aristotle's system. The following is one of those types of arguments:

SAMPLE ARGUMENT

If either Terry wins or Pat loses, then Jane will be disappointed. Either Hank campaigns harder or Pat will lose. If Jane is disappointed, then she will not contribute to Lucinda's next campaign. Either Jane contributes to Lucinda's campaign or Lucinda has no chance of winning. Hank is too busy to campaign harder and Terry wins. It follows that Lucinda has no chance of winning and Pat loses.

In this chapter we will look at the *truth-functional* logic of sentences (sentential logic) due largely to Russell. It is a tremendously elegant and powerful system of logic with applications in computer science, economics, politics, philosophy, and more. Sentential logic is often called symbolic logic or mathematical logic because it develops its own "language," that is, its own way of exhibiting the logical structures of arguments. This language is called the "PM notation" after the *Principia Mathematica,* which was its major introduction.

The language of sentential logic

As developed by Russell, the PM notation will have *sentence variables*, *logical constants*, and *grouping symbols*.

Sentence variables

A variable is a symbol that can represent different examples of its type, so a sentence variable is a symbol that can represent different sentences. We will use upper case letters (X, Y, Z, A, B, C, etc.) as sentence variables. The above argument can be broken down ultimately into simple sentences such as:

T = Terry wins.   P = Pat will lose.   J = Jane is disappointed.

A *simple sentence* is a claim that is not composed of any other claims. Note that the above variable T does NOT stand for "Terry" but for the entire sentence, "Terry wins," and P stands for the entire sentence, "Pat will lose."

Logical constants

Simple sentences are connected to make compound sentences. This "connecting" is accomplished by logical connectives. A *compound sentence* is one that contains a logical connective. The simpler sentences that make up a compound are its *components*. Examples of compound sentences are,

(1) "**If** Jane is disappointed, **then** she will not contribute to Lucinda's next campaign."
(2) "**Either** Hank campaigns harder **or** Pat will lose."
(3) "Hank is too busy to campaign harder **and** Terry wins."

The three compound claims above were created by connecting the components by using the *logical connectives*,

(1)   if *** then ---

(2)   either *** or ---

(3)   both *** and ---

In ordinary English we often leave off the "either" and the "both" in #2 and #3, but clarity is improved if we include them. Since a compound is any sentence that contains a logical connective, we can also create a compound claim by simply negating a sentence. For example, we can take the simple claim, "Terry wins," and negate it, to produce "Terry does not win" or "It is not the case that Terry wins." Here the logical connective is,

(4)   "It is not the case that ---"

A logical connective is a word or phrase that operates upon simpler claims (or components) to create more complex claims (or compounds). The four logical connectives are represented by symbols that are constants. A constant is a symbol that represents some determinate or unchanging entity. A *logical constant* is a symbol that represents some particular logical connective. So we have:

logical connectives	logical constants	sentence variables with constants
if *** then ---	*** → ---	P → Q
either *** or ---	*** v ---	P v Q
both *** and ---	*** & ---	P & Q
it is not the case that ***	~ ***	~ P

The use of these artificial symbols allows us to rewrite ordinary compound sentences in such a way as to exhibit their compound logical structure. Assuming that W = "Terry wins" and L = "Pat loses," then the English sentence,

"Either Terry wins or Pat loses"

is written,

"Either *** or ——"

or as,

"*** v ——"

or finally as,

"W v L"

Since sentences are represented by variables, it makes no difference whether we write "W v L" or "X v R" or "A v B," as long as we are consistent in representing the same sentence with the same variable. But since logical connectives are represented by constants, it does make a difference if we write "W v L" or "W & L."

In Aristotle's logic the different structures of simple sentences can be exhibited, for example, by rewriting "All philosophers are logicians" as "All Q is R," and "Some philosophers are logicians" as "Some Q is R." In sentential logic the logical structure of simple claims remains hidden, while only the structure of compounds is exhibited. So "All philosophers are logicians" could be written as Q, and "Some philosophers are logicians'' as R, with the sentence variables Q and R exhibiting none of the difference in logical structure. [Russell did go beyond the notation of sentential logic to quantification so that ''All people are mortal'' could be written, ''(x)(Px → Mx),'' to be distinguished from ''Some people are mortal,'' written as, ''(∃x)(Px & Mx)'']. For our purposes, which are limited to sentential logic, if we build logically different compounds out of these simple sentences, then those logical differences will be clearly exhibited, for example, as the following.

''If all philosophers are logicians, then some philosophers are logicians''

is written as: "Q → R"

Whereas,

''Either not all philosophers are logicians or some philosophers are logicians''

is written as: "~Q v R"

The symbolic rewriting clearly exhibits the logical differences between the two compounds.

Grouping symbols

The first compound sentence of our sample argument reads:

''If either Terry wins or Pat loses, then Jane will be disappointed.''

We could represent this as:

$$"T \ v \ P \ \rightarrow \ J"$$

But this would be ambiguous. If we showed this structure to someone who reads PM notation, she would not know whether to read it as:

''If either T or P then J''

or as:

''either T or if P then J''

The two different readings must be distinguished, and the ambiguity eliminated, by the use of grouping symbols. We will use parentheses (. . .), brackets [. . .], and braces { . . . } as our grouping symbols. We can use parentheses to eliminate the ambiguity in our first formulation.

$$\text{"(T \ v \ P) } \rightarrow \text{ J"}$$

Grouping the (T v P) together clearly indicates that in the English sentence as written, the ''If . . . then ***'' is the major connective.

The major connective of a compound = df the connective which, after having linked the components of the compound, leaves nothing remaining.

In the sentence ''(T v P) → J'' the ''v'' connects ''T'' with ''P'' but leaves the ''→ J'' remaining. The ''→'' connects the ''(T v P)'' with the ''J''—leaving nothing remaining. So the ''→'' is the major connective. In reading a sentence from PM notation into English, the major connective indicates which word to say first. Here are some examples:

formula	translation	major connective
~P v Q	Either not P or Q"	"v"
~ (P v Q)	Not either P or Q"	" ~ "
~ (P & Q) v R	Either not both P and Q or R	"v"
(~P & Q) v R	Either both not P and Q or R	"v"
~P & (Q v R)	Both not P and either Q or R	"&"
~[~P & (Q v R)]	Not both not P and either Q or R	" ~ "

We are now able to formulate our sample argument in PM notation.

prem #1	(T v P) → J
prem #2	H v P
prem #3	J → ~C
prem #4	C v ~L
prem #5	~H & T conclusion ~L & P

First exercises

A. Translate the following English sentences into PM.

1. Either the test is difficult or I will pass the course.

2. If the test is not difficult, then I will surely pass the course.

3. If I pass the course, then either the test was not difficult or the teacher graded kindly.

4. If either the teacher graded kindly or the test was not difficult, then if I did not really bomb the final then I will pass.

5. It is not the case that if the test was difficult, then either I did not fail or I really bombed the final.

B. Make up English sentences for the sentence variables and translate the following PM formulas into English sentences.

1. (Y v ~ T) → M
2. ~ Y → (M & ~ T)
3. ~ [Y → (M & ~ T)]
4. ~ (M v ~ Y) → (~ T → Z)
5. (~ (~ M) → Y) v ~ (~ M → Y)

The meaning of "truth-functional"

Sentential logic will present techniques for evaluating the validity of arguments involving compound claims. These techniques, however, are limited to compounds that are truth-functional.

A compound sentence "S" is truth-functional = df there is a rule that determines when "S" is true or false based only upon the truth or falseness of the simple claims that make up "S".

Suppose that we define the *truth value* of a claim as whether it is true or false. So the truth value of "Julius Caesar was a Greek" is "false," and the truth value of "Socrates was a Greek" is "true." When a *compound* is truth-functional you can always determine its truth value just by knowing the truth value of its *components*. An example is worth a thousand definitions, so here's an example.

(1)
"I am wet **and** it is raining"

(2)
"I am wet **because** it is raining"

In the first case you know that the entire compound is true just in the case where the simple claims "I am wet" and "it is raining" are both true, and you know that the compound is false in all other cases. So, as long as you know the truth value of the two simple claims, you will know the truth value of the compound. In the second case this is not so. Suppose that "I am wet" is true and that "It is raining" is also true. You still do not know whether the rain caused my wetness (I sometimes shower on rainy days), and so you do not know whether "I am wet because it is raining" is true or false.

Since our four connectives are truth-functional, we will need to know the four rules that determine the truth value of the compounds, given the truth values of the components. Suppose that L = "Pat loses" and W = "Terry wins"; then the sentence "Pat loses and Terry wins" can be written "L & W". This sentence is describing a possible world in which:

world #1: both "Pat loses" is true and "Terry wins" is true.

What is called here "world #1" is not just one possible world, of course, since there are in fact an infinite number of possible worlds in which both "Pat loses" is true and "Terry wins" is also true. For example, there could be a world in which "Pat loses and Terry wins and it's cold in Detroit," or a world in which, "Pat loses and Terry wins and it's warm in Detroit." These are two different worlds, even though Pat loses and Terry wins in both of them. World #1 could be thought of, then, as *the set of all possible worlds* in which both "Pat loses" is true and "Terry wins" is also true. Alternately, you could think of "world #1" as one of the *relevantly possible ways* that the world could be with respect to the sentence, "Pat loses and Terry wins." In this way of speaking, there are three other relevantly possible ways (or sets of possible worlds) that the world could be:

world #2: both "Pat loses" is true and "Terry wins" is false.

world #3: both "Pat loses" is false and "Terry wins" is true.

world #4: both "Pat loses" is false and "Terry wins" is false.

The reason that there are only four possible worlds for this sentence is that there are only two distinct sentence variables.

The rule for the number of possible worlds: If "*n*" = the number of distinct sentence variables, then the number of possible worlds, possible combinations of true and false, = 2^n.

Since there are only four combinations of truth values for the simple sentences, we need a rule that will tell us the truth value of the entire compound whose major connective is "&" for each of these four cases.

The Rule for the "and": Where "x" and "y" can be any sentence variable (A, B, P, Q, etc.), "x & y" is true when both "x" is true and "y" is true; otherwise "x & y" is false.

The results of the rule for the four worlds can be summarized in the following "truth table."

WORLDS			L	&	W
world #1	T	T	T	T	T
world #2	T	F	T	F	T
world #3	F	T	F	F	T
world #4	F	F	F	F	F

So, in world #1 both the "L" and the "W" have a "T" under them (and so are both true), and in this case there is a "T" under the major connective "&", indicating that the entire compound is "T" (or true). In the three other worlds (rows) the "&" has an "F" under it, indicating that the entire compound is false.

It is very important to realize that the "x" and the "y" in this rule for the "&" are variables that can stand in for any claims, both simple and complex. Thus it follows from the rule for the "and" that "~R & S" is true when both "~R" is true and "S" is true; otherwise "~R & S" is false. The rules for our four connectives can best be summarized in the following truth table.

WORLDS			"and"	"or"	"if/then"	"not"
	x	y	x & y	x v y	x → y	~ x
world #1	T	T	T	T	T	F
world #2	T	F	F	T	F	F
world #3	F	T	F	T	T	T
world #4	F	F	F	F	T	T

We should understand clearly what the above truth table describes. Note first that there are only two sentence variables "x" and "y". This means that there are only $2^2 = 2 \times 2 = 4$ possible combinations of true and false for these variables, which are:

world #1: "x" is true and "y" is true

world #2: "x" is true and "y" is false

world #3: "x" is false and "y" is true

world #4: "x" is false and "y" is false

These four possibilities are listed under "WORLDS" in the truth table. Each horizontal row is a possible combination of true and false (a possible world). Following the row across to the right, you will find whether the compound is true or false in that world. For example, in the world where "x" is false and "y" is true (world #3), "x & y" is false; "x v y" is true; "x → y" is true; and "~x" is true. We can now state the rules for all four connectives.

RULES DEFINING THE LOGICAL CONNECTIVES

The rule for the "and": "x & y" is true when both "x" is true and "y" is true, otherwise "x & y" is false.

The rule for the "or": "x v y" is false when both "x" is false and "y" is false, otherwise "x v y" is true.

The rule for the "if/then": "x → y" is false when the left hand side of the "→" is true while the right hand side is false, otherwise the "x → y" is true.

The rule for the "not": " ~ x" is true when "x" is false, and " ~ x" is false when "x" is true.

In English "either/or" sometimes is taken in the *exclusive* sense to mean that the compound sentence is true when only one side is true and not when both sides are true. Our "or" is the *inclusive* "or" in which the compound is true if either one or both sides are true. The rule for the "→" is not a natural translation of the English "if/then". The relationship designated by the "→" is called "material implication" and was developed by Russell for the purposes of analyzing mathematical expressions. Still, it almost always yields the correct answer when Bertie's logic is used to evaluate the validity of arguments stated in English or some other natural language.

We are now able to determine for any possible truth-functional compound sentence whether it is true or false, based only upon whether its components are true or false. Let's suppose that:

> P is true
> Q is false
> and, R is true

and we want to determine the truth value of:

$$\sim P \quad v \quad (Q \quad \rightarrow \quad \sim R)$$

Here are the steps:

1. Number the logical constants with "1" designating the major connective of the entire compound, "2" designating the major connective of each of the sentences that "1" connects, "3" designating the major connectives of what "2" connects, and so forth, until all connectives are numbered.

2   1   2 3
~ P v (Q → ~ R)

2. Put in the truth values given above for each of the simple sentences.

2   1   2 3
~ P v (Q → ~ R)
  T   F   T

3. Begin with the largest numbered constant and determine the truth value of the sentence for which it is the major connective by using the rules for the connectives given above. Put that truth value under the number, as well as all other truth values not affected by that connective.

2   1   2 3
~ P v (Q → ~ R)
  T   F   T
level #3:   T   F   F

Note that since "R" is given as true, the "~R" will be false, and we repeat the values of the unaffected truth values.

4. Do the same for the constants on the next level.

2   1   2 3
~ P v (Q → ~ R)
  T   F   T
level #3:   T   F   F
level #2: F   T

Note that since the "P" is given the value of true, then "~P" is given the value of false. And since "Q" is given the value of false on the third level, and since "~R" is given the value of false on that level, then "(Q → ~R)" is given the value of true. This follows the rule for the "→".

5. Do the same for the final level, the level of the entire compound's major connective.

```
          2     1    2    3
          ~ P v (Q → ~ R)
            T   F       T
level #3:   T   F     F
level #2: F           T
level #1:       T
```

The truth values for each level are found by applying the rules for the logical connectives to the truth values at the level with the next greater number. The conclusion is that in the world where "P" is true, "Q" is false, and "R" is true, the compound "~P v (Q → ~R)" is true. Since there are three distinct variables in this compound, there will be a total of $2^3 = 8$ possible worlds. We have just determined the truth value of the compound for *only one* of these eight. It would be very time consuming to go through the same procedure for each of the others, and so much quicker to do it all at once by putting the compound on a large truth table. Below is a truth table for this compound.

WORLDS			2	1		2	3	
P Q R			~ P	v	(Q	→	~ R)	
world #1	T T T		F T	F	T	F	F T	
world #2	T T F		F T	T	T	T	T F	
world #3	T F T		F T	T	F	T	F T	
world #4	T F F		F T	T	F	T	T F	
world #5	F T T		T F	T	T	F	F T	
world #6	F T F		T F	T	T	T	T F	
world #7	F F T		T F	T	F	T	F T	
world #8	F F F		T F	T	F	T	T F	

Here is how the truth table was constructed.

Step #1: Place the distinct variables for the formula on the left, and list all the possible worlds for the formula. Since there are three distinct sentence variables, you know that there will be eight worlds or horizontal rows on the table. Start with the right-most variable and alternate every other *one* until there are eight rows. Move to the left and double the one, alternating every other *two*; then double the two alternating every other *four*, etc. If there had been four variables, there would sixteen worlds or rows. This procedure assures that you will have a list of every relevantly possible way that the world might be, with no relevantly possible world listed more than once.

Step #2: Mark the compound's major connective with a "1", the major connective of what the #1 connects with a "2", and so on until there are no remaining connectives.

Step #3: Put all of the truth values for each sentence variable in columns under the variable. These can be taken from the list under "WORLDS."

Step #4: Using the rules for the connectives, assign a "T" or an "F" in the columns under the logical connectives, beginning with the largest numbered connective and working down to #1. The column under #1, which was got from the two columns under #2, is the column for the major connective and will indicate the truth value of the entire compound for any possible world.

To be sure that you understand where the column under the major connective came from, the table is below with just the final step indicated. You will remember that the "v" is false when both sides are false; otherwise it is true.

WORLDS			2	1		2	3
P	Q	R	~ P	v	(Q	→	~ R)
world #1 T T T			F ---> F		< -----	F	
world #2 T T F			F ---> T		< -----	T	
world #3 T F T			F ---> T		< -----	T	
world #4 T F F			F ---> T		< -----	T	
world #5 F T T			T ---> T		< -----	F	
world #6 F T F			T ---> T		< -----	T	
world #7 F F T			T ---> T		< -----	T	
world #8 F F F			T ---> T		< -----	T	

Recall that in our earlier example we were dealing with the case where "P" was true, "Q" was false, and "R" was true. This is world #3 on the truth table, and in that world there is a "T" under the major connective just as we had found earlier.

Second exercises

A. Fill in the columns for the truth tables and formulas below to decide what worlds make the formulas true and what worlds make them false.

1.

WORLDS	~ P → ~ H
world #1 T T	
world #2 T F	
world #3 F T	
world #4 F F	

2.

WORLDS	~ (L & F) v ~ F
world #1 T T	
world #2 T F	
world #3 F T	
world #4 F F	

252   *Chapter Ten*

3.

WORLDS	M & [(~ M → ~ L) v ~ L]
world #1 T T	
world #2 T F	
world #3 F T	
world #4 F F	

4.

WORLDS	~ R v ~ (T & ~ S)
world #1 T T T	
world #2 T T F	
world #3 T F T	
world #4 T F F	
world #5 F T T	
world #6 F T F	
world #7 F F T	
world #8 F F F	

5.

WORLDS	[~ S & (R → D)] → ~ R
world #1 T T T	
world #2 T T F	
world #3 T F T	
world #4 T F F	
world #5 F T T	
world #6 F T F	
world #7 F F T	
world #8 F F F	

B. Determine by using a truth table all of the worlds in which the following formulae are false.

6.   Y → F
7.   ~F & (Y → F)
8.   [~F & (Y → F)] → ~Y
9.   [(T V M) & ~M] → (T V R)
10.   ~~F V [~G → (M → F)]

Using Truth Tables to Test for Validity

The concept of a valid argument was defined earlier as one with a structure such that there is no possible world in which all premises are true while the conclusion is false. One of the things that a truth table does is provide a list of all possible worlds. So a truth table can be used to test whether an argument is valid or not. Below are two arguments:

ARG #1   ARG #2

A → C   A → C
A   concl C   C   concl A

Each argument has two premises and a conclusion, where the conclusion is placed to the right of the "concl" sign. Each argument has only two sentence variables and so there are only $2^2 = 4$ possible worlds. Below is a truth table with both arguments on it. The premises and the conclusion are labeled. A major column exists for each sentence (premise and conclusion), and so a "true" or "false" for each sentence is given for each of the four possible worlds. Let's see if either or both are valid. All you need to do is check to see, for the two arguments, whether there is a possible world in which all the premises are true and the conclusion is false.

WORLDS		ARGUMENT #1			ARGUMENT #2		
		prem	prem	concl	prem	prem	concl
A	C	A → C	A	C	A → C	C	A
w #1 T	T	T	T	T	T	T	T
w #2 T	F	F	T	F	F	F	T
w #3 F	T··	T	F	T	T	T	F
w #4 F	F	T	F	F	T	F	F

If we look at argument #1 there is only one world (w#1) in which all the premises are true, and in that world the conclusion is also true. There is no possible world in which all premises are true while the conclusion is false. Argument #1 IS valid.

Things are different in argument #2. Here there is a world in which all premises are true while the conclusion is false, namely world #3. Argument #2 is NOT valid. Do not make the error of saying that argument #2 is not valid in world #3. Argument #2 is not valid (period!) since there exists a possible world (world #3) in which all premises are true while the conclusion is false. Let's see if the following argument is valid:

> Either Peter is not a carpenter or Connie has made a mistake. But Connie never makes mistakes. If Jim is telling the truth, then Peter is a carpenter. It follows, then, that Jim is not telling the truth.

We will assign sentence variables as: P = "Peter is a carpenter," C = "Connie has made a mistake," J = "Jim is telling the truth." The argument can now be put into PM notation.

ARG #3

prem #1   ~P v C
prem #2   ~C
prem #3   J → P   concl ~J

There are three distinct sentence variables, P, C, and J, and so there are $2^3 = 8$ possible worlds for this argument. Below is the truth table for the argument with columns under only the major connectives. Be sure you understand how those columns were derived, and then check to see if the argument is valid.

WORLDS					PREM $\sim P \vee C$	PREM $\sim C$	PREM $J \rightarrow P$	CONCL $\sim J$
world #1	T	T	T		T	F	T	F
world #2	T	T	F		T	F	T	T
world #3	T	F	T		F	T	T	F
world #4	T	F	F		F	T	T	T
world #5	F	T	T		T	F	F	F
world #6	F	T	F		T	F	T	T
world #7	F	F	T		T	T	F	F
world #8	F	F	F		T	T	T	T

Is there a possible world in which all the premises are true while the conclusion is false?

As a method of checking validity, the truth table has two important positive qualities. The first is that it is algorithmic in the technical sense that there is a step by step procedure that will always provide you with the result. The second is that it is able to determine either validity or invalidity. The drawback is that it is boring and cumbersome.

Third exercises

A. Determine on truth tables if the following arguments are valid or not.

1.

WORLDS				PREM	PREM	PREM	CONCL
				R v ~ T	T	Y → ~ R	Y
world #1	T	T	T				
world #2	T	T	F				
world #3	T	F	T				
world #4	T	F	F				
world #5	F	T	T				
world #6	F	T	F				
world #7	F	F	T				
world #8	F	F	F				

2.

WORLDS				PREM	PREM	PREM	CONCL
				A → (F → ~ Z)	A	Z	F
world #1	T	T	T				
world #2	T	T	F				
world #3	T	F	T				
world #4	T	F	F				
world #5	F	T	T				
world #6	F	T	F				
world #7	F	F	T				
world #8	F	F	F				

3.

WORLDS				PREM	PREM	PREM	CONCL
				T v M	~ M	~ T	F
world #1	T	T	T				
world #2	T	T	F				
world #3	T	F	T				
world #4	T	F	F				
world #5	F	T	T				
world #6	F	T	F				
world #7	F	F	T				
world #8	F	F	F				

B. Beneath each of the following, construct truth tables to determine their validity.

4. T v ~M
  T concl M

5. ~P → ~Z
  Z concl P

6. Y → (~M → L)
    T v (K & ~G)   concl ~G

7. ~T
    ~L & Y   concl ~ ~M

The Forced Invalidity Method Of Proving Invalidity

The following is an invalid argument, as can be seen from the truth table beneath it.

$$\sim P \rightarrow Q$$
$$P \qquad \text{concl} \quad \sim Q$$

WORLDS			PREM	PREM	CONCL
	P	Q	$\sim P \rightarrow Q$	P	$\sim Q$
world #1	T	T	T	T	F
world #2	T	F	T	T	T
world #3	F	T	T	F	F
world #4	F	F	F	F	T

World #1, in which P is true and Q is true, indicates that the argument is NOT valid. But surely we should have been able to find W#1, the invalidating world, without constructing the entire table! Here is a method, the forced invalidity method, recalling that it is a method of proving INVALIDITY only.

Step #1: Write the argument with a list of all the sentence variables next to it.

     <— prem #1 $\sim P \rightarrow Q$ P —>

     <— prem #2 P   concl $\sim Q$ —>   Q —>

Step #2: Assign a T or an F to the variables in the conclusion in such a way that the conclusion becomes *false*. Put these assignments above the sentence variables in the argument and next to the variables on your list.

<— prem #1   ~ P → Q   F T   P —>

<— prem #2   P   concl ~ Q —> F   Q —> T

Since we were trying to make the conclusion ~Q *false*, we assigned a *true* to Q.

Step #3: In the same way, assign a T or an F to the rest of the sentence variables, forcing all the premises to become *true*. Be sure that once you have assigned a T or an F to some sentence variable, you maintain that same assignment throughout the argument.

                 F T T T

T <— prem #1   ~ P → Q   P —> T

                  T   F T

T <— prem #2   P   concl ~ Q —> F   Q —> T

Since we are trying to make all premises *true*, we assign a true to P, maintaining the true we assigned to Q, and the premises are all true. We have found a world in which all the premises are true and the conclusion is false, and so we have proven the argument to be NOT valid. We have also found the same world that the truth table identified, the world where both variables are true.

Step #4: In case you have not found an invalidating world, check if there is another way to make the conclusion false. If so, make new assignments to the premises. If not, then perhaps the argument is not invalid (is valid), in which case you may want to try the natural deduction method of proving validity that is described in the next section.

Fourth exercises

A. Prove that the following arguments are not valid, using the forced invalidity method.

   1. P → ~ G   2. ~ H v ~ G

       G   concl P   ~ ~ H   concl G

3. K → (F & T)
    T & K   concl ~ F

4. Y & [P → (K → ~M)]
    ~P → ~Y
    M   concl K

5. W & ~H
    ~H → T   concl ~T & W

6. K v [T & (L → ~H)]
    ~K   concl ~T

A natural deduction system for proving validity

The forced invalidity method will fail if the argument is valid. That is, you will not succeed in finding an assignment where all premises are true while the conclusion is false. When you fail to find such an assignment, can you conclude that the argument is valid? Not unless you have tried every possible assignment to the premises in every possible case that the conclusion is false. In this case you will have come quite close to having done a truth table. The *natural deduction* method to be described is a way of proving *validity only*. If an argument is NOT valid, then the method will fail. In this section we will present a system of natural deduction, which we will call "ND." Using ND relies upon your ability to recognize identical logical patterns. For example, the five arguments below all have identical logical patterns (structures).

... → ***	### → $$$	A → C
... concl ***	### concl $$$	A concl C

(Y v T) → M	~F → ~(R & S)
(Y v T) concl M	~F concl ~(R & S)

How should we describe the pattern? In all cases the major connective of one of the premises is the arrow; there is only one other premise and that premise is the left hand side of the arrow, and the conclusion is the right hand side of the arrow. So we could describe the structure as, "Left hand side – arrow–right hand side, left hand side again, conclude the right hand side." Here is another example of the same pattern.

$$\sim(\sim P \text{ v} \sim T) \to \sim\sim Y \text{ v L}$$
$$\sim(\sim P \text{ v} \sim T) \quad \text{concl} \sim\sim Y \text{ v L}$$

Since these arguments, as different as they look, all have the same logical structure, and since validity is determined by logical structure, then as long as one of them is valid, they all must be valid. In fact we already proved that argument #1 is valid, using the truth table method. This means that the six argument structures above are valid as well, since they are identical to argument #1. The argument pattern that we are discussing is so common that it has a name, *the rule of detachment* (RD). Where "x", "y", and "z" are variables that can denote any sentence, simple or complex, RD can be stated:

$$\text{RD} \quad x \to y$$
$$x \quad \text{concl } y$$

It is important to note that the validity of RD does NOT rest upon the order of the premises. The following is also a case of RD and so is valid.

$$\sim T$$
$$\sim T \rightarrow \sim (N \rightarrow F) \quad \text{concl} \sim (N \rightarrow F)$$

Let's suppose that we had the following argument.

prem #1 $\sim H \rightarrow (P \rightarrow F)$
prem #2 $\sim H$
prem #3   P   concl F

It does not look like RD; for example, it has three premises. But parts of it do resemble RD, in particular, prems #1 and #2 resemble the first two lines of RD. So we should be able to draw a conclusion from them by using RD. If we did, it would look like the following.

prem #1 $\sim H \rightarrow (P \rightarrow F)$
prem #2 $\sim H$
prem #3   P   concl F
    #4 $(P \rightarrow F)$ from #1 and #2, using RD

And note how prem #3 and line #4 also look like RD, so we should be able to do the following.

prem #1 $\sim H \rightarrow (P \rightarrow F)$
prem #2 $\sim H$
prem #3   P   concl F
    #4 $(P \rightarrow F)$ from #1 and #2, using RD
    #5   F   from #3 and #4, using RD

Since "F" was the original conclusion, and "F" has been derived from the three original premises by using the valid argument form of RD, then we have proven that the original argument was valid. It is important to note that we could NOT have used prem #1 and prem #3 to derive "F" since RD must be applied to whole lines. The "$\rightarrow$" between "P" and "F" in prem #1 is not the major connective of prem #1. When it became the major connective of line #4, then RD could be applied.

You will probably have guessed that RD is not the only valid argument pattern that we could use. Another common argument form is *disjunctive syllogism* (DS).

DS $x \vee y$ $x \vee y$
     $\sim x$ concl y   or $\sim y$ concl x

One of the differences between the "→" on the one hand and the "v" and "&" on the other hand is that with the arrow it makes a difference whether a variable is on the left or the right side. This is not the case with the "wedge" or the "ampersand." In other words, "P → Q" is not the same as "Q → P" while "P v Q" and "P & Q" are the same as "Q v P" and "Q & P" respectively. So with DS it makes no difference which side of the "v" is negated; you are able to write the other side. The following is a proof using both RD and DS.

prem #1	~P v F		
prem #2	~F		
prem #3	~P → T	concl T	
#4	~P	from #1, #2 using DS	
#5	T	from #3, #4 using RD	

So far our system, ND, contains two valid argument patterns, RD and DS. We will add others below. But we will include, in addition to argument patterns, equivalencies. Two compound sentence patterns are *equivalent* if they are true or false in exactly the same worlds, that is, they have the same truth table. The relation of equivalence will be marked by the bidirectional arrow, "↔". If two compounds are equivalent then one can be substituted for the other in a proof, either in a whole line or in part of a line. Check the truth table below to determine if the two compounds are equivalent.

WORLDS		EQUIVALENCIES		
X	Y	~ (X & Y)	↔	~ X v ~Y
world #1 T	T	F		F
world #2 T	F	T		T
world #3 F	T	T		T
world #4 F	F	T		T

This equivalence is a form of a distribution rule known as DeMorgan's rule (DM). The same name is given to another similar equivalence: ~(X v Y) ↔ (~X & ~Y). Below is a proof in ND using DM.

prem 1. $\sim(P \& Q) \rightarrow F$
prem 2. $T \vee (\sim P \vee \sim Q)$
prem 3. $Y \rightarrow \sim T$
prem 4. $S \vee Y$
prem 5. $\sim S$ concl F
    6. $T \vee \sim(P \& Q)$ from 2, DM
    7. Y   from 5 and 6, DS
    8. $\sim T$ from 3 and 7, RD
    9. $\sim(P \& Q)$ from 6 and 8, DS
    10. F   from 1 and 9, RD

The concept of a proof

Let's be clear what has been proven. We have NOT proven that "F" is true. We have proven that in every possible world where prems #1–#6 are all true, then F will be true; that is, we have proven validity. If we were to put argument #14 on a truth table there would be $2^6 = 64$ possible worlds (rows), and in every one where all the premises are true, the conclusion will be true. We can give a more formal definition of "proof" as follows.

A proof of "x" from prems #1–#n in ND =df a series of sentences of which "x" is the last, and in which every sentence is either a member of prems #1–#n or is derived from previous sentences following the valid argument patterns of ND.

Valid argument patterns and equivalencies

The valid argument patterns and equivalencies of ND are given in the table on page 266, where "x", "y", and "z" are variables for any sentences either simple or complex. The abbreviations are as follows: DS = disjunctive syllogism, MT = *modus tollens*, SP = simplification, DN = double negation, RD = rule of detachment, CJ = conjunction, AD = addition, DM = DeMorgan's rule, MI = material implication, and CP = contrapositive.

VALID ARGUMENT PATTERNS
AND
EQUIVALENCIES OF ND

DS	*x v y* *~x concl y*		*RD*	*x → y* *x concl y*
MT	*x → y* *~y concl ~x*		*CJ*	*x* *y concl x & y*
SP	*x & y* *concl x*		*AD*	*x* *concl x v y*
DN	*x ↔ ~ ~x*		*DM*	*~ (x & y) ↔ ~x v ~y* *~ (x v y) ↔ ~x & ~y*
MI	*(x → y) ↔ (~x v y)*		*CP*	*(x → y) ↔ (~y → ~x)*

The logic behind several of these valid patterns may not be obvious. In the case of AD, recall that when the major connective is the "v", the sentence is true as long as at least one side is true. So if "x" is true, then (x v ***) will be true no matter what "***" is. Conversely, in the case of SP, "x & y" will be true only when both sides are true. So if both sides are true, then either side must be true. Finally, CJ says that if you assume that "x" is true and that "y" is true, then "x & y" must be true since "x & y" is true when both sides are true. If you have any doubts about whether the patterns above are valid, the way to resolve those doubts is to test their validity on a truth table.

Fifth exercises

A. Below are two proofs in ND. See if you can fill in the blank lines with the patterns and equivalencies that are used to justify the steps in the proof.

1.

1. $(\sim P \ \& \ \sim Q) \to T$
2. $\sim (P \ v \ Q) \ v \ M$
3. $\sim T$
4. $M \to (\sim F \ v \ R)$
5. $\sim R$ concl $\sim F$
6. $\sim (\sim P \ \& \ \sim Q)$ 1, 3
7. $\sim \sim P \ v \sim \sim Q$ 6,
8. $P \ v \ Q$ 7,
9. $\sim \sim (P \ v \ Q)$ 8,
10. M 2,9,
11. $(\sim F \ v \ R)$ 4, 10,
12. $\sim F$ 5, 11

2.

1. $(P \ v \ Z) \to (M \to T)$ 9. $P \ v \ Z$
2. $M \ \& \ \sim S$
3. $\sim P \to S$
4. $M \ v \ (Q \to H)$
5. $\sim T$ concl $(Q \to H)$
6. $\sim S$ 2,
7. $\sim \sim P$ 3, 6,
8. P 7,
9. $\sim \sim (P \ v \ Q)$ 8,
10. $(M \to T)$ 9, 1,
11. $\sim M$ 5, 10,
12. $(Q \to H)$ 4, 11,

B. Below are two more proofs in ND. See if you can fill in the blanks with both the line numbers and the patterns and equivalencies. Note that the formulas up to and including what is to the left of the "concl" are premises and what is to the right of the "concl" is the conclusion that you are trying to prove.

3.
1. ~T → Q
2. T → [P → (M v ~F)]
3. ~Q & P
4. F   concl M
5. ~Q
6. ~T
7. T
8. P → (M v ~F)
9. P
10. (M v ~F
11. Z
12. M

4.
1. ~S → ~T
2. ~T → ~R
3. ~(S v M) v Z
4. R   concl (Z & S)
5. ~ ~R
6. ~ ~T
7. ~ ~S
8. S
9. S v M
10. ~ ~(S v M)
11. ~ ~F
12. Z & S

C. Prove the following arguments valid by using the system ND. Be sure to include both the lines and the justifications.

5.
1. Y → (H → Z)
2. Y & H   concl Z
3.
4.
5.
6.
(four steps and you've got it!)

6.

1. Y → (H → ~ Z)
2. Y & H
3. T v Z   concl   T
4.
5.
6.
7.
8.
(five steps and it's yours!)

7.

1. Y → (H → Z)
2. M v ~ (H → Z)
3. ~ M   concl   ~ Y

8.

1. Y → (H → Z)
2. M v ~ (H → Z)
3. ~ M & (Y v ~ F)
4. D → Y   concl   ~ D

9.

1. L & ~ D
2. T → ~ L   concl ~ T & ~ D

10.
1. T
2. (W v Y) → ~L
3. T → W   concl ~L

11.
1. (K v L) → M
2. (M → T) & ~T   concl ~L

12.
1. (S → T)
2. ~T   concl S → M

13.
1. Y v ~P
2. G → [S v (R → P)]
3. ~G → ~F
4. ~S & F
5. ~S → R   concl Y

14.
1. (Y v T) & ~Y
2. (~R → T) & ~R concl L

D. Recall the sample argument from the beginning of the chapter. Supplied below are the justifications for the lines of the proof. You supply the missing lines in the deduction.

15.   SAMPLE ARGUMENT

If either Terry wins or Pat loses, then Jane will be disappointed. Either
Hank campaigns harder or Pat will lose. If Jane is disappointed then
she will not contribute to Lucinda's next campaign. Either Jane con-
tributes to Lucinda's campaign or Lucinda has no chance of winning.
Hank is too busy to campaign harder and Terry wins. It follows that
Lucinda has no chance of winning and Pat loses.

        1. $(T \lor P) \rightarrow J$
        2. $H \lor P$
        3. $J \rightarrow {\sim} C$
        4. $C \lor {\sim} L$
        5. ${\sim} H \& T$ concl ${\sim} L \& P$
        6.
        7.
        8.
        9.
      10.
      11.
      12.
      13. ${\sim} L \& P$

E. Prove the following arguments valid or not valid by using any
method you wish.

16. If Mary is successful, then Brad loses. Either Frank is successful or
Mary is successful. Frank is never successful. Either Brad does not lose or
Terry is bankrupt. It follows that Terry is bankrupt.

17. Philosophers are theoretical and chemists are practical. If philosophers
are theoretical, then philosophical theories are not applicable. Either
chemists are not practical or chemists are boring. If philosophical theories
are not applicable and chemists are boring, then I will study archaeology.
It follows that I will not study archaeology.

18. If I am not an agnostic, then I must believe in something. Either religion is reasonable or I will be an agnostic. It is not the case that if I am an
not agnostic, then religion is reasonable. It seems to follow that I should
be a Rotarian. But, it also seems to follow that I should not be a Rotarian.

19. It is not the case that either France has the greatest food or Great
Britain has uninspired cuisine. If Great Britain does not have uninspired
cuisine, then the Roy Rogers fast food chain should not do well there.

Either the Roy Rogers chain does well in Great Britain or my investments will not grow. It follows that my investments will grow.

20. Colleges are charging more for tuition. If colleges are becoming less able to teach students, then they are not charging more for tuition. If colleges are not becoming less able to teach students, then colleges should not eliminate requirements. It follows that colleges should not eliminate requirements.

What is wrong with contradictions?

To contradict oneself is the most serious sin of logic, the sin that will consign you to an eternity of constructing truth tables. Think of the following conversation.

Terry: "Is it raining today? I don't know whether to bring an umbrella."

Fran: "It's beautiful out. It rained yesterday, I doubt that it will rain for another week."

Terry: "That's great, then how about a picnic for dinner tonight?"

Fran: "That's not so smart, a picnic in the rain."

Terry: "I said tonight, for a picnic."

Fran: "I heard you."

Terry: "But you said it won't rain for a week."

Fran: "So?"

Terry: "Let's start over. Is it going to rain today or not?"

Fran: "How would I know?"

Terry: "Oh God!"

To contradict oneself is to assert something and then to deny that same thing. Who is guilty of the sin of contradiction in the dialogue? One of the things wrong with contradiction is that it makes communication impossible. What's Terry to do? In sentential logic you get the contradictory of a sentence simply by putting a "~" in front of it. So the contradiction of P is ~P. For me to contradict myself, then, is for me to assert "P & ~P". Another thing wrong with contradictory statements like "P & ~P" is that they are *always false*, in every possible world. Let's do a truth table of "P & ~P".

WORLDS		CONTRADICTION				
	P	P	&		~	P
world #1	T	T	F		F	T
world #2	F	F	F		T	F

There's a third thing wrong with contradictions, namely that if you start with a contradictory theory or set of premises, then *anything at all* can be validly derived. The following is a valid argument.

It was the best of times and it was not the best of times,
so the Red Sox will win the World Series.

Supposing that B = It was the best of times, and R = the Red Sox will win the World Series, our argument looks like this.

prem 1. B & ~B   concl R

There is no problem proving that "R" (or anything else, for that matter) follows from the premise.

1. B & ~B   concl R
2. B   1, SP
3. B v R   2, AD
4. ~B   1, SP
5. R   3,4 DS

As a lifelong Red Sox fan, should I be thrilled at the result? Have I any reason to think that finally, once in my lifetime, the Red Sox will be the champions? No, because although the proof shows that whenever the premise is true then "R = the Red Sox will win the World Series" will be true, the premise will never be true in any possible world. Furthermore, if you are a Yankees fan, you can just as easily prove that the Red Sox will NOT win the World Series "~R" (or even that the Dallas Cowboys or Boston Celtics will win the World Series).

6. B v ~R   2, AD
7. ~R   4,6 DS

For a theory or a set of premises in an argument to contain a contradiction is a fatal flaw, requiring at the very least some changes. In sentential logic there are two ways to determine if some set of premises contains a contradiction. One way is to put the premises on a truth table and check to see if there is no possible world in which all the premises are true. If there is no such world, then the premises are contradictory. This is exhibited below.

1. P → ~T
2. T & ~R
3. P v R   concl ??

WORLDS			PREM	PREM	PREM
P	T	R	P → ~ T	T & ~ R	P v R
world #1 T	T	T	F	F	T
world #2 T	T	F	F	T	T
world #3 T	F	T	T	F	T
world #4 T	F	F	T	F	T
world #5 F	T	T	T	F	T
world #6 F	T	F	T	T	F
world #7 F	F	T	T	F	T
world #8 F	F	F	T	F	F

There is no possible world in which all the premises are true, so they are contradictory. The contradiction in the premises can also be shown by deriving an explicit contradiction of the form "x & ~x" from them by using the system ND.

1. P → ~T
2. T & ~R
3. P v R   concl ??
4. T   2, SP
5. ~ ~T   4, DN
6. ~P   1,5, MT
7. ~R   2, SP
8. P   3,7, DS
9. P & ~P   6,8, CJ

Famous Contradictions

The Liar's Paradox

Sentences in ordinary languages like American English, even sentences that seem straightforward, can contain contradictions, particularly when the language is used in a self-referential way. A statement is self-referential if at least part of what it is referring to is the sentence itself. So the sentence by Connie, ''Whatever I say is a lie,'' is self-referential, since that sentence is something that Connie says and so is part of what the sentence refers to. Think about the sentence in the box below.

> The sentence in this box is false.

Let's call the sentence in the box S. Since S says that it is false, it follows that if S is true, then S must be what it says it is, namely false. On the other hand, if S is false, then since that's what it says it is, it must be true. What we have is: If S is false then it must be true and if S is true then it must be false. We could write this:

$$(\sim S \to S) \ \& \ (S \to \sim S)$$

This certainly seems to be an odd result, but is it a contradiction? Suppose we make the above formulation a premise and see what can be derived from it.

1.	$(\sim S \to S) \ \& \ (S \to \sim S)$	
2.	$\sim S \to S$	1, SP
3.	$S \to \sim S$	1, SP
4.	$\sim \sim S \lor S$	2, MI
5.	$S \lor S$	3,4, DN
6.	S	5, $x \leftrightarrow (x \lor x)$
7.	$\sim S \lor \sim S$	3, MI
8.	$\sim S$	7, $x \leftrightarrow (x \lor x)$
9.	$S \ \& \ \sim S$	6,8, CJ

The derivation of the contradiction makes use in lines #5 and #7 of an equivalence that is not on our list. You can test it on a truth table.

Russell's paradox

Occasionally contradictions are discovered in theoretical systems, even in formal systems. Bertrand Russell discovered that set theory, a formal logic of class inclusion, contained a contradiction. A *set* S is a group of elements that share some property P. Every member of the set of all trees shares the property of "being a tree," and every member of the set of all complex things shares the property of "being a complex thing." Some sets are *subsets* of other sets. A is (properly) a subset of B means that every member of A is a member of B and there is at least one member of B that is not a member of A. There is a logic to the idea of sets (or classes). For example, the following principle seems true about sets: If A is a subset of B and B is a subset of C, then A is a subset of C. The theory of sets is a formal theory of the logical relations among sets or classes. It is usually taught in mathematics courses, though it is often taught in courses of modern logic as well.

Bertrand Russell had the idea that all of mathematics could be derived, proven to follow logically, from the theory of sets. This would explain why mathematical sentences seemed so obviously true: mathematics would be just a branch of logic. The German philosopher/logician Gottlob Frege was working on the same problem. The shoulders of the theory of sets would have to be very strong if they were to carry the weight of the certitude of mathematics. But disaster struck for the theory of sets. As Russell was thinking about a famous proof by the mathematician Cantor that there is no greatest positive integer, he happened to think of the fact that some classes are members of themselves. For example, the class of all complex things is itself a complex thing. Some classes are NOT members of themselves. For example, the class of all trees is not a tree (it's a class!). The class of all dogs is not a dog. The class of all logic exams is not a logic exam, and so forth. You have just had three examples of classes that are not members of themselves. Now think of the class of ALL such classes. Think of:

N = The class of all classes that are not members of themselves.

All the classes in N share the property of "not being members of themselves." The theory of sets implies that N exists. Suppose that the symbol "ϵ" means "is a member of"; then we can define N as follows:

Given any set (S),   (S $\in$ N) $\leftrightarrow$ ~(S $\in$ S)

This means that any set S is a member of N if and only if it is not a member of itself. So for the set D of all dogs we can say, (D ϵ N) $\leftrightarrow$ ~(D ϵ D). And for the set T of all trees we can say, (T ϵ N) $\leftrightarrow$ ~(T ϵ T). But here is the problem. N is itself a set, as much a set as D or as T. So we can ask whether N is a member of itself. In other words:

$$(N \in N) \leftrightarrow \, \sim(N \in N)$$

Suppose that S = (N $\in$ N), then the above would be stated:

$$S \leftrightarrow \, \sim S$$

There is an equivalence that states:

$$[x \leftrightarrow y] \leftrightarrow [(y \rightarrow x) \, \& \, (x \rightarrow y)]$$

If we substitute "S $\leftrightarrow$ ~S" for [x $\leftrightarrow$ y], it becomes:

$$[(\sim S \rightarrow S) \, \& \, (S \rightarrow \, \sim S)]$$

from which, as we have already seen in the case of the liar, an explicit contradiction can be derived. Russell wrote Frege a short letter describing his discovery, and Frege is said to have replied, "Arithmetic totters." There have been numerous attempts in the presentation of set theory to escape Russell's contradiction, but none is considered entirely satisfactory.

The voting paradox and the logic of relations

The word "democracy" derives from the Greek suffix *"cracy"* meaning "rule of" and the word *"demes,"* which refers to the neighborhoods of the ancient Greek city-states where the common people lived. Generally, then, we can think of democracy as a society ruled *by* the people and *for* the people. We can think of the society as a whole having preferences, as for example when a society prefers to build a bridge "b" over the river rather than a tunnel "t" under it or a road "r" around it. And we can also think of the individuals of the society each having preferences. For example, James prefers the road since the bridge and the tunnel were both planned to cross his property. Since democracy is a rule by and for the people, it can be thought of as a social decision procedure that somehow translates individual preferences into societal preferences. Such a democratic social decision procedure would be different from a dictatorial social decision procedure that would translate the preferences only of the leader into societal preferences. The most common, though not the only, democratic social decision procedure is majority rules. Unfortunately, the majority rules social decision procedure contains a contradiction.

In Aristotle's logic we dealt with sentences of the form, "All people are large." The term "people" is the subject of the sentence, and the term "large" is the predicate. In this sentence "large" is a one-place predicate, meaning that it describes only one thing at a time—people. Predicates can also be more-than-one-place, that is, two-place, three-place, etc. In the sentence, "Dogs are larger than mice," the predicate "larger than" is a two-place predicate. Predicates that are not one-place are called "relations." Here are some relational predicates with a suggested notation.

A NOTATION FOR RELATIONS

1. aGb for "a" is the grandfather of "b"
2. aRb for "a" is to the right of "b"
3. aJPb for "a" is preferred by James to "b"
4. aSIb for Society is indifferent between "a" and "b"
5. aSPb for Society prefers "a" to "b"

There are certain standard logical properties that any relation will either have or not have. So any specific relation will have some set of these properties. These properties of relations are listed below, where "R" stands for any possible two-place relation, and x, y, and z stand for any elements that can enter into a relation. Finally, the "v" connective should be interpreted as exclusive, ruling out the possibility that both are true. It follows that: x v y

$$x \quad \text{concl} \quad y$$

is now a valid argument (call it EX).

PROPERTIES OF RELATIONS

xRx	reflexivity
~(xRx)	irreflexivity
xRx v ~(xRx)	nonreflexivity
xRy → yRx	symmetry
xRy → ~(yRx)	asymmetry
xRy → [yRx v ~(yRx)]	nonsymmetry
(xRy & yRz) → xRz	transitivity
(xRy & yRz) → ~(xRz)	intransitivity
(xRy & yRz) → [xRz v ~(xRz)]	nontransitivity

Let's check the relation "is in the same college class as." It is reflexive since everyone is in the same class as herself; it is symmetric since if Jane is in the same class as Jim, then Jim is in the same class as Jane; and it is transitive since if Jane is in the same class as Jim and Jim is in the same class as Pat, then Jane is in the same class as Pat. Why would it be true to say that the relation "is an enemy of" is nonreflexive, nonsymmetric, and nontransitive? Check which properties the ten relations listed above have.

For the relation, "society prefers a to b" we will write "aSPb", and for the relation "person Q prefers a to b" we will write "aQPb". And we would expect that both of these relations should have the following properties:

irreflexivity	~(xPx)
asymmetry	xPy → ~(yPx)
transitivity	(xPy & yPz) → xPz

We can now see how the majority rules decision procedure is contradictory. For simplicity, suppose that we have a three-person society made up of James, Fran, and Connie. And let us suppose as well that this society must decide whether to build a bridge "b," tunnel "t," or road "r" across, under, or around the river. If the decision procedure is majoritarian, then any option that represents the preferences of two or more citizens will become the societal preference. Here are the preferences of our three citizens:

CITIZEN PREFERENCES

JAMES	FRAN	CONNIE
bJPt	tFPr	rCPb
tJPr	rFPb	bCPt
bJPr	tFPb	rCPt

Note that none of the citizen preferences violate the properties of the preference relation. There are, for example, no intransitivities of individual preference. Let's use the majoritarian decision procedure and the accepted properties of the preference relations to derive the societal preference.

DERIVATION OF THE SOCIETAL PREFERENCE

1.	tSPr	majority, (James, Fran)
2.	rSPb	majority, (Fran, Connie)
3.	tSPb	1,2 transitivity of "SP"
4.	~(bSPt)	3, symmetry of "SP"
5.	bSPt	majority, (Connie, James)
6.	bSPt & ~(bSPt)	4,5 CJ (CONTRADICTION!!)

This voting paradox, attributed to the French philosopher the Marquis de Condorcet (1743–1794), was generalized and made much more powerful as a critique of the logic of democratic decision rules by the 1972 Nobel economist Kenneth Arrow (1951).

Sixth exercises

A. For Terry to have "rational preferences" for apples (a), cherries (c), oranges (o), and peaches (p), economists tell us that the preferences (P) would have to be transitive, asymmetric, and irreflexive; that the indifference relation (I) needs to be transitive, symmetric, and reflexive; and that Terry's preferences need to be "complete" in that for any two fruits, x and y, either xTPy or yTPx or xTIy, where the "or" is exclusive. (There is a wonderful discussion of these matters in Patrick Suppes' *Introduction to Logic*, 1957, ch. 10.)

1. We ask Terry to state the preferences in pairs, and Terry answers: aTPc, cTPo, oTPp, cTPp, pTPa. Prove that Terry's preferences are not rational.

2. Terry changes preferences and adds indifferences:
aTPc, cTPo, oTPp, cTPp, aTPp
oIPa, aIPo, pIPa

Prove that Terry's preference/indifferences are still not rational.

Indirect Proof

Before continuing the exercises, there is one further proof technique to describe. Suppose that the argument

prem R
prem S   concl C

was known to be valid. This means that if we put it on a truth table, in every world where R and S are both true, then C will be true. If we added ~C to the premises, then in every world where both premises are true, ~C would be false. In other words, there would be *no possible world* in which both premises are true and ~C is also true. Adding ~C to the premises when C is a valid conclusion from those premises creates a contradiction. This means that had we not proven that C was a validly drawn conclusion, we could prove it by adding ~C to the premises and deriving a contradiction. This is called the *method of indirect proof*.

The method of indirect proof = df to prove that x can be validly derived from some set of premises, add ~x to that set of premises and derive a contradiction.

Seventh exercises

1. Prove that the following argument is valid by the method of indirect proof.

1. $\sim Y \rightarrow \sim (Q \lor \sim G)$
2. $\sim (\sim Q \ \& \ G)$ concl Y
3.
4.
5.
6.
7.   (CONTRADICTION!!)

2. When economists define rational preference, they like to do it elegantly, which involves using the fewest principles needed. So they usually include only two principles as follows: for all items x, y, and z,

1. $(xPy \ \& \ yPz) \rightarrow xPz$ (transitive)
2. $xPy \rightarrow \sim (yPz)$ (asymmetric)

The irreflexivity of preference, $\sim(xPx)$, can be derived from these two principles by indirect proof, that is, by showing that adding a principle of reflexivity of preference, (xPx), would lead to a contradiction. Provide that proof. Hint: You will need to consider the case where x = y.

3. Show by the same method that the reflexivity of indifference, xIx, can be derived from the symmetry of indifference which states: for all x, y, 1. $xIy \rightarrow yIx$. Hint: You may need to use the equivalence, $(x \rightarrow x) \leftrightarrow x$.

Solutions to Selected Problems

Chapter 3

First exercises

C, 5. (D) Since the weather is beautiful (B) and the people are more relaxed, (A) Santa Barbara, California is a better place to start a business than Long Island, New York. (E) They say that there are on average 160 days of sunlight per year in Santa Barbara. (C) It's also true that Santa Barbara provides a very good business environment, since (F) the taxes are low and (G) labor is not expensive. (H) The average hourly rate for unskilled labor in Santa Barbara is $5.25.

Second exercises

A, 1.

$$\{ \text{S} \}$$

↓

$$\{ \text{M} \} \qquad (\text{CP})\{ \text{T} \}$$

↓ ↓

$$\{ \text{N} \} \quad \{ \text{O} \} \quad \{ \text{P} \} \quad (\text{CP})\{ \text{R} \}$$

↓ ↓ ↓ ↓

_____

$$\{ \text{Q} \}$$

A, 4.

   (CP){ G }

       ↓

{ J } { A } (CP){ F } (CP){ E } { C } (CP){ M }

 ↓   ↓   ↓   ↓   ↓   ↓

{ I } (CP){ B }   (CP){   D   }   (CP){ L } { K }

 ↓   ↓   ↓   ↓   ↓

───

                        { H }

B, 9.

                    (CP){ U } (CP){ V }

                        ↓   ↓

            { Q } { R }   { T } (CP){ X }

             ↓   ↓   ↓   ↓

            { N } { O }   (CP){ S } (CP){ W }

             ↓   ↓   ↓   ↓

───
                    { M }

Chapter 6

First exercises
5. "You have sold too many things!"
8. "You are in trouble."

Second exercises

3. reportive by example
6. stipulative by enumeration
12. reportive by synonym (unfamiliar terms)
14. reportive by enumeration
15. reportive by synonym (circular)

Third exercises

nuclear exchange = euphemism for mutual nuclear bombing
Dept. of Human Kinetics = euphemism for Physical Education
landfill = euphemism for dump
negative economic growth = euphemism for recession

Chapter 7

A, 4. small sample
A, 6. circular reasoning
A, 8. straw person
A, 20. invalid sample test
A, 24. biased sample

B, 27.   ACADEMIC QUESTIONS

It has become increasingly the practice of college teachers to use multiple-choice and true/false exams. They argue that these are valid measures of student learning when in fact they measure only memorization of facts, [*and the real reason that teachers argue this is because these exams are so easy to grade* (**ad hominem—circumstantial**)]. [*Statistics will show that since "multiple-guess" exams have become widely used students' reasoning skills as measured by LSAT exams have declined. It's ironic that colleges have joined the public schools in the attack against reason* (**post hoc ergo propter hoc**)]. Another reason why multiple-choice tests are not valid as measures of learning is that they give the same score to the student who selects the "wrong, but almost right" answer as to the student who selects the absurd answer when their level of learning is very different. Some faculty argue that they don't have time to grade essay exams because they are teaching seven or eight courses, but no faculty member can ever adequately teach more than five courses. [*I know this because I once tried to teach six courses and failed miserably* (**small sample**)]. In some colleges they have tried to encourage non-multiple-choice testing and yet it continued, so informal measures are of no use; only a formal ban on true/false and multiple-choice tests will solve the problem. Some argue for such exams on the basis that students like them. But the only reason that students like true/false exams is that [*they have an even chance of getting a correct answer (true or false)* (**fallacy of equiprobability**)] and that's not a very intelligent reason.

E, 42. YES: "[Since the beginning of time, moral teachers and clergy have tried everything they could think of to get married people to practice sexual exclusivity. Extramarital affairs still continue, showing that no amount of moral persuasion is going to have any influence (**false denial of a cause**). The simple fact is that the practice of [utilizing the benefits of supplemental relationships (**euphemism**)] is [gaining wider and wider acceptance (**ad populum**). [Those who try to oppose this phenomenon are just acting out their repressed sexuality that stems no doubt from having reached sexual maturity in an uptight culture (**ad hominem–circumstantial**). [I didn't see this until I myself underwent analysis and finally got in touch with my true feelings (**small sample**)]."

43. NO: "We are no doubt living in a time of great moral decay. [To advocate sexual promiscuity (**straw person**)] in such a time is irresponsible. [Since it is wrong, as everyone knows, to break one's promises of sexual faithfulness to the one to whom one has pledged such faithfulness, then extramarital sexual relationships ought to be condemned on moral grounds (**circular reasoning**). [Besides, the 1920s were a time of great moral and sexual decay and were followed by a great depression and a world war. I don't think that we want that repeated (**post hoc**)]."

Chapter 9

First exercises

1. Some sailboats are sloops. U or [P]; [A] or N; [T] or F
4. No fire is a cause of heat. [U] or P; A or [N]; T or [F]

Second exercises

10. Since, some E are B ——> F

   So, some E are not F ——> T   VALID

Third exercises

A, 3. maj prem: Some W are not [M]   O
      min prem: Some P are M   I

     concl: Some P are not [W]   O

Fourth exercises

A. 2. maj prem: All [S] is D   A
      min prem: Some P is S   I   1st figure, NOT VALID - R #2

     concl: All [P] is D   A

Fifth exercises

2. maj prem: All C are P
   min prem: [All D are C]   VALID

     concl: All D are P

Chapter 10

First exercises

A, 2. $\sim D \to P$

4. $(K \vee \sim D) \to (\sim B \to P)$

B, 2.   If yellow is not my color, then both Mary is right and Tom is not color-blind.

Second exercises

A, 1.

WORLDS			$\sim$ P	$\to$	$\sim$ H
	P	H			
world #1	T	T	F	T	F
world #2	T	F	F	T	T
world #3	F	T	T	F	F
world #4	F	F	T	T	T

Third exercises

A, 2. Not valid—world # 7

WORLDS	PREM		PREM	PREM	CONCL
	A → (F → ~Z)		A	Z	F
world #1 T T T	F	F	T	T	T
world #2 T T F	T	T	T	F	T
world #3 T F T	F	F	T	T	F
world #4 T F F	T	T	T	F	F
world #5 F T T	T	F	T	T	T
world #6 F T F	T	T	T	F	T
world #7 F F T	T	T	T	T	F
world #8 F F F	T	T	T	F	F

Fourth exercises

3. K → (F & T)
    T & K   concl ~ F

K ——> T; F ——> T; T ——> T   so, not valid

5. W & ~H
    ~ H → T   concl ~ T & W

W ——> T; H ——> F so, not valid

Fifth exercises

B, 3

1. $\sim T \rightarrow Q$
2. $T \rightarrow [P \rightarrow (M \vee \sim F)]$
3. $\sim Q \& P$
4. F concl M
5. $\sim Q$ 3, SP
6. $\sim\sim T$ 1,5, MT
7. T 6, DN
8. $P \rightarrow (M \vee \sim F)$ 2,7 RD
9. P 3, SP
10. $(M \vee \sim F)$ 8,9 RD
11. $\sim\sim F$ 4, DN
12. M 10,11 DS

C, 6.

1. $Y \rightarrow (H \rightarrow \sim Z)$
2. $Y \& H$
3. $T \vee Z$ concl T
4. Y 2, SP
5. $(H \rightarrow \sim Z)$ 1,4 RD
6. H 2, SP
7. $\sim Z$ 5,6, RD
8. T 3,7, DS

Bibliography

Arrow, Kenneth J. 1951. *Social Choice and Individual Values*. New York: Wiley.

Benedict, Ruth. 1934. *Patterns of Culture*. New York: Penguin.

Bridgman, Percy W. 1927. *The Logic of Modern Physics*. New York: Macmillan.

Brown, Roger. 1986. *Social Psychology*. Cambridge, England: Cambridge University Press.

Catholic University of America. 1967. Marriage. *New Catholic Encyclopedia*, vol. IX. New York: McGraw Hill.

Copi, Irving. 1965. *Symbolic Logic*. 2nd ed. New York: Macmillan.

Dawes, Robin. 1988. *Rational Choice in an Uncertain World*. New York: Harcourt Brace.

Festinger, Leon A. 1957. *Theory of Cognitive Dissonance*. Evanston: Row Peterson.

Giere, Ronald N. 1979. *Understanding Scientific Reasoning*. New York: Holt, Rinehart and Winston.

Gordon, Daniel. 1991. Female Circumcision and Genital Operations in Egypt and the Sudan: A Dilemma for Medical Anthropology. *Medical Anthropology Quarterly* 5(1):2–14.

Hanson, Norwood R. 1965. *Patterns of Discovery*. Cambridge, England: Cambridge University Press.

Kahneman, Daniel, Paul Slovic, and Amos Tversky. 1982. *Judgment Under Uncertainty: Heuristics and Biases*. Cambridge, England: Cambridge University Press.

Kahneman, Daniel, and Amos Tversky. 1972. On the Psychology of Prediction. *Psychological Review* 80:237–51.

Kierkegaard, Soren. 1841, 1989. *The Concept of Irony*. Trans. Howard V. Hong and Edna H. Hong. Princeton: Princeton University Press.

Kierkegaard, Soren. 1849, 1968. *Sickness Unto Death*. Princeton: Princeton University Press.

Lichtenstein, Sarah, Paul Slovic, and Baruch Fischhoff. 1978. Judged Frequency of Lethal Events. *Journal of Experimental Psychology.* 551–58.

McElroy, Ann, and Patricia Townsend. 1989. The Meaning of Adaption. In *Medical Anthropology in Ecological Perspective.* 2nd ed. ch.3. Boulder: Westview.

Mullen, John D., and Byron M. Roth. 1991. *Decision Making: Its Logic and Practice.* Savage, Maryland: Rowman and Littlefield.

Mullen, Kimberly B. 1994. *Using a Professional Consultant Model to Teach Parents Functional Assessment.* Unpublished Master's thesis. University of California at Santa Barbara.

Putnam, Hilary. 1977. Remarks. In Frederick Suppe, ed. *The Structure of Scientific Theories,* 438. Chicago: University of Illinois Press.

Ross, Lee, and Craig Anderson. 1982. Shortcomings in the Attribution Process. In *Judgment Under Uncertainty: Heuristics and Biases.* Ed. Daniel Kahneman, Paul Slovic, and Amos Tversky. Cambridge, England: Cambridge University Press.

Shaughnessy, J. Michael. 1981. Misperceptions of Probability. In *Teaching Science and Probability.* Washington, D.C.: Yearbook of the National Council of the Teachers of Mathematics.

Sowell, Thomas. 1984. *Civil Rights: Rhetoric or Reality.* New York: William Morrow.

Suppes, Patrick. 1957. *Introduction to Logic,* ch. 10. Princeton: D. Van Nostrand.

Tannen, Deborah. 1986. *That's Not What I Mean.* New York: Ballantine.

Taylor, Shelly E. 1982. The Availablity Bias in Social Perception and Interaction. In *Judgment Under Uncertainty: Heuristics and Biases.* Ed. Daniel Kahneman, Paul Slovic, and Amos Tversky. Cambridge, England: Cambridge University Press.

Williams, Bernard. 1972. *Morality: An Introduction to Ethics.* New York: Harper and Row.

Wong, David. 1991. Relativism. In Peter Singer, ed. *A Companion to Ethics,* 442–50. Cambridge, Massachusetts: Basil Blackwell.

Wright, George. 1984. *Behavioral Decision Theory.* Beverly Hills: Sage.

Index

About the Author

JOHN D. MULLEN is Professor of Philosophy at Dowling College in Oakdale, New York. He received a B.S. degree from the College of the Holy Cross and his M.A. and Ph.D. degrees in philosophy from Boston University. Dr. Mullen has written in the areas of preference logic, critical thinking, and decision theory. He is the author, with Byron M. Roth, of *Decision Making: Its Logic and Practice*. His widely read *Kierkegaard's Philosophy: Self-Deception and Cowardice in the Present Age* will be reissued in 1995 by University Press of America.